Due Return	Due Return
Date Date	

GISSING IN CONTEXT

GISSING
IN
CONTEXT

Adrian Poole

ROWMAN AND LITTLEFIELD
Totowa, New Jersey

First published in the United States 1975
by Rowman and Littlefield, Totowa, N.J.

First published in the United Kingdom 1975
by The Macmillan Press Ltd

Library of Congress Cataloging in Publication Data

Poole, Adrian.
    Gissing in context.

    Bibliography: p.
    Includes index.
    1. Gissing, George Robert, 1857–1903 – Criticism
and interpretation. I. Title.
PR4717.P6   823'.8   75-16367
ISBN 0-87471-744-2

Printed in Great Britain

FOR REGINE

Contents

Preface

This book is based on the conviction that George Gissing's work occupies a peculiarly central position in the last two decades of the nineteenth century, through its dramatisation of some of the deepest imaginative patterns of the time. Gissing's writing is still often referred either to an excessively specific context (his personal temperament and misfortunes) or to an excessively vague one (a general atmosphere of late-Victorian malaise). I propose to relate his work to that of some of his predecessors and contemporaries with more precision than has usually been attempted.

It will become clear that one of the assumptions behind my argument is the indissolubility of the two terms in the title, Gissing and his 'context'. I should explain the limits and emphasis of the word 'context' here. Gissing's work will be examined from a primarily literary and imaginative perspective, to which the consideration of factors and issues biographical, sociological, ideological and historical will be subordinate. The extent to which Gissing's versions of class conflict or the literary world coincide with and deviate from available historical evidence is certainly not ignored. But such tests of the novels' naïve mimetic accuracy are themselves instruments for defining rather than passing judgement on the deeper imaginative vision. This leads to the more positive emphasis behind the term 'context'. For one of the greatest values of Gissing's work is its ability to encourage us towards the definition of those shared images and forms that go to make up a particular historical consciousness. The preposition 'towards' is carefully chosen, for it is clearly more a question of directing a flow of critical interest than of establishing a triumphant and exhaustive prospect. Several people have suggested to me that the cumulative impression of Gissing conveyed by my argument is that of a writer of considerably greater imaginative energy and literary craftsmanship than most unprejudiced readers have been able to perceive. This seems to me a reasonable criticism, directed against a liability inherent in my particular approach. In order to guard against misunderstanding, therefore, let me say here that it is not my intention to extol Gissing as *the* novelist most attuned to the central experiences of his age and most successful in articulating them, thereby ignoring his palpable inferiority to Meredith, Hardy and James in terms of creative scope, ingenuity and skill. The 'context' which I hope to establish is offered as *one* possible way of reading and judging Gissing's work, just as Gissing's work is offered as one possible way of reading and judging his context.

Since my argument takes as its scope the elucidation of those elements in Gissing most relevant to a more general analysis of the literature of his time, it has been necessary to select some of the novels for detailed discussion, and to exclude from consideration a large part of his total output. Much of the later work, though eminently efficient and often attractive, was found not to contribute significantly to the furtherance of the argument.

The novels studied are grouped under three headings: the early social novels; the writer and society; desire, autonomy and women. Though this grouping is primarily thematic, it will be noticed that with the minor exception of *Isabel Clarendon*, it also follows a chronological scheme. As with all such categorisation, there is some distortion in this, since *In the Year of Jubilee* (1894) and *The Whirlpool* (1897) are as much concerned with the analysis of a general social condition as *Demos* (1886) and *The Nether World* (1889), just as *Demos* and *The Nether World* are as concerned with marriage and identity as the two later novels. Nevertheless, given the need for selection and emphasis, this patterning was felt to do the least violence to the integrity of the individual novels.

This is essentially a work of critical reinterpretation. The only unpublished material that has been used is Gissing's Holograph Diary (1887–1903), in the possession of the Berg Collection, New York Public Library (soon to be published as *London and the Life of Literature in Late Victorian England*). I am grateful to Mr Alfred C. Gissing and to the New York

Public Library for permission to quote from this. In recent years Gissing has benefited from the studies of a number of scholars, among whom the indeflectable Pierre Coustillas is pre-eminent, and I have had no qualms in availing myself of their findings. I acknowledge a general debt to the basic works of biography: Morley Roberts, *The Private Life of Henry Maitland* (1912); Mabel C. Donnelly, *George Gissing: Grave Comedian* (Cambridge, Mass., 1954); John D. Gordan, *George Gissing 1857–1903: an exhibition from the Berg Collection* (New York, 1954); Jacob Korg, *George Gissing: A Critical Biography* (1965), and the excellent handbook to the National Book League Gissing Exhibition by John Spiers and Pierre Coustillas, *The Rediscovery of George Gissing* (1971). I should also mention Gillian Tindall's *The Born Exile: George Gissing* (1974), which appeared after the writing of this book was more or less completed. I can fairly record here, however, that her approach and aims differ from mine in virtually every respect.

There are two particular critics whose general influence on the shape and scope of this book I would like to acknowledge: Raymond Williams and John Goode. Raymond Williams's comparatively brief discussions of Gissing are to be found in *Culture and Society 1780–1950* (1958), *The English Novel from Dickens to Lawrence* (1970), and *The Country and the City* (1973). John Goode has made the single most important contribution to a detailed critical reassessment of Gissing, in his essays on *The Nether World*, in *Tradition and Tolerance in Nineteenth-Century Fiction*, by D. Howard, J. Lucas and J. Goode (1966), and on *Demos*, in *Victorian Studies*, XII (Dec 1968).

I am very grateful to Professor Raymond Williams for his advice and encouragement in his capacity as my research supervisor, and to the following for many various helpful criticisms and suggestions: Mr Richard Allen, Mrs Gillian Beer, Professor Bernard Bergonzi, Dr Patrick Parrinder, Mr Leo Salingar, and Mr Graham Storey. Finally, I would like to thank Richard Allen and Graham Odd for reading the proofs.

Introduction: Gissing and the Victorian Novel

None of Gissing's work is unflawed by his merely personal prejudices and temperament, but to focus attention on them as Virginia Woolf did when she described him as a writer with whom 'we establish a personal rather than an artistic relationship',[1] can obscure the objective achievement. The brief biographical account that follows, therefore, offers a critical introduction to some of the elements in Gissing's life that shaped his imaginative outlook, rather than an explanation to the terms of which all his work can be reduced.

Gissing was born in the industrial town of Wakefield in Yorkshire on 22 November 1857. His father was a dispensing chemist, with literary and botanical enthusiasms, his mother the daughter of a solicitor. In later years, Gissing made this note that suggests the acute sense of status of the lower-middle-class family:

> My childhood was somewhat solitary, — apart from society of schoolfellows. I think the Hicks were the only *family* with whom we habitually associated ... we *never* came in contact with the families of other shopkeepers; so that we hung between two grades of society, — as I have done ever since in practical life.[2]

It is a characteristic image, of being helplessly stranded between two possible spheres of community, belonging to neither, yet connected tenuously to both. In *The Woodlanders*, Hardy refers to Grace Melbury's equivocal social status in similar terms; she hangs 'as it were in mid-air between two storeys of society'. For both writers, this state of poised ambivalence becomes a central image for personal and social relationship — the sense of dislocation that results neither in the clean break nor in the new commitment, but provides only paradoxes of simultaneous release and restriction.

Direct reflections of Gissing's own childhood and family relationships are conspicuous by their comparative absence from his novels.[3] Indeed there is a general recession in the later Victorian novel from the preceding emphasis on child—parent and family ties as referential images and analogues for adult relationship. For Dickens, the images of salvation and damnation provided by child—parent relationships are so strong as to make it difficult for adult relationship to resist their gravitational pull. Gissing too has his problems in freeing women from his own restrictive definitions of saint or prostitute, but he differs radically from Dickens and other earlier writers in being unable to refer back these and other images to formative childhood relationships, tyrannical or benevolent fathers, possessive or idealised mothers. Many of his characters are simply 'without parents', rather than positively orphans. There are important exceptions to this statement (Mutimer in *Demos*, Peak in *Born in Exile* and Nancy Lord in *In the Year of Jubilee*), but the list of 'parentless' central characters is long: Waymark, Kingcote, Egremont, Kirkwood, Reardon, Rhoda Nunn, Harvey Rolfe. Even Arthur Golding, the Oliver Twist of Gissing's first novel, does not feel the fact of his being orphaned as a decisive, originating deprivation. Of the orphans of an earlier period, Charlotte Brontë's Lucy Snowe is perhaps the only one similarly to accept a general sense of deprivation as a matter of course.

This sense of blankness, therefore, is the version of his childhood adopted by Gissing. In his *Commonplace Book*, he makes some pertinent comments on this absence of an original home to which the adult can look back. He is recording the sensations aroused by revisiting the scenes of his early down-and-out years in London.

. . . my early years in London were a time of extraordinary mental growth, of great spiritual activity . . . The indelible impressions which other men receive in their earliest years seem in my case to have been postponed until after I was twenty. My childhood is of no practical use to me; it was passed in mere comfort.[4]

This is important for the very fact of its being Gissing's

interpretation to himself. 'Mere comfort' simply cannot be an
adequate description of a childhood in which he was left as
head of the family at the age of thirteen, on the death of his
father. But as is well known, Gissing was to have good reason
for wanting to cut off the past. There are many instances of
this denial of continuity in his life and work. In *Isabel
Clarendon*, Kingcote exclaims: 'I deny identity . . . The past
is no part of our existing self; we are free of it, it is buried.'
In a letter of 1894, we find this gesture of ablution provoked
by those same London streets celebrated for their memories
in the *Commonplace Book:*

> . . . how strange a thing it is when, in walking about the
> streets of London, I pass the streets where I lived in those
> days of misery! Of course *that man* and *I* are not identical.
> He is a relative of mine, who died long ago; that's all.[5]

When we come to examine the narrative patterns of
Gissing's work, one of the most striking features will be their
abandonment of confidence in the progressive, sequential
development of character and event. Identity is not supported by a past and a future; it balances precariously on the
pin-point of the present. This image of being voluntarily or
involuntarily cut off from the past was shared by other
writers of the time. James Thomson ('B.V.'), for example,
made this entry in his diary for 4 November 1869, after
burning all his old papers and letters. The image of being
stranded in mid-air links suggestively with those of Hardy and
Gissing.

> I felt myself like one who, having climbed half-way up a
> long rope (thirty-five on the 23rd inst.), cuts off all
> beneath his feet; he must climb on, and can never touch
> the old earth again without a fatal fall. The memories
> treasured in the letters can never, at least in great part, be
> revived in my life again . . .[6]

The treasure-trove of memory to which Ruskin eloquently
refers in *Modern Painters,*[7] seems now to be *more* inacces-
sibly buried than it had been for a previous generation.

The testimony of friends such as Wells and Morley Roberts
was to Gissing's affectionate and admiring memory of his

father. Theirs has been described as 'an unusually intense relationship'.[8] It is all the more striking, therefore, that the dominant impression one gets from his work is of the absence of a father or fathers. There is nothing as dynamic, as temporally specific as loss. Just as there was no original belonging in a social sense, so also is there no Parent, no primal Authority, to be rediscovered or rejected. The false fathers of Dickens, whatever form their tyranny takes (Murdstone, Dombey, Dorrit), demand resistance, conflict, transformation. There are no such sharp, specific presences in Gissing. When parents and homes are represented in his work (as in *A Life's Morning* and *Born in Exile*), they feature less as originating forces or locations, than as the more or less arbitrary embodiment of generalised conditions. This is usually the case in Hardy also. Tess's parents are, as it were, accidental. No animus can be returned on their heads for the false illusions with which they fill her before she sets off to her 'cousin's'. Subject to the same social and natural forces as their children, parents are no longer responsible.

One of Gissing's rare references to his father occurs in his *Commonplace Book*.[9] Two or three times a year, the note reads, he dreams of his father, always with this condition, that — 'he is invariably, for a reason unknown, held beyond the possibility of intimate association'. He has dreamt of a dinner in some hotel, when his father arrived just as he was leaving. He has had another dream where his father 'seemed to be living in the same house, but hopelessly shut away'. He has often felt 'a passionate desire to approach him', but has never met with any response. These are images of seminal value. For the critical patterns in Gissing's experience, social, personal, sexual and artistic, depend on just these feelings of being painfully near, yet still excluded from intimacy. The desire and the possibility of sharing the feast are never destroyed but never fulfilled.

With the rest of his family Gissing maintained a cordial but reserved correspondence throughout his life. Again, it seems a typical pattern of participation without enthusiasm, but revulsion from the sharp, irrevocable break.[10] Yet a sharp break was exactly what he *did* suffer at Owens College, Manchester. His natural ability and fanatical self-application had brought him brilliant success in the Oxford Local Examination for 1872 and subsequently at Owens. Such great expectations as these student days must have encouraged were rudely cut short by his arrest, conviction and expulsion from the College. On 31 May 1876, he had been caught stealing money from some cloakrooms — to help a prostitute, as it turned out. The minutes of the meeting of the Owens College Disciplinary Council recording his expulsion, conclude with these words: 'The Principal further stated that Gissing had also been leading a life of immorality and dissipation.'[11] This curt dismissal must have caused incalculable hurt, burning into him the sense of stigma and exclusion from social success and recognition.

This image of a critical fall or dislocation from a state of security and order becomes a familiar one in other writers around this time, such as Wells and Conrad. But there is one particularly exact analogy with Gissing's actual experience in the life of a writer — whose name is indeed often linked with Gissing's, though all too vaguely. William Hale White ('Mark Rutherford') suffered dismissal from his theological training college in London for a similar flouting of established authority, in this case, an heretical questioning of the orthodox interpretation of Biblical inspiration. He was put on trial before the college authorities in a manner which could still rouse him to extreme and uncharacteristic bitterness, sixty years later.[12] For both Gissing and Rutherford this sudden amputation of their expected futures was to become a dominant imaginative element in their fictional patterns. Nevertheless it is important to see the way in which, for Gissing at least, it is not so much the image of the fall itself that permeates his work, as the state of *having fallen*. The crisis has already taken place, there are no great expectations to begin with, no illusions to lose. Austin Harrison, who was taught by Gissing as a boy, recorded this impression: 'Unlike other men, he practically began life with no disillusions to face.'[13]

The three decisive emotional relationships in Gissing's life can be described briefly. There was first the catastrophic marriage with the prostitute whom he had tried to 'save', Nell Harrison. In his relationship to her, Gissing found all his

complicated personal feelings focused: compassion, responsibility, guilt and revulsion. After some years of separation, Nell
died in squalor in 1888. Edith Underwood, whom he married
in 1891, for all her initially placid appearance, turned out to
be a virago of the same appalling dimensions as Nell, but
without the latter's compensating appeal as a victim of
society. Gissing fled again, but the hapless Edith lived on
until 1917; for the last fifteen years she was in an asylum. In
1898, however, Gissing met a Frenchwoman, Gabrielle
Fleury, who at last provided him with some of the cultural
equality and reciprocal affection he so deeply desired.

We should note here one of the features of Gissing's
temperament, to which many of the people who knew him
testify — his apparently exaggerated sensitivity and painful
incapacity to sustain the ordinary frictions of everday life. In
a collection of brief memoirs in *The Bookman* in 1915, one
of the shrewdest comes from A. C. Benson, who only met him
once. He was struck by 'an almost unnecessary dignity and
remoteness, as if he were walking in a world of foes, or at
least of possible foes'.[14] There is a revealing photograph of
Gissing taken in company with Wells, Conan Doyle and E. W.
Hornung, when they met on holiday in Rome in March
1898.[15] Gissing is the only one of the four not standing in an
informal and relaxed pose, but erect, stiff, alert, apart from
the spirit of the group. This reticence and defensiveness
characterised his attitude to the outside world. It was his
inability to match outward gesture to inner feeling that, as he
himself recognised, produced that familiar, corrosive frustration. An intolerable German called Plitt, with whom
Gissing was characteristically foolish enough to go on holiday,
prompted him to this reflection.

> Strange that I, all whose joys and sorrows come from
> excess of individuality, should be remarkable among men
> for my yieldingness to everyone and anyone in daily
> affairs . . .[16]

In another diary entry, he reveals some of the social
implications of this reserve. During the Bryant and May
match-girls' strike of 1888, he went to strike meetings on Mile
End Waste and Regent's Park to hear such speakers as Annie

Besant, John Burns and Cunninghame Graham. He records giving a shilling twice in one day, 'rather, I'm afraid, because I was ashamed to give nothing at all, in my bourgeois costume'.[17] Anything to avoid trouble.

We shall see later the more general significance of this extreme tentativeness about the practical display and exertion of the will, its potential intersection and confrontation with the will of another. Meanwhile we can sum up as follows the most important constituent forces, tensions and needs in Gissing's personal life, evident in his attitude to childhood, family, women, and general relationship. On the one hand, there is the sense of enforced participation in relationships at best disappointing or blank, at worst, viciously painful; on the other, the fear of irrevocable isolation, the clean break. This complex fusion of contradictory desires, for autonomy and connection, withdrawal and integration, is the emotional matrix on which his creative writing draws.

Of the sense of crisis experienced by all the major late-Victorian writers, Gissing was one of the cognoscenti. He was less well padded and bolstered than most others, less well equipped to duck and swerve and accommodate. In his work we can see the fragments of earlier Victorian assumptions, ideals and aspirations in an advanced state of erosion. It is no wonder that *New Grub Street* has been likened to 'a Victorian *contre-roman*'.[18] Some account, therefore, of the preceding problems and achievements of the mid-Victorian novelists is imperative.

The central achievement of these novelists can be defined as a radical investigation of the relationship between an observed social reality, and the intuited experience of the individuals within and comprising that reality. The essential confidence informing this project was that, however illusory the expectations of the available satisfactions offered by society, it was both possible and necessary to discover connections and effect reconciliations between desire and actuality. In Dickens, the mutual sustenance and interaction of the two spheres of 'inner' desire and 'outer' reality is the ideal towards which the narrative structure and idiom aspire. Thus, the objective social world of facts, forms, appearances

and institutions is remade in counterpoint to the clarification
and chastening of the inner world of desire and imagination.
The familiar rhythm of the narrative — of *Jane Eyre* and
Middlemarch, as well as of *Great Expectations* — is of the
progressive qualification and refining of the initial inordinate
desire of the individual through repeated, progressively
significant confrontations with the restrictive forces of social
forms. 'Progressive significance' is indeed the characteristic
project of the mid-Victorian novel, based as it so often is on
the theme of 'lost illusions', the progress of an individual
(and of the reader with him) through the bewildering,
delusive phenomena of social appearances and offered relationships, towards the climactic penetration to a hidden,
secret 'reality' — a reality that is characteristically at the same
time a personal experience and relationship and also a social
commitment, namely, marriage. The centrality of the notion
of marriage to any analysis of the assumptions underlying the
Victorian novel cannot be over-estimated. Marriage is the
point of intersection of the infinite desire with the temporal
reality, the confirming sanction of the reciprocity between
experience in its most secret and private aspect, and the
public, visible, declared social forms. By the 1880s, marriage
has become a conscious, contentious issue for many
writers — Meredith, Gissing, Hardy (who provoked Mrs
Oliphant's article, 'The Anti-Marriage League').
    The crisis to which the later writers testify is, in its
broadest terms, one of faith in the possibility of healing the
schism between the two areas of experience loosely
conceived as 'private' and 'public'. Clearly, any adequate
historical perspective of this schism would stretch back at
least to the Romantics. This is a continuous crisis, the terms
and interpretations of which vary throughout the nineteenth
century and our own. Gissing and the other late Victorians
share in a specific historical consciousness, the key to which
is the sense of an unprecedented *intransigence* in the terms of
the opposition between the inner, personal and subjective,
and the outer, public and objective. In political, social, and
economic spheres, the move towards corporation reflected a
general sense of the massing of forces, the taking of sides in a
world of decreasing options and manoeuvrability. In the

literary world, both writers and publishers organised bodies to protect their interests; nations became increasingly conscious of their boundaries; writers such as Kipling thrived on their ability to define 'us' and 'them'. All these external phenomena testified to deep and complex changes in consciousness.

For the earlier Victorians, the crossing of boundaries had been more important than their defence. This attitude embraced both the incursions of imperialist expansion, and middle-class efforts to cross class-barriers, to understand and help the poor. It is significant that the metaphors associated with the latter activity were taken over from the former, the slums equated with darkest Africa, and missionary zeal accepted as a general sanctification.[19] For the novelists too, it was the movement towards connection that informed their work, the personal connections of marriage and the recovery of lost relationship, and the social connections between rich and poor, secure and degraded, the Lady Dedlock at one end of the scale, and the crossing-sweeper Jo at the other.

It is to the novelists we turn in this respect, since it is in them that we find explored creatively the relationship between apparent dichotomies and oppositions, rather than in the discursive writers such as Carlyle. For these latter the stress is on discrimination, both as observed fact and as prescribed necessity, rather than on integration. The distinction drawn by Newman, for example, between opposing modes of cognition, 'notional' and 'real' assent, becomes itself incorporated as the object of the novelist's interrogative and transforming narrative, rather than its preceding thesis. The project is to articulate, actually or potentially, the interaction between these two spheres of knowing, an interaction that can only be revealed as part of a creative process. Again, it is the confidence underlying the narrative that needs to be stressed; the confidence that, however disillusioning and frustrating is the discrepancy between the intuitive knowledge of the individual and the mysterious opacity of objective 'reality', the *possibility* of reconciliation is permanently available or renewable. Thus, for example, the process by which a Pip or a Dorothea Brooke is divested of his or her 'illusions', leads not to a private and non-shareable

'knowledge' (as, say, Marlowe's 'knowledge' at the end of
Heart of Darkness is only shareable with us, the readers), but
back to questions of active and actual relationship.

There are two novels that will help to qualify these
suggestions and project discussion forward to the later
Victorians. The first is Dickens's *Our Mutual Friend* (1865).
Here the aspiration to a vision of total human interdependence that had in various ways animated Dickens's previous
major novels, finally buckles under the pressure of a
deepening scepticism. For the stress in this novel is on the
virtually total divergence between the individual's inner
progress through discovery and revelation to salvation, and
the brute, unchanged intractability of society at large.
Eugene Wrayburn simply leaves an empty place at the
dinner-tables of Society. His hosts, the Veneerings, can
dissolve back into oblivion, causing scarcely a ripple. Particular people are now incidental to this massive abstraction of
Society. Only the individual can be healed and made whole,
and that too by a sharp dislocation that prefigures the image
of the 'fall' for later writers. But the shattering of Wrayburn's
personal 'mirror' leaves the mirrors of the Veneerings and
Podsnaps blandly intact. There is no longer even potential
connection between the salvation of the individual and
society at large. It is no wonder that readers seize on the
metaphors of the river and the dung-heap. They have to do
more work here than in any previous novel, since the
connections between people and areas of society have
become less demonstrable through action and event, have
withdrawn in the direction of the symbolic and metaphysical.
The permanent facts of disease and death that 'unite'
humanity, are seen less as actively immanent forces illuminating and transforming the social vision, than as vast,
indifferent presences that threaten to render the actual
complexities of human life ultimately irrelevant.

The increasing difficulty of reconciling spatial and
temporal perspectives will become a major theme for Hardy,
Conrad and others. For the inner space and inner time of
particular individuals no longer interact with historical and
social space and time. It is in a sense prophetic that the
imaginative energy of the novel focuses more and more on

Bradley Headstone, the type of the exile who will dominate the novels of Gissing and Conrad. The sense of the 'trap' that Dickens conveys here in visual terms, corresponds to their vision of the confines of the single consciousness, exiled both from 'society' at one level, and from the world of objective historical reality itself at another.

> In the distance before him lay the place where he had struck the worse than useless blows that mocked him with Lizzie's presence there as Eugene's wife. In the distance behind him, lay the place where the children with pointing arms had seemed to devote him to the demons in crying out his name. Within there, where the light was, was the man who as to both distances could give him up to ruin. To these limits had his world shrunk.[20]

But the shrinking carries with it an intensity that severely disturbs the proposed equilibrium of the conventional marriage settlements. The lonely, private experience of Headstone disrupts as that of Bill Sykes never did.

The other novel that adumbrates, in a very different way, some of the issues beneath Gissing's work is *Villette* (1853). It seems strange that more has not been made of Gissing's acute sense of affinity with Charlotte Brontë. The contrast, for example, between the obscurity of most of her life, and her subsequent fame, struck a responsive chord:

> These revenges of time are very palatable to me. I think of such cases with a sort of exultation over oblivion, a rebellious triumph over the world's brute forces.[21]

In the figure of the governess, so central to Charlotte's life and work, we can see some close connections with Gissing, his intimacy and identification with the traumas of the vulnerable, exposed, but grimly determined individual. Wanda Neff has described the social ambivalence of the governess,[22] supposed to be of gentle birth (preferably the daughter of a clergyman or ruined gentleman), often in servitude to families her social inferiors. The peculiar isolation of her position could not have been more intense, treated with a mixture of respect and contempt both by the employing family and by the servants below stairs, relegated

to a room at the top of the house, her only company the
children. Gissing must have been drawn to such a figure,
belonging and not belonging, hovering at the edge of
communal groups, attracted and repelled, her energies
devoted to watching, waiting, listening. There are numerous
admiring references to Charlotte in his letters, Diary, and
Commonplace Book — far more uniformly admiring than to
Dickens, for example. His enthusiasm even carried him to
this, by modern standards, heretical comparison:

> I am reading again *Villette*. Charlotte Brontë I find more
> and more valuable. She is the greatest English woman after
> Mrs. Browning. George Eliot is poor in comparison with
> her . . .[23]

And he noted in his *Commonplace Book*: 'In no modern
writer have I such intense *personal* interest as in Charlotte
Brontë.'[24]

It is in her articulation of a pattern of desire that differs
from most of her contemporaries' that Charlotte Brontë
looks forward to Gissing. There is first of all the absence of
any initial sense of belonging, any primal point of reference
such as even David Copperfield or Pip can look back to. Both
Jane Eyre and Lucy Snowe start from a more total state of
loneliness than any Dickensian orphans. One of our first
images of Jane is of her enshrining herself with a book in the
window-seat 'protecting, but not separating' her from the
outside. This immediately presents us with an image that will
be central to the novel, but it also adumbrates many images
of equivocal withdrawal in the work of Gissing, Hardy and
James. Hardy's hidden watchers and James's trapped spec-
tators are similarly cut off but still involved, hovering
between self-exposure and self-effacement. Charlotte seems
to differ from her immediate contemporaries in her acceptance of this initial isolation. The individual starts on the
defensive, withdrawn but not excluded from the possibility
of observation or even of active relationship — the drawing
back of the curtain. Charlotte's significance, in the context of
the present argument, is her feeling for this state of
maximum ambivalence, between the desire to connect and
the desire to withdraw: thus, Jane Eyre, who wants to

cherish her private inner world yet still be able to look outwards, and Lucy Snowe, who wants to be 'a mere looker-on at life', and yet finds herself not unwillingly forced to play a part in the school theatricals.

The tension here between simultaneous and equal desires is crucially different from that more linear rhythm of desire in Dickens and George Eliot, that is a modification through disillusionment towards final equilibrium. Though still present, this linear rhythm is greatly attenuated in force. For one thing, Lucy Snowe has virtually no 'great expectations'. Her 'desire' does not follow the process of the child's desire being moulded into adult maturity, which is the actual or analogous process through which Pip or Dorothea pass. The nexus of ambivalent desire is present in her from the start, permanent and infinite. It is this sort of pattern of desire that we shall find in Gissing and Hardy, one that relies on the notion of equal and opposite forces knotted together. In Charlotte Brontë, the reverberating images are less those of active, positive desire, than of intense, lonely, passive *waiting* — desiring yet fearing the intrusion of connection. How striking in the following extract from *Villette* is the sense of vulnerability; it is not the vision of the connection that once made is permanent. The suggestion here is of risk, threat, and potential pain, and it carries the tempting corollary, that to avoid suffering, one must avoid connection.

> How often, while women and girls sit warm at snug fire-sides, their hearts and imaginations are doomed to divorce from the comfort surrounding their persons, forced out by night to wander through dark ways, to dare stress of weather, to contend with the snow-blast, to wait at lonely gates and stiles in wildest storms, watching and listening to see and hear the father, the son, the husband coming home.[25]

Waiting, watching, listening; the anxiety, fear and desire almost take on an autonomous significance, quite separate from the possibility of fulfilment, the actual arrival and connection with father, son, husband. Gissing, too, is obsessed with waiting and watching, though for something less tangible than father, son or husband. It is out of this sort

of sense of exiled, self-absorbed consciousnesss that the
altering narrative patterns of the late-Victorian novel are
drawn. No longer is there the same confidence in the gradual
expansion and sharing of consciousness between narrator,
character and reader. It is with the traumatic ebb and flow
within the exiled Bradley Headstones and Lucy Snowes that
the narrative energy will begin to identify.

If we look at the two major novelists dominating the
1860s and 1870s, George Eliot and Meredith, we can see the
way in which some of these issues develop. In George Eliot,
the paramount but supremely difficult duty of extending
consciousness involves the burden of increasing strains and
incipient divorces. At the heart of her ethical and artistic
beliefs is a humidity before the Otherness of an objective,
external world, 'that religion which keeps an open ear and an
obedient mind to the teachings of fact'.[26] Dorothea has to
struggle out of the 'moral stupidity' that projects the patterns
of selfish desire onto the outside world. The vision projected
by Self can only ever be the perversion of 'fact', never
positive creation. The condition of health can only be
guaranteed by perfect, hygienic severance of Self and Other.
Through the ordeal of marriage to Casaubon, Dorothea is led
to recognise 'with that distinctness which is no longer
reflection but feeling — an idea wrought back to the directness of sense, like the solidity of objects — that he had an
equivalent centre of self . . .' The implications behind the
cryptic 'feeling' need pursuing. There is one moment in
Middlemarch when Will Ladislaw is gazing at Dorothea and
his feelings are recorded as 'perfect'; it is a moment in which
'love is satisfied in the completeness of the beloved object'.
This is the point of pure admiration, the suspension of desire
in the recognition of perfect Otherness, but it must of
necessity belong outside time, if the beloved is to escape the
liabilities of being an 'object'. This 'feeling', so crucial to
George Eliot, holds ambiguities that run deep — ambiguities
that we all experience, if we think, for example, of the
acquiescence in difference after argument with others, the
feeling that can embrace genuine tolerance or relieved
dismissal, expansion or contraction.

The risk in the demand that we perceive a solid, objective

world is that it may produce only a world of solid objects, and it is thus in the face of this threat, and in partial contradiction of the implied ethic, that George Eliot labours not only to make us recognise the multiple, indeed infinite 'centres of self' in the world, but also to share them. But which ones? It is simple enough in the one-to-one relations where we can exclaim, 'but why always Dorothea?' The narrator can claim the right, the duty, to move the centre of self in the narrative, but it can only be effectively moved to one place at a time. (Of the image which she uses of a candle creating patterns out of the otherwise arbitrary scratches on a mirror, we can note similarly that there is only one candle.) The terrors of this infinite sequence of self-centres can only be contained by the tenacious mediation of the all-knowing and all-forgiving narrator, who is forced to poise between concealing and admitting that her *choice* of who and what we see and hear is dictated by desire, enthusiasm, belief, prejudice, fear, as much as by obedience to 'the teachings of fact'.

> If we had a keen vision and feeling of all ordinary human life, it would be like hearing the grass grow and the squirrel's heart beat, and we should die of that roar which lies on the other side of silence. As it is, the quickest of us walk about well wadded with stupidity.[27]

We close our ears and eyes in order to survive, yet how can we justify this refusal to see and feel and hear the squirrel's heartbeat out of anything other than the pressure of Self? For on the other side of silence, within the walls of the solid object, reverberates the roar that cannot be heard across the chasm of perfect severance between Self and Other.

These anomalies in the theory and practice of 'realism', in seeing the world 'as it really is' with the detached clarity of scientific observation, are drawn out of George Eliot's deepest sense of the discontinuity between history and the private experience of the individual. For the prescription of resignation, that one cannot and should not interfere, is shaped by the feeling that history, like other people, is beyond one's control. In 1851, George Eliot was writing with fervour of 'the presence of undeviating law in the material and moral world — of that invariability of sequence which is acknowledged to be the basis of physical science'.[28] Though she was to mitigate the rigour and the enthusiasm, she would never abandon the basic assumption that, as she wrote in 1868, 'Wisdom stands outside of man and urges itself upon him . . .'[29] In her hands, it can be a noble, rich concept, but it sets a sharp interdiction on man's positive creation and transformation of 'wisdom'. The 'finely-touched spirit' of a Dorothea is not entirely wasted, but it can only work in secret. The 'growing good of the world is partly dependent on unhistoric acts, . . . [on those] who lived faithfully a hidden life'. It is the word 'growing' in these famous lines from the close of *Middlemarch*, that the course of the narrative conspicuously fails to justify. The 'finely-touched spirit', the current of energy, has to go underground, into a 'hidden life', because belief in its historical efficacy must now be a question of religious faith: not just that the 'good of the world' depends on it, but the '*growing* good of the world'.

The good of the world and the good of particular individuals can only be connected by this sort of blind, but moving assertion. All the real energy of the narrative goes into registering the divorce between an inner world of desire and imagination, and an outer world of facts, forms, communications. The introduction to *Felix Holt* stresses the intolerable privacy of the pain and loneliness, when 'vibrations that make human agonies are often a mere whisper in the roar of hurrying existence'. The introduction closes with the parable of the enchanted forest in the underworld.

> The thorn-bushes there, and the thick-barked stems, have human histories hidden in them; the power of unuttered cries dwells in the passionless-seeming branches, and the red warm blood is darkly feeding the quivering nerves of a sleepless memory that watches through all dreams. These things are a parable.

It is an image of frozen, communal subjection that will be picked up and examined in the next chapter, but the point here is in the emerging belief that the 'unuttered cries' and the 'pain that is quite noiseless' belong to a different, and more important, sphere of reality than the external world of mere event, of mere Reform Bills. It is not a wood that will ever arise and march on Dunsinane. In the absence of any inherent potency to dissolve the enchantment, the daunting burden falls (more heavily than in Dickens) on the anxious, exposed narrator — the narrator who provided this memorable definition of her problem in the epigraph to Chapter XVI of *Daniel Deronda*.

Men, like planets, have both a visible and an invisible history. The astronomer threads the darkness with strict deduction, accounting so for every visible arc in the wanderer's orbit; and the narrator of human actions, if he did his work with the same completeness, would have to thread the hidden pathways of feeling and thought which lead up to every moment of action, and to those moments of intense suffering which take the quality of action — like the cry of Prometheus, whose chained anguish seems a greater energy than the sea and sky he invokes and the deity he defies.

The 'hidden pathways of feeling and thought' that lie beneath or behind the public process of history, of speech, action and movement, are felt now to carry a complexity to which the mediating writer tries in vain to do justice.

In order to hold together the centrifugal forces threatening to tear the coherence of the narrative apart, Marian Evans had to create the figure of a massive, omnicompetent Self-beyond-Self, 'the narrator of human actions' — George Eliot. Meredith threw himself with more abandon right to the heart of the vortex, acting out with studious fury the conflict between human imagination and the stubborn and subtle forms of social, psychological, material obstruction. *Beauchamp's Career* (1876) presents a world locked even further into intransigence than Dickens's in *Our Mutual Friend*. The narrator makes clear *his* lack of illusions about the possibility of Nevil Beauchamp's lofty dreams of changing society. It is a 'simple truth' that has to be told:

... how he loved his country, and for another and a broader love, growing out of his first passion, fought it; and being small by comparison, and finding no giant of the

Philistines disposed to receive a stone in his fore-skull, pummelled the obmutescent mass, to the confusion of a conceivable epic.[30]

The prime effect of the narrative, both here and in *The Egoist*, is perfectly conveyed by that image of frustrated desire pummelling an 'obmutescent mass'. We watch the desires and aspirations of Beauchamp and Clara Middleton continually being blocked, deflected, repressed and contained, not only by 'society', but by the narrative itself. What *seems* to be the main action or the crucial scene so often takes place off-stage, round the corner or in the distance. In *Beauchamp's Career*, the two key scenes of violence are never actually seen (the thrashing of Shrapnel and the duel in France). An apparently vital scene of confrontation between Beauchamp and Romfrey can only be seen from a distance through Rosamund's watching eyes. The narrative itself imitates the infuriating difficulty of direct confrontation between will and the world. Of course this conveys wonderfully the effective ethos of the whole society in which Nevil is trapped, shackled by the polite suavities, courtesies and rituals of country-house life.

By the time of the late and, even for Meredith, venomously idiosyncratic *One of Our Conquerors* (1891), the simultaneous collusion and enmity between the activity of the narrative and the opacity of the experience represented has been pushed to infamous lengths. Like *Beauchamp's Career*, this can be read as a 'condition of England' novel, but the society portrayed here is no longer dominated by the country houses of an earlier generation, so much as by the more incorporeal power of immense Capital, dramatically acquired and magically manipulated. Victor Radnor, the millionaire 'conqueror' of the title, belongs with James's Milly Theale and Wells's Ponderevo, as the embodiment of a spectacular contemporary image, that draws on and excites expectations and terrors of almost divine power. It is the sense of this power that is behind the elusive 'Idea' that haunts Victor (and us) through the novel: the vision of a regenerated world, inspired by himself, and involving not just a society and a nation, but ultimately the physical world itself. Victor sees himself as the conqueror who will redeem the divorces between man and man, rich and poor, mind and matter — *how*, he has no idea. The novel's central irony is that it is Victor himself who is supremely responsible for these divorces, through his rigid belief in the primacy of material, public and external achievement, in the ludicrous country house he builds, in the social marriage he plans for his daughter and the Parliamentary seat for himself. Meredith's own attitude towards him is extemely complex, admiring, mocking, condescending, compassionate, horrified. At one level, he seems to share Victor's barely grasped aspiration that money should be transformed into music, matter into mind. But what of the means to this radiant end? Victor relies on a blind faith in mutation, and the most explicit positive force Meredith offers, the pure rebellious 'Nature' of Victor's warrior daughter, 'burning Nesta', remains a subject for hectic celebration rather than significant activity. It would seem that the discomfort of the hostile intimacy with Victor *can* only be relieved by the dispersal of Meredith's own presence into the complementary extremes of cynicism and sentimental faith, embodied in the acrid satirist, Colney Durance, and the idealised Nesta.

The central contradictions between faith, belief and scepticism can be located in a passage describing one of Victor's walks through London. At first the city presents itself as a magnificent operatic spectacle — 'immensity, swinging motion, collision, dusky richness of colouring', 'a noble harmony of heaven and the earth of the works of man'. But — and here Meredith implicitly exposes the willed selectiveness of the modish nineties' raptures over London's 'poetry' — the moment cannot last; 'the dinnerless, the weedy, the gutter-growths' can no more be summarily ignored than the banana-skin that brought Victor crashing to the ground at the bizarre opening of the novel.

A moment of satisfaction in a striking picture is accorded, and no more. For this London, this England, Europe, world, but especially this London, is rather a thing for hospital operations than for poetic rhapsody; ... Mind is absent, or somewhere so low down beneath material accumulations that it is inexpressive, powerless to drive the ponderous bulk to such excisings, purgeings, purifyings as might — as may, we will suppose, render it acceptable, for a theme of panegyric, to the Muse of Reason; ultimately, with her consent, to the Spirit of Song.[31]

'The ponderous bulk' — of London, of English society, of matter itself — it is against this that Meredith pits the writhing, contorted energies of the narrative, in furiously dissilient harness with Victor. For as an ally, Victor is a terrifying and comic absurdity, whose actual achievements in the end encompass only silence, madness and death. Yet as we can see in the hesitations of the above passage 'as might — as may, we will suppose . . . ultimately'), Meredith himself still retains a remote, tensile faith in the possibility of Song, with an obstinacy equal to that of the obstruction. Nevertheless, the true emotional centre of the novel cannot be found in this faith; it is to be found in the appalling withdrawn suffering of Nataly, the woman who has lived with Victor as his wife for twenty years, and in the unbridged, indeed exacerbated divorce between the two sounds that Nesta hears, when, at a public meeting for Victor's proposed candidature, news of her mother's death reaches her.

> The words of her mother: 'At peace when the night is over', rang. Along the gassy passages of the back of the theatre, the sound coming from an applausive audience was as much a thunder as rage would have been. It was as void of human meaning as a sea.[32]

Between the lonely cry and the public roar, the silence and the noise, 'music' can be only a matter of bitter, hopeless or sentimental faith.

For writers of Gissing's generation — and Meredith, born nearly thirty years before Gissing, lived to *become* a member of that generation in the eighties and nineties — the relationship between form and feeling has reached a stage of acute crisis. The imbalance was indeed becoming almost intolerable between an expanding interior world of consciousness, of complex, delicate sensitivities and velleities, and an apparently narrowing and rigidifying external world of peremptory self-assertion. It is no wonder that these years produce so many versions of a sharp polarisation between will, success, vulgarity and pragmatism on the one hand, and will-lessness, failure, imagination and self-consciousness on the other. The keen dichotomies bear witness to an unprecedented anxiety about the relationship between Self and Other. The late years of the century saw an enormous complication and expansion of imaginative perspective, social and psychological, spatial and temporal. It was only gradually that the geological time-scale opened up by Lyell's *Principles of Geology* (1830—3), for example, began to pass into conscious currency. But by the end of the century this sort of reorientation of the consciousness of time has become only one of many pressures forcing man into new and strange relationships with history, other people and himself. In the notorious *Degeneration* (1895), Max Nordau was in no two minds about the effects of technological change. Man had developed methods of communication that dislocated and accelerated space and time to such an extent that his emotional reactions were left lagging disastrously behind.

> The humblest village inhabitant . . . [if] he do but read his paper . . . takes part, certainly not by active interference and influence, but by a continuous and receptive curiosity, in the thousand events which take place simultaneously in all parts of the globe, and he interests himself simultaneously in the issue of a revolution in Chili, in a bush-war in East Africa, a massacre in North China, a famine in Russia, a street-row in Spain, and an international exhibition in North America.[33]

The last item, the international exhibition, is a revealing concession to the possibility of more positive extensions of consciousness than are suggested by the apocalyptic congruity of revolutions, bush wars, massacres, famines and street rows. Yet Nordau was only expressing in extreme form the deep anxieties naturally aroused when objects, events and experiences that had seemed remote and hence controllable, suddenly lunge into terrifying proximity.

In this sort of world, it has become increasingly difficult to say with certainty where and hence who 'I' am, in relation to 'him', 'us', 'you' or 'them'. This bewilderment is certainly at the heart of many of the paradoxes that Gissing character-istically presents. It provoked a more general crisis in the credibility of such conventional ethical notions as that of 'sympathy'. Olive Schreiner, for example, who suffered more than her fair share of the neurotic traumas of the age, testified to the terror of being forced to give more than she could afford:

> People with sympathetic natures like mine must shield themselves from their own sympathies or they must be cruelly crushed and life's work left undone.[34]

It was a feeling familiar enough to Gissing. But this is a problem that permeates all the important fictional writing of this time, the problem of *how far* to extend the flow of sympathetic identification, where and how to cut it off. George Eliot had set herself the magnificent, impossible ideal of a total sympathy, ('the same completeness' as the astronomer). For Gissing and most others of his generation, neither her universal embrace nor Dickens's more impetuous gestures of inclusion and exclusion could satisfy. Gissing revealed his own uncertainty about sympathy and distance by his extraordinary identification with Uriah Heep in the Dickens *Study*. If ever a fictional character was intended by his author to be kept at a distance, it is surely Uriah Heep; but Gissing has lost all such confidence (or naïveté) in the naming of angels and villains.

In this respect, the phenomenon of Kipling's popularity during the 1890s is of great significance. He is the one writer of major talent who *does* essay a Dickensian confidence about naming. The results can be unnervingly erratic — and dangerously exhilarating. *The Light that Failed* (1891), for example, is almost entirely based on a wilful pattern of embrace and rejection. The artist-war correspondent, Dick Heldar, arrogantly rejects the world of 'culture' and relation-ship with women, and embraces the masculine world of action, violence and camaraderie. The confidence (or smug-ness) about who 'we' are is necessarily complemented by the naming and dismissal of 'them' — editors, aesthetes, the reading public, women in general, and of course the marauding Sudanese on the battle-front. The novel is written looking down a gun-barrel.

Lionel Trilling, C. S. Lewis and others have written well about the excitement for Kipling of the power of the 'word', the secret cult, its rituals and sanctions. It is an appeal, familiar to childhood, of secure, quasi-magical fortifications from which Others are excluded. In a limited sense, Kipling *is* Dickens's successor; but this creation of images of belonging and rejection has become totally divorced from any larger, objective vision. The satisfaction of naming has become a dangerously unearned gratification, isolated from the educative process in a Dickens novel. There, it is only by first learning the discrepancy between names and things that a true concordance can eventually be reached. But in Kipling we find only the magical correspondence between names and things that satisfies man's desire for perfect control over the Other. It does not matter particularly who or what the Other is; in fact, the vaguer the threat the better (as the Russians in *Kim*, for example). It is the reciprocal assurance of initiation and commitment to an organisation, a club, an Empire, that is the real motive. One has to go to Conrad for the radically disturbing questions, 'what is the club, the machine, the Empire *for*?' Engrossing, hypnotic, therapeutic as the perfect internal functioning of the machine or the ship may be, it still has significance beyond itself, ports and products. But while Gissing, Hardy, James and Conrad are all in their various ways examining the disastrous consequences of man's propensity for nailing the living and moving into fixity, Kipling is *celebrating* the fictions of an absolute control that finds its political justification in the idioms of imperialism.

It is significant that Kipling rose to popularity on the wings of the short story, for the emergence of the short story as a dominant narrative form in the 1890s is the index to some critical modulations of consciousness. In the 1880s, the narrative patterns of the English novel were still dependent on conditions of publication and distribution established for and suited to the reading habits and expectations of an earlier generation. These will be discussed in more detail later. Gissing saw himself as 'a notable victim of the circulating-library system',[35] and his struggles with the notorious three-decker are painfully apparent in the almost uniform inferiority of his Volume IIIs to his Volume Is. But it was not a lack of merely personal energy that made it difficult for him to sustain the drive of the narrative over such a long span. The downfall of the three-decker was certainly caused by the economic and social pressures on the publishing and distributing institutions, as outlined by Guinevere Griest in her recent history of Mudie's.[36] But it was also a question of dissolving confidence in the assumptions underlying the notion of evolutionary moral development, on which the earlier Victorian novel had been based.

Dissatisfaction with the three-decker, as Miss Griest shows, had been at work for longer than is usually supposed. As early as 1853, Charles Reade had condemned it as hopelessly outmoded in a letter to the publisher Bentley.

> ... the forms go with the age which is intelligent & rapid & has learned the value of time and space. The Novels lag behind the age — .[36]

But the three-volume form lasted for a good while yet. The pattern it proposed, in its crudest form, of hope (Volume I), disillusionment (Volume II), and reconciliation (Volume III), still apparently corresponded to the 'consciousness' of writer and reader alike. It was only in June 1894 that the form finally expired. The discrediting and effective death of the three-decker in the 1890s is matched by the ennobling of the short story. For this form is felt to 'go with the age' in showing experience that is perceptible and controllable only in small quantities, glimpses and fragments. A collection such as Derek Stanford's *Short Stories of the 'Nineties*[38] suggests the emergence of some shared imaginative patterns. For the theme of almost all these stories is the shattering of the dream or illusion by contact with a more or less rude reality. Here we see a crucial reorientation of the relation between dream and actuality articulated by the mid-Victorians. For instead of the necessary, energising confrontation between desire and actuality, there is only the progressive erosion of the former by the latter, only reduction and depletion. Instead of a *series* of crises in which desire and actuality are brought into ever closer concord, there is only the single, but all-embracing débâcle. Value becomes consequently located not in the adaptation but in the renunciation of desire, for there is no possibility of re-engagement.

Time can no longer be trusted as a linear, sequential process. The familiar images confirming Time's presence and activity, from the old man with sickle to the ringing grooves of change, even the natural cycle of night into day — they have all become hollow. This terror of time standing still, of time ceasing to *function*, is central to the age, and a recurring obsession in Gissing's work. In *The Unclassed*, as Ida Starr waits in prison for the dawn to rise, 'It was as though the sun should fail one morning to rise upon the world, and men should stand hopeless of day for ever.' Time becomes trapped, destroyed as flux and movement, and reduced to a subsidiary analogue of Space. And the fear of some ultimate state of darkness that weaves in and out of the *fin de siècle* and *fin du globe* myths is of course exactly complemented by the ultimate state of light dreamed of by the Utopian writers. The relation between 'now' and 'then' that is the problematic centre to *News from Nowhere* or *The Time Machine* must be swathed in gruesome or colourful fantasy, precisely because the morning after the night cannot be grasped as a communal expectation.[39]

It is, perhaps unexpectedly, from Reading Gaol and Oscar Wilde that we receive one of the most moving descriptions of the annihilation of Time.

> Suffering is one very long moment. We cannot divide it by seasons. We can only record its moods, and chronicle their return. With us time does not progress. It revolves. It seems to circle round one centre of pain. The paralysing immobility of a life every circumstance of which is regulated after an unchangeable pattern, so that we eat and drink and lie down and pray, or kneel at least in prayer, according to the inflexible laws of an iron formula: this immobile quality, that makes each dreadful day in the very minutest detail like its brother, seems to communicate itself to those external forces, the very essence of whose existence is ceaseless change.[40]

The literal prison, and its experience, become an image for the age.

These deep, shifting anxieties about Time are vital factors in the shaping of the late Victorians' fictional structures, as we realise from the perceptible congruities between writers as dissimilar in so many ways as Hardy and Gissing. In their novels we can see three overlapping, but clearly distinguishable, rhythms or patterns of desire. There is first the traditional, essentially rectilinear pursuit of desire, the staple rhythm of the nineteenth-century novel, that finds its consummation in death (*Le Rouge et le Noir*) or marriage (*Jane Eyre*) or both (*Anna Karenina*). Godwin Peak and Jude Fawley trudge a well-beaten track from provincial innocence towards the promise of urban maturity. This rhythm is still present in the work of Gissing and Hardy, but there is far less sense of 'significant progression'. For both Jude and Godwin are turned away at the city gates. They meet only blank walls, brute impenetrability — Meredith's 'obmutescent mass'. Thus is initiated the second and most characteristic rhythm of desire, as they turn away in frustration. This rhythm tends to be repetitive and circular, and moves in short, sharp bursts of energy suddenly frustrated. This is the essential movement in *The Mayor of Casterbridge*, for example. Every positive movement of volition on Henchard's part is immediately checked. As soon as he confides to Elizabeth-Jane that she is his daughter, he opens his wife's letter to discover that she is not. It is a cruel parody of earlier Victorian patterns of desire; instead of the gradual interaction and reconciliation, only peremptory, vicious amputation. For all the differences of setting, style and temper, *The Mayor of Casterbridge* and Gissing's *The Nether World* grow out of a shared sense of the quality of suffering, of intense desire deflected and introverted at every twist and turn. In *Jude*, this violent syndrome of frustration is played out in the relationship betweeen Jude and Sue, in the perpetual oscillation between attraction and repulsion, Sue summoning from a distance, repelling in proximity. It is usual in Gissing and Hardy, however, for the two rhythms to coexist, even if ironically. The ever-decreasing circle of frustration suffered by Henchard or Reardon is balanced by the traditional linear movement of Farfrae and Milvain.

The third 'rhythm' that enters has become hardly a rhythm at all, since it provides the vision of time as totally spatialised, in which only pattern can exist. This is the view of 'the one fact of inconceivable duration' that Godwin Peak discovers. It is the perspective of Lyell's 'geological time', that reduces the human and specific to microscopic elements in a vast, indifferent scheme. For the philosophical justification, it was natural to turn to Schopenhauer.[41] Repeated frustration prompts the assimilation of desire into a larger metaphysical or evolutionary pattern. The function of the child in *Jude*, Father Time, is precisely to lift the narrative out of its particular context into the realm of the timeless.

Yet at their best, Hardy and Gissing hold these three temporal patterns firmly in tension. One of Hardy's most typical stylistic effects is the controlled alternation between two of the spatially analogous perspectives, a painless, liberated distant view and the intense, involved 'close-up'. In *Tess*, we see two women working in a field from a lofty, aerial vantage point one moment, and in close physical identification the next; from a tiny, distant object, a mere 'fly', to a specific, suffering human being, feeling 'the creep of rain-water, first in legs and shoulders, then on hips and head, then at back, front and sides'.[40] The rhythm of the prose itself enacts the sense of identification seeping into the reader. The moving energy of the narrative in Hardy is generated precisely in this space between the perspective from which particular, variegated humanity with its complex desires and needs is seen in close and passionate proximity, and the perspective from which it is dissolved into the ceaseless ebb and flow of non- or trans-human existence. There is always an acute sense of the point at which the tiny human figure, such as we glimpse at the beginning of *The Return of the Native*, rising up from the dome of the distant barrow 'like a spike from a helmet', disappears, and we can see only the heath. But for both Hardy and Gissing, the viewpoint from which suffering humanity can be observed with perfect aesthetic (or rather anaesthetic) detachment, must remain only a relative perspective, if the positive act of relationship and communication, the writing of novels, is to continue. It is arguable that it was exactly this balance between identification and withdrawal that Hardy felt he could no longer sustain within the terms of the novel.

Nothing is more problematic in the study of these late-Victorian years than the nature of the critical changes of consciousness, reflected in the altering perspectives, rhythms and styles of the dominant fictional forms. In Gissing's own case, the patterns of contradictory and frustrated desire reflect both the personal, inner proclivities previously suggested, and the objective issues of class and sexual relationship studied within the narrative. We shall go on to study the working of these contradictions through the specific novels.

Part I

THE CITY, CLASS AND 'CULTURE'

1 The Writer and the City

Historians and sociologists have made us familiar with the social and economic implications of the unprecedented scale of urbanisation in the nineteenth century. This chapter and the specific studies of Gissing's early novels that follow will be concerned with the human consciousness of the city, as it finds expression in various writers and works throughout the century. In the changing experience and interpretation of life in the city are concentrated several interrelated images and issues that become in the end inseparable: the visual images of the city, of physical scenes and locations, rooms and streets; images of individuals, crowds, masses, classes and communities; problems of relationship, and the desire for knowledge and love; and beneath all these, the issue of language, of finding words and styles to explain these experiences to oneself and to others.

In 1862 Henry Mayhew introduced a survey of London's prisons (written in collaboration with John Binny) with a chapter entitled 'London Considered as a Great World'. Carrying through this image with characteristic relish, he wrote:

> Viewing the Great Metropolis, therefore, as an absolute world, Belgravia and Bethnal Green become the opposite poles of the London sphere — the frigid zones, as it were, of the Capital; the one icy cold from its exceeding fashion, form, and ceremony; and the other wrapt in a perpetual winter of withering poverty.[1]

It is a vision that suggests the basic contradiction in the human response to the changing experience of the city at this time. On the one hand, there is the sense of the city as an absolute, unified entity, organism or world; on the other, the sense of this world as a manifestation of some of the most absolute oppositions and disconnections between human

31

beings. The city is felt to pose the most perplexing problems of identity, and to provide the most extreme, but at the same time representative, experiences of dislocation. But if life in the city becomes imbued with the connotations of a 'Fall' from a prelapsarian state of innocent integration (rural or provincial), it carries also the potential consolations of a Fortunate Fall. If one continuing impulse is towards the nostalgic return to a provincial Eden, it is counterbalanced by a desire to accept the challenge and subdue the mystery, with its threats, promises and solicitations. It is this *desire* to understand with which we shall be concerned, the desire to penetrate through the bewildering appearances, masks and façades, to a hidden 'reality' that will redeem the fallen world and the fallen Self.

It is of inestimable importance that in literary terms, 'the city' invariably meant London. The new industrial cities of the north, above all of course Manchester, did indeed have an enormous imaginative impact, especially through their images of stark and extreme class confrontation. But the Manchester of Mrs Gaskell, the Preston of *Hard Times*, are primarily places to be visited, out of conscience, duty or fear. London, the seductive, the magical, is to be lived in. Against the new and simplified images of the 'mass' projected by the actual conditions of work in the large-scale factories of the northern industrial city, London offered the more difficult but more enticing images of subtle and mysterious differentiation, of the peculiar, the unique, the eccentric. When Arnold Bennett refers at the end of the century to the 'imperious fascination' exercised on his young provincial aspirant by the metropolis, he is setting his first novel, *A Man from the North* (1898), in the traditional perspective.

At the beginning of the century we see a critical pattern emerging in Wordsworth's well-known Book VII of the *Prelude*, 'Residence in London'. There is the challenge and threat of London's 'blank confusion', but this is met by the observer — narrator's desire to find coherence and significance, to see 'the parts/As parts, but with a feeling of the whole'. We find a more innocent, but equally instructive perspective in Pierce Egan's *Life in London* (1821), which belongs to a continuing genre based on the exhilarating variety and 'colour' of urban life. This sort of celebration of boisterous urban roguery goes back at least to the Elizabethans, to Greene's *Coney-Catching Tracts* and Dekker's *Gull's Horn-Book*. But even in Egan we can see the celebration receiving some prophetic qualifications. Before conducting his three gentlemen tourists round the 'sights', Egan offers a general view of London's characteristics. Above all, London is the place where men can find out the *truth* about themselves. It is the place of tests, trials and decisions, the place 'where all can view themselves at full length, affording innumerable opportunities either to push forward, to retreat, to improve or to decide'. It is the images of confrontation and competition that he stresses.

> It is in London, too, that almost at every step, TALENT will be found jostling against TALENT — and greatness continually meeting with greatness, — where ABILITY stares ABILITY full in the face — and where *learning*, however extensive and refined, is opposed by *learning* equally erudite and classical. *Intellect* also meets with a formidable opponent in *intellect*. *Independence* likewise challenges *independence* to its post. And where *superiority* on the one side always operates as a check upon *superiority* on the other, that *self-importance* may be humbled and *egotism* pulled down and exposed.[2]

The last sentence is particularly revealing, for the notion of the city as a self-regulating moral organism, in which conflicting interests maintain a natural and moral balance of power, grows out of the same rationalised optimism as the 'laws' of the classical economists. And yet, despite the naïveté, Egan is expressing a permanent, continuing aspiration here — that the city *can* be a moral organism, that harmony and unity can be achieved, beyond the evident separations. For Egan is certainly aware of these: 'The next door neighbour of a man in London is generally as great a stranger to him as if he lived at the distance of York.' On a larger scale, he can see the city as the manifestation of extremes of difference, but these can be seen and stated only in abstract and moral terms: 'The greatest love of and contempt for money are equally conspicuous . . .' It is a

vision miraculously untainted by particularities of class and
social condition. For his three tourists the city's variety is a
raucous, gaudy, but innocent carnival. We move with them,
without evident sense of irony, from palace to slum, from
Newgate to the Royal Exchange. If Dickens drew, as he
clearly did, on a tradition on which Egan set his colourful
imprint, it was precisely to emphasise and exploit the larger
significance of the continuities and discontinuities revealed
by such movements. For the descent into Newgate in
Pickwick marks the break with the tourist's innocence. We
might note that Egan does at least feel the need to provide
his tourists with the snug security of a 'camera obscura' view
of the Metropolis, by virtue of its possessing 'the invaluable
advantages of SEEING and not being *seen*'. There is a
disarming frankness about this confession, to which so much
writing about the city later in the century is less than prone.

Both Mayhew and Dickens extend the basic tension
between felt multiplicity and desired unity, by which in their
very different ways Wordsworth and Egan are both im-
pressed. Perhaps there seems little advance on Egan, when
Mayhew writes of London as 'essentially a city of antithesis — a city where life itself is painted in pure black and
white'. But the emphasis is changing. Mayhew can still refer
to the extremes in terms of moral abstraction ('that strange
conglomeration of vice, avarice, and low cunning, of noble
aspirations and humble heroism . . .'), but the virtue and the
vice are now beginnning to be located in relation to specific
social and human relationships. The contrast between wealth
and poverty is illustrated by a precise instance. The London
docks are the centre of world trade; through them pass
enormous concentrations of wealth and power. Against this
knowledge is set the physical scenes of the dock-labourers,
queuing up in the early morning, and desperately scrabbling
for work at the gates. Here is the real originality, the fusion
of the analytical and the imaginative, the intermingling of
aesthetic delight in the city's sights and sounds with a desire
to understand their origins and ends. Instead of Egan's coy
camera obscura, Mayhew offers us a view of London from a
balloon — a view of grand emblematic significance, since it
provides the literal vantage-point for the imaginative vision of

human totality to which Dickens aspires, and against which subsequent writers continue to define themselves.

> ... as the intellect experiences a special delight in being able to comprehend all the minute particulars of a subject under one associate whole, and to perceive the previous confusion of the diverse details assume the form and order of a perspicuous unity; so does the eye love to see the country, or the town, which it usually knows only as a series of disjointed parts ... become all combined, like the coloured fragments of the kaleidoscope, into one harmonious and varied scene.[3]

Extrapolated from its context, this could be one of the first (and shrewdest) recognitions of the essential imaginative patterns beneath Dickens's novels.

For the images consciously marshalled by Mayhew provide Dickens with the dramatic energy of the narrative in its search for a human unity beneath the evident disconnections. Instead of a contradiction baldly stated, there is a progressive interplay between the desire to find knowledge and love, and the subtly resistant phenomena and experiences of the city. The desire and the resistance are forces equally matched, locked in a titanic struggle, that neither precludes nor guarantees a final resolution. First there is the apparent sense of absolute disconnection, of every sight and sound, every scene and person being irredeemably strange, unknown and unknowable. The city is a landscape of strangers and secrets, its buildings, inhabitants and relationships frozen and locked, never to be entered, understood or possessed. Here, in this great passage from *A Tale of Two Cities*, Dickens gives memorable expression to the initial and perhaps ultimate terror, that in its permanent unknowability, the city is the City of Death, or of Death-in-Life.

> A wonderful fact to reflect upon, that every human creature is constituted to be that profound secret and mystery to every other. A solemn consideration, when I enter a great city by night, that every one of those darkly clustered houses encloses its own secret; that every beating heart in the hundreds of thousands of breasts there, is in

some of its imaginings, a secret to the heart nearest it!
Something of the awfulness, even of Death, is referable to
this. No more can I turn the leaves of this dear book that I
loved, and vainly hope in time to read it all. No more can I
look into the depths of this unfathomable water, wherein,
as momentary lights glanced into it, I have had glimpses of
buried treasure and other things submerged. It was
appointed that the book should shut with a spring, for ever
and for ever, when I had read but a page. It was appointed
that the water should be locked in an eternal frost, when
the light was playing on its surface, and I stood in
ignorance on the shore. My friend is dead, my neighbour is
dead, my love, the darling of my soul is dead; it is the
inexorable consolidation and perpetuation of the secret
that was always in that individuality, and which I shall
carry in mine own to my life's end. In any of the
burial-places of this city through which I pass, is there a
sleeper more inscrutable than its busy inhabitants are, in
their innermost personality, to me, or than I am to them?[4]

It is one of the most moving passages in all Dickens, and it
concentrates some of the central images with which we shall
deal, the image of the lonely night-walker set over against a
massive sleeping community, the image of the receding or
unreachable hidden secret (the 'buried treasure'), and the
interchange between separation, ignorance, inscrutability and
death.

Yet if the terror of this absolute reification can never be
wholly abolished, it *is* possible to unlock some secrets,
discover some connections, and thus melt the frozen labyr-
inths in which human vitality is incarcerated. There are two
radically different movements towards the revelation of unity
beneath diversity; it is a continuing, perhaps permanent
ambiguity. For on the one hand, there is the progressive
perception that we are all subject to the same conditions and
laws. We are all trapped in the fog, and all susceptible to the
disease, that dominate *Bleak House*. This is of course at
best a negative or passive unity, but it can be used for very
different purposes. In so far as it points to a shared humanity
according to which we are all the subjects of Time and Death,

it can serve to affirm a passive and metaphysical unity, a unity discoverable only in symbols that refer to planes of experience beneath or beyond consciousness, in myth or death. In *Our Mutual Friend*, the river provides exactly this focus for the recognition of a shared humanity; but it can only be experienced subjectively, and, symptomatically, by a violent and quasi-religious purgation. Eugene Wrayburn's baptism into new life is by means of descent to a plane of experience (the fall into the river, and the marriage to the working-class girl, Lizzie Hexam) that remains fixed outside or beyond the level of 'ordinary' existence. The heart of darkness and truth can only be visited. The knowledge and love discovered there can only provide a subjective and extra-ordinary consolation amid the continuing oppressive disconnections of Podsnapland.

On the other hand, this discovery of a passive unity can be interpreted less in terms of the private oracular wisdom attained by the individual, than in terms of active threat to the stability of society as a whole. And this perspective leads to a different image of unity and community. For the violent blow that sends Wrayburn crashing into the river can be envisaged as the fate of a whole society. From this point of view, the violence and disease to which a whole society is vulnerable can prompt a vision not so much of communal suffering as of communal destruction. But the destruction can then be seen as the prelude to a communal rebirth, physical and spiritual. This is the import of the famous passage in *Dombey and Son*, 'Oh for a good spirit who would take the house tops off . . .':

> Bright and blest the morning that should rise on such a night: for men, delayed no more by stumbling-blocks of their own making, which are but specks of dust upon the path between them and eternity, would then apply themselves, like creatures of one common origin, owing one duty to the Father of one family and tending to one common end, to make the world a better place![5]

This is the third main aspect of Dickens's response to the city, the vision of an actual human unity being born out of the destruction and suffering of the present negative community.

For now there is a space between the passive sharing of 'one common origin' and 'one common end' in which men can act together as well as suffer together.

The major shift in consciousness between Dickens and later Victorian writers is in the recession of this confidence in the 'blest morning'. The city still epitomises the challenging unknown, but the balance of power has been radically altered between perceiver and perceived, Self and Other. Instead of the active assault, the attempt to survive; instead of progressive understanding and connection, the acquiescence in ignorance and isolation.

Gissing had suffered in Manchester and Chicago before he came to London in the autumn of 1877. Four years later he was able to write to his sister Ellen with a peculiarly intimate knowledge of the struggle for survival that was, for him, the central experience of life in the city.

> . . . this huge wilderness of a town, where no one has any friends and where one doesn't even know by sight — a fact — the people who live in the same house. Struggling for a living in London is very much like holding yourself up, after a shipwreck, first by one floating spar and then by another; you are too much taken up with the effort of saving yourself, to raise your head and look if anyone else is struggling in the waves, and if you do come into contact with anyone else, ten to one it is only to fight and struggle for a piece of floating wood.[6]

Gissing's London is as empty as Dickens's was full, a world of chronic want that will be mostly fully dramatised in *The Nether World*.

In an even more memorable image than Gissing's one of shipwreck, Hardy expressed this sense of continuing crisis and exposure.

> In the City. The fiendish precision or mechanism of town-life is what makes it so intolerable to the sick and infirm. Like an acrobat performing on a succession of swinging trapezes, as long as you are at particular points at precise instants, everything glides as if afloat; but if you are not up to time — .[7]

The trapeze and the floating spar — given the different elements of air and water, they are curiously similar images. For these are the only objects the city seems to provide for the sustaining of identity, the perilous floating or floundering. It is interesting to find this image of the acrobat and the trapeze being used by Arthur Symons in a volume of short stories entitled *Spiritual Adventures* (1905) — dedicated to Hardy. In the superb story 'Christian Trevalga', the concert pianist of the title imagines the mechanical activity of his performance to be similar to that of the trapeze-artist, and then projects the image beyond this to characterise his whole public identity.

> For ever on the trapeze of sound, his life, the life of his reputation, risked whenever he went through his performance before the public; yes, he was only an acrobat, doing tricks with his fingers.[8]

Though Gissing's image typically refers to a state in which the individual has *already* in some sense fallen, for all three writers the maintenance of identity is associated with a perilous edge of survival. Beyond the edge of the spar or the trapeze, there is only vacancy, as Symons's artist discovers in his progressive absorption into a disembodied inner world.

The Self is now embattled, anxious and defensive with a desperation unknown to Dickens. In a note just preceding the one quoted above, Hardy wrote:

> London appears not to *see itself*. Each individual is conscious of *himself*, but nobody conscious of themselves collectively, except perhaps some poor gaper who stares round with a half-idiotic aspect.
>
> There is no consciousness here of where anything comes from or goes to — only that it is present.[9]

It is the same negative community of insulated, self-engrossed egos as Gissing suggested. And if it is only the 'poor gaper' who is conscious of this general condition (an ironic version of the young provincial aspirant), there is a deep scepticism about even his ability to penetrate to specific meanings. The poor gaper at least desires to understand, but his vision is arrested at the level of the immediate, the apparent, the

present. The initial excitement of the strange phenomenon
does not lead to a growing perception of its origins and ends,
its 'historical' significance, but instead to a deepening pessimism about the possibility of *any* knowing.

One of the most revealing expressions of this sort of
scepticism is made by Henry James in his preface to *The
Princess Casamassima*, written for the collected New York
edition, 1907–9. Describing the genesis of the novel in his
first year of prolonged residence in London (1877), James
talks of the 'assault' made by the great city on his
imagination. We note that in contrast to Dickens, it is,
unequivocally, the city that is now the aggressor. And yet, it
is a deliberate connection that James seems to be making
with Dickens, when he goes on to talk of London's secrets
and mysteries, of

> . . . a mystic solicitation, the urgent appeal, on the part of
> everything, to be interpreted and, so far as may be,
> reproduced . . .
> . . . to a mind curious, before the human scene, of
> meanings and revelations, the great grey Babylon easily
> becomes, on its face, a garden bristling with an immense
> illustrative flora.[10]

'Interpretation', 'reproduction' — these are key words in
James's critical vocabulary, 'reproduction' standing custom-
arily for the uncritical, 'naturalistic' recording of objective
reality, in opposition to the 'representation' that is the more
accredited shaping of that reality into a distilled 'interpretation'. There is something curious about James's use of the
words here; it would be more expected to find, 'the urgent
appeal . . . of everything, to be reproduced, and, so far as
may be, interpreted'. But James the prestidigitator is in full
flight here, juggling with the most provocative of dis-
crepancies between the curiosity of the 'interpreting' observer and the intractability of the phenomena to be
'reproduced'. This is why the interpretation has to *precede*
the reproduction. It is this anomaly that James tries to
resolve when he suggests a defence against the charge of
vagueness in his picture of London.

Shouldn't I find it in the happy contention that the value I wished most to render and the effect I wished most to produce were precisely those of our not knowing, of society's not knowing, but only guessing and suspecting and trying to ignore, what 'goes on' irreconcilably, subversively, beneath the vast smug surface?[1 1]

The '*value*' of 'not knowing'? The word is, typically, restricted to its technical (painting) sense. James is pressing towards a perverse defiance, in which the artist effectively aligns himself with society's smugness — presumably out of a reluctance to align himself with Hardy's poor gaper. But the calculated belligerence clearly has its source in the same concern with survival as the other writers.

What it all came down to was, no doubt, something like *this* wisdom — that if you haven't, for fiction, the root of the matter in you, haven't the sense of life and the penetrating imagination, you are a fool in the very presence of the revealed and assured; but that if you *are* so armed you are not really helpless, not without your resource, even before mysteries abysmal.[1 2]

It is bold to claim this as 'wisdom', for it is a mystifyingly generous gift to the imagination to call it '*penetrating*' when James has just previously admitted, and is just going on again to admit, the impenetrability of 'mysteries abysmal'. Whatever else the imagination can be called, it cannot be called 'penetrating'. For James has implied an absolute divorce between the subjective world of imagination and knowledge, and the sphere of objective reality, whether it be 'the revealed and assured' or 'mysteries abysmal'. The gift of imagination enables the privileged owner not in fact to penetrate, but to survive. The fear of 'not knowing' can thus be contained, since the imagination can, in the case of emergencies, supply its own reality.

If we place Gissing's London directly beside Dickens's, it is the evident absences and depletions that we notice first. The city has been drained of its epistemological excitement; the blank streets, the gritty light, the coarse sounds, seem to provoke sullen resignation rather than vigilant expectancy; we have been tramping around all day with an increasing conviction that today, like yesterday and tomorrow, will bring neither food, lodging, nor human companionship. And yet, beneath the insistent gloom, there is a voice and an attitude that does make connection, however remote, with Dickens. The point of contact is with the image of the wakeful watcher in the passage from *A Tale of Two Cities*. Both there and in the passage from *Dombey and Son,* the city was seen shrouded in darkness and, apparently, in sleep. Dickens's stress is characteristically on the active desire to penetrate the darkness, and take the house-tops off. With Gissing, on the other hand, we have become far more concerned with the anxiety of the lonely watcher, still desiring knowledge and connection, but becoming progressively sceptical about their fulfilment, about a literal or metaphorical dawn. Through the mouth of Henry Ryecroft, Gissing recalls how little comfort the dawn used to bring when it did come. 'Waking at early dawn used to be one of the things I most dreaded.'

As Raymond Williams has suggested in his recent book, *The Country and the City* (1973), Gissing's vision of the City of Night is close to that of James Thomson ('B.V.'). In his early poem, 'The Doom of a City' (1857),[13] less well known than the later 'The City of Dreadful Night', we can see some pertinent connections. This extraordinary visionary poem is built around a contrast between the isolated, stigmatised consciousness of the wakeful poet, and the secure, frozen fixity both of the 'real' city and its inhabitants, which he leaves, and the imagined city of stone to which he sails. The insomnia is now deliberate and significant. The watcher is no longer accidentally awake, as it were, just happening to 'enter a great city by night', as in *A Tale of Two Cities*. The watcher, embedded already deep within the city, cannot get to sleep. His difference from the rest of slumbering humanity is stressed, and the ambiguity about the consequent stigma and privilege of his wakefulness becomes crucial.

The mighty City in vast silence slept,
Dreaming away its tumult, toil, and strife:
But sleep and sleep's rich dreams were not for me . . .

In the last year of a life that surpassed even Gissing's in physical and mental misery, Thomson devoted a whole magnificent poem to this experience of 'Insomnia' (1882),[14] in which all the exile's sense of exclusion from normality erupts into bizarre images of distorted time. Eventually he can stand it no longer, and with a movement that will become familiar, he gets up to pace the deserted streets. These are images, central to the later Victorian years, of solitary, brooding consciousness, exiled from the slumbering security in which the mass of humanity, perhaps civilisation itself, is steeped.

In Thomson's early poem, the ambiguities of this exile and of the apparent security are driven through to apocalyptic proportions. The nightmare 'Mausolean City' to which he sails is frozen to stone:

> The vigorous heart and brain and blood and breath,
> Stark, strangled, coffined in eternal stone.

Yet the waking dreamer registers more than simple horror at this total arrest of life. Wherever he looks, he finds

> . . . all this blissful human kind
> Lifted up from clay's corruption into marble firm and fair.

His admiration for this freedom from vicissitude alternates with an instinctive repulsion to create a characteristic emotional pattern, one that we shall find in Gissing. On the one hand, the isolated individual cherishes and clings to his lonely wakefulness; he alone is alive, awake and conscious. But on the other hand, he feels a deep guilt at his separateness, and consequent attraction to the obliterating community, to absorption into the frozen mass, of communal sleep or death. The second of the poem's four sections ends with this direct expression of longing for absorption.

> Thank God, I soon shall cease to be alone;
> My mad discordant life is nearly blended
> With all this realm's unsuffering death of stone.

The rest of the poem describes the destruction of the Mausolean City, and the dreamer's return to the old city. But the relation between the two cities, as the meaning of the destruction, is held in doubt. For the destruction that

overtakes the city of stone seems to carry with it a vision of
transcendent spiritual life to which the stony figures can now
attain, a vision from which the lonely dreamer is as excluded
as he was previously from their petrifaction. Has he therefore
witnessed a communal redemption from a *general* human
condition of spiritual arrest, or the prophetic destruction of a
particular society's disastrous fixity? For when he returns to
the old city, he finds difference as well as similarity. Though
it is dark and oppressive, 'Its dark suggestions were of Life,
not Death'. *This* city is absorbed in sleep, not in death. The
dreamer is overcome with a sense of human compassion and
of the possibility of an active human community, as opposed
to the transcendent redemption of the stony city.

> A flood of awe and fear and love and pity
> Swelled in my heart and overflowed my eyes
>   With unexpected tears . . .

Yet the dreamer now has a responsibility, to proclaim the
warning and convert the threat of the stony city's negative
community into the positive and living community.

It is instructive to find another writer using very similar
images in a short, little-known poem, a few years earlier. In
1851 Meredith published his first book of poems. The one
that concerns us is called 'The Sleeping City'.[15] Again the
central theme is the contrast between a lonely wakeful
observer, and the general and ambiguous community of sleep.
The narrator compares himself to the princess 'in the eastern
tale', who paces through 'a marbled city pale'. She alone is
awake and alive — 'Herself the only child of change'. Everyone and everything else is frozen — 'The seemingness of
Death, not dead'. It is then the contradictory emotion of the
isolated individual that connects so strikingly with
Thomson's poem. The princess feels herself succumbing to
the general sleep, and feels first alarm — 'Her alien heart
shrank from the charm' — but then expansion and peace:

> Yet as her thoughts dilating rose,
> Took glory in the great repose.

The poet thus identifies his own contradictory emotions as
he paces the empty city streets:

Like such a one I pace along
This City with its sleeping throng;
Like her with dread and awe, that turns
To rapture, and sublimely yearns;

Again it is the double movement of dread and rapture, with
the unresolved energy of 'yearning'. The sleep from which he
is exiled then receives various interpretations, sleep as peace,
sleep as respite from passion, sleep as the therapeutic
expression of secret aspirations. Yet the crucial ambiguity
about the nature of this community is the same as in
Thomson's poem. For just as the poet seems to build up to a
climactic revelation of human connection ('Now while dumb
nature owns its links,/And from one common fountain
drinks') the vision is projected, with a harsh disappointment,
into the frozen images of the transcendent and eternal. This
community cannot be translated into speech (*'dumb*
nature'), action, movement; it is arrested, petrified as if by
Medusa. We are back in the princess's 'marbled City'.

The energies and movements of these poems are very close
to those that shape Gissing's response to the city in his early
novels. Gissing's is a City of Night, in which the separated,
wakeful individual gnaws restlessly at the problem of his
separation from the mass of humanity. With alternating pride
and shame, he nurses the sense of his superiority to and
exclusion from the community of literal and metaphorical
sleep in which ordinary men are sunk. Yet the *desire* to
transform this exile into something more positive is continually reborn, even if it is as regularly frustrated.

Rooms and streets — these are the dominant locations in
Gissing. The single room is set against the streets as the locus
for all the most intense emotions. It is the scene of those
characteristic dramas of married hell, in which all human
energies are narrowed down to the bitterest confrontations.
In Gissing's first novel, *Workers in the Dawn* (1880), Arthur
Golding finds that marriage has trapped him in just this way.
'For six months the single room which he occupied with his
wife was the sole scene of his existence.' The presence of
another person complicates without relieving the essential
loneliness of this single room. Again and again we find

Gissing's characters alone in their rooms at night, waiting and watching. In this extract from *Workers in the Dawn*, we see a paradigmatic situation of expectancy. Arthur Golding has just returned from rescuing his alcoholic wife from a pub brawl. While she lies in a drunken stupor (an ironic parody of the 'normality' of sleep), he stands brooding beside her. Big Ben strikes midnight.

> In a garret on the opposite side of the street a dull light was burning, and it was now the only light visible in the houses around. Arthur began to find employment for his thoughts in speculating as to the cause of the light. Most likely some one was lying in the garret ill, perhaps dying; or perhaps it was only a husband or a wife sitting in all but hopeless expectation for the loved one to return, even though it were in a condition which it was agony to picture. With such watchers as these Arthur felt that he should henceforth have a keen sympathy. Then, as he thus pictured imaginary scenes, a far-off shriek, piercing even though so distant, seemed to cut through the night. Here was a fresh horror, a fresh exercise for the thoughts. Was it the mere yell of a drunken woman being dragged through the streets? Was it a scream to awaken the neighbourhood to the terrors of fire? Or was it midnight murder? He heard the policeman who had been tramping steadily along the street below suddenly pause and listen. But there was no second cry, the policeman continued to tramp on, and Arthur's thoughts wandered away to other themes.[16]

It is exactly at the point of *speculation* that we are arrested along with Arthur, the state of 'not knowing' so deliberately invoked by James in his preface to *The Princess Casamassima*. For Gissing, only the desire to know the hidden, inner meaning of the light and the shriek maintains the attenuated possibility of fulfilled knowledge. There *are* still signs to be interpreted, 'public' shareable events and experiences. The individual is not yet so imprisoned within the subjectivity of his own consciousness as to renounce the possibility of shared knowledge. But the signs are themselves arbitrary and commonplace, the everyday phenomena of depressed urban life; they contain no promise of transforming revelation, or buried treasures. For they are not, as they would be in Dickens, mysterious, but simply and neutrally opaque.

Yet there is a genuine commitment in the passage. It is not towards the deciphering of the signs themselves, but, characteristically, towards the shared, passive community of the 'lonely watchers', whom Arthur imagines in a similar position to his own. It is the most tentative and tenuous sort of community imaginable, as negative and hypothetical as any glimpsed in the previous examples – so it would seem from this passage at any rate. Yet we shall find that this notion of a shared but isolated wakefulness can become invested with such powerful allegiances as to put its 'negativeness' in doubt. John Addington Symonds, for example, made one of the most powerful and precise formulations of this commitment.

> In this age it is almost the greatest faith to have *no* faith, for the old faiths are passing away and the new one has not come, and the men of this generation are like travellers before daybreak, the majority asleep, the few awake and watching anxiously in darkness.[17]

This goes as deep as any single statement about the essential beliefs and feelings of a whole generation, that reached its fullest self-expression in the 1880s. For Gissing and Rutherford and Hardy as for Symonds, 'wakefulness' becomes a positive activity. Though never actually to be attained here and now in the City of Night, knowledge can and must still be desired.

Gissing's image of the lonely room finds corroboration among other writers of the time. There is another poem of Thomson's, 'In the Room',[18] that seems to connect with Gissing, in its intimation that the experience of the lonely room (here, a suicide's room) is coming to replace the Dickensian movements, meetings and recognitions, as the most pressing phenomenon of life in the city. Yet this sense of the lonely room is shared by a writer as remote from Gissing in temperament as Thomson is close. In his *Autobiography* (1902), Walter Besant describes his life as a student in London lodgings. Although the time to which he is referring is the mid-fifties, the experience he records corresponds exactly to that which Gissing associates with life in the

city in the eighties. Indeed, when Besant talks of the
constraints imposed by the absence of places to meet people
of the opposite sex, he could be describing the conditions
that must have weighed on the young Gissing in his own
student days in Manchester.

> No one appeared to know how desperately miserable an
> evening all alone in lodgings may be. I have sat with my
> books before me while the silence grew more and more
> intolerable, rising up all round as a cloud hiding the rest of
> the world. When my nerves would stand it no longer, I
> have taken my hat and rushed out into the streets.[19]

How familiar this sort of feeling is from Gissing! And Besant
sees it as a general condition.

> Why, there were clerks and students all round me; every
> house in my street was filled with them; every man sat in
> his own dismal cell and listened to the silence till his
> nerves could stand it no longer. Then he went out into the
> street.[20]

Yet the single room and the isolated watcher acquire this
sort of significance only in relation to the larger experience
of the city as a whole. In this respect, the dominant images
associated with the city as a totality in the 1880s are those of
intransigence, of immoveable and impenetrable relationships
and structures. When H. G. Wells looked back on the
muddled, emergent Socialist activity of the eighties, it was to
define his sense of distance from a time when men were
shackled by the 'persuasion that we were up against
essentially immutable institutions'. Even at Morris's Hammer-
smith meetings, to which the young Wells and his friends
enthusiastically trooped — 'There they all felt and spoke as if
they were in an absolutely fixed world . . .'[21] Morris himself,
in his lectures at least, was under no illusions about the 'vis
inertiae', the 'solid front of resistance' to change. For Gissing,
as for many others, this sense of intransigence was suggested
and apparently confirmed by the experience of the city, the
unyielding solidity of physical conditions of poverty and
squalor, and the equally unyielding conditions, as he saw it,
of the mass of human ignorance and egotism. For outside the

sphere of the single room, it has become increasingly difficult to see human beings other than in the mass — in this sense Gissing's London is closer to the northern industrial towns of mid-Victorian fiction that to Dickens's London. The people we do see in the streets can no longer merge in and separate out from a continuing flow as they do in Dickens. They are seen more sharply, *either* in the mass, *or* separately. Henry Ryecroft testifies to this vision, though with a smug sententiousness of which the earlier Gissing was rarely capable.

> Nothing is more rooted in my mind than the vast distinction between the individual and the class. Take a man by himself, and there is generally some reason to be found in him, some disposition for good; mass him with his fellows in the social organism, and ten to one he becomes a blatant creature, without a thought of his own, ready for any evil to which contagion prompts him.[22]

We note that the word is not 'connection' nor even 'contact', but *'contagion'* — the choice of a sour dogmatism.

There were plenty of physical manifestations of this 'mass' for Gissing to observe in the eighties. We know that Gissing was an avid observer on occasions such as the huge mass demonstrations in Hyde Park and Trafalgar Square, and the more regular mass meetings on Clerkenwell Green. Yet, while most readers have focused on the emotions of revulsion or compassion that are attached to this observation, it is the method and implications of Gissing's way of seeing that are crucial. For if one half of his deepest response to the city is his understanding of individual loneliness, the other half is his ability to diagnose and record a general condition of subjection and suffering. The following extract from a well-known passage in *Demos* exemplifies the most character-istic and eloquent style that can be found within this idiom of 'mass' observation. It is, symptomatically, a description of a cemetery.

> Not grief, but chill desolation makes this cemetery its abode . . . Here lie those who were born for toil; who when toil has worn them to the uttermost, have but to yield

their useless breath and pass into oblivion. For them is no
day, only the brief twilight of a winter sky between the
former and the latter night. Indistinguishable units in the
vast throng that labours but to support life, the name of
each, father, mother, child, is as a dumb cry for the
warmth and love of which Fate so stinted them.[23]

Here we see the connection with Thomson's City of Stone
and Meredith's sleeping city. For here too, the observer is set
over against a vast, silent, motionless community. It is a
revealing element in Gissing that the observer's compassion
should reach its climax in response to an absolute, arrested
passivity; for this is, at least primarily, a scene of actual
death, rather than of Thomson's death-in-life or Meredith's
sleep. Yet, as the passage makes clear, the other meaning is
not excluded — this is an analogue for the condition of
death-in-life in which the mass of humanity is trapped.

If this deep compassion represents the most positive
emotion available within this structure of relationship, of the
lonely individual set over against the generalised mass, it is
important to see the 'negative' response of extreme revulsion
as a necessary, or at least logical, corollary. In *Demos*, we see
the other version of the mass, in its active condition of brutal
violence, as well as in its passive condition of subjection and
death. The mob riot that emerges from the temporary
control of a mass meeting mocks the would-be Socialist
leaders' aspirations to organise this terrifying natural force.

The meeting was over, the riot had begun . . . Demos was
roused, was tired of listening to mere articulate speech; it
was time for a good wild-beast roar, for a taste of
bloodshed . . . Demos was having his way; civilisation was
blotted out, and club law proclaimed.[24]

In retrospect, we recognise the significance of the 'dumb cry'
that speaks from the tombstones. For, whether in passive
suffering or violent action, the single most important
characteristic of this 'mass' is that it has no articulate voice of
its own. There can be no dialogue between observer and
observed, when there is such an absolute barrier of articulate-
ness and consciousness between them.

Yet it is precisely Gissing's appalled awareness of this barrier that acquires such a caustic distinction when we place his work beside most of the other kinds of writing about the city at this time. There emerged in the 1890s, as one of its initiates later noted, 'quite a cult of London and its varied life, from costers to courtesans'.[25] This cult extended from a group of writers that has been called the 'Cockney school' at one extreme, to the aesthetic connoisseurs who followed Whistler's lead at the other. (It is Holbrook Jackson who suggests Whistler as the key figure, who 'taught the modern world how to appreciate the beauty and wizardry of cities'.)[26] In fact, the similarities between the 'naturalistic' and 'aesthetic' attitudes are in the end far more instructive than the differences.

In a recent book on the representation of the working-classes in Victorian fiction,[27] P. J. Keating has made some unexpected claims for the 'Cockney' writers' success in recording working-class experience 'in its own terms' (recorded in its own language and judged according to its own values). Another writer, H. J. Dyos, has talked of 'the authentic literature of the slums' produced by Morrison, Whiteing and the others, in which 'something of the rhetoric of both the dignity and degradation of life in the slums' is captured.[28] It is true that a break-through of sorts was achieved by Kipling's gift for mimicking some of the idioms, the rhythm, pace and wit of 'ordinary', and specifically Cockney, speech. But this localised verisimilitude can be grossly misleading, if we elevate it as Keating does:

> ... the eccentricities which turned a class of people into a caricature are removed and a way of life is expressed in the speech.[29]

In fact the mania for phonetic accuracy whan carried to its extremity by a Barry Pain virtually obstructs the expression of anything at all, let alone anything as grandiloquent as a 'way of life'.

> The other dye I 'appened ter pick up a extry 'alf-thick-un throo puttin' money on my opinyun of the Gran' Neshnal.[30]

Perhaps the most relevant question is: who is this being
written *for*? It relies on the assurance that the narrator, a
Cockney bus-conductor, will stick unremittingly to his role as
a colourful foreigner, spinning anecdotes in his mangled
English for the amusement of the reader-tourist. Throughout
the slum-fiction of the nineties, working-class characters are
invariably returned to the strictest theatrical conventions
governing the narration of the jape, the joke, the clever ruse.
For the limited extensions of experience and gains in
verisimilitude made by Kipling and Morrison at the highest
point, and Pain, Pugh, Pett Ridge and Rook at the lowest,
are invariably based on a comfortable divorce between
observer and observed that is all the more crippling for its
lack of acknowledgement. The quality of this divorce is
determined by the fact that the observer's judgements on
working-class experience are not, as Keating claims, generously withheld, but have become, insultingly, *unnecessary*.

The perniciousness of the notion that these or any other
writers somehow record an unmediated 'way of life' that is
allowed to 'speak for itself' really deserves more detailed
exposure. As so often, one way of testing such claims is to
look for a point of crisis.

> 'Liza', he said again, his voice growing hoarse and
> thick — 'Liza, will yer?'
> She still kept silence, looking away and continually
> bringing down her fist. He looked at her a moment, and
> she, ceasing to thump his hand, looked up at him with
> half-opened mouth. Suddenly he shook himself, and
> closing his fist gave her a violent, swinging blow in the
> belly.
> 'Come on', he said.
> And together they slid down into the darkness of the
> passage.[31]

This is the single most important moment in Maugham's first
novel, *Liza of Lambeth* (1897) — Liza's seduction by her
married admirer: but the narrator's studied 'impartiality'
becomes, at such a point, a criminal evasion of narrative
responsibility. One looks in vain for a language capable of
representing experiences that lie outside or beneath the limits

of the suspiciously ritualised 'way of life', the bank-holiday outings, the street brawls and so on. The best of these writers can indeed *gesture* towards such experiences — the hysteria beneath the jaunty stoicism of Kipling's soldiers, the lonely vulnerability of Morrison's children, even the somewhat sentimentalised passions in Nevinson's *Neighbours of Ours* (1895). But the disruption is only a threat. Reader and narrative remain essentially immune; we are back with the camera obscura.

In other sorts of contemporary writing concerned with class and the city, we can watch a similar consolidation of the distance between observer and observed, even or especially within an idiom of apparent concern or tolerance. Booth's social investigations provide a classic instance. They are indeed based on a deep concern, but it is a concern that with the same methods and motives as those of the Fabians, reduces the complex and human reality of what is observed to a set of controllable 'facts'. Thus fixed and circumscribed the life and the labour become a recognisable 'problem', to be solved, scientifically, by the detached planners. The 'objectivity' of the approach effectively neutralises the possibility of any human threat or interaction between the faceless, recording observers, and the slums, the dirt and disease.

> At the outset we shut our eyes, fearing lest any prejudice of our own should colour the information we received. It was not till the books were finished that I or my secretaries ourselves visited the streets amongst which we had been living in imagination.[32]

But the 'information' is of course already prejudiced by a way of seeing, for it is culled by the representatives of authority, the school board visitors, the investigators and officials of Charity.

> With the insides of the houses and their inmates there was no attempt to meddle. To have done so would have been an unwarrantable impertinence.[33]

The concepts of 'meddling' and 'impertinence' belong, for all the honourableness of the intention, not to an ideal sphere of pure objectivity as Booth believes, but to a specific way of seeing, that assumes the universal primacy of the virtues of courtesy and tact in the conduct of face-to-face relationships.

At the other extreme from Booth's studied impartiality is the hectic, overtly rhetorical idiom of the literature of 'exposure', of Mearns's *The Bitter Cry of Outcast London* (1883) and Jack London's *The People of the Abyss* (1903). The paradoxes of this idiom are still very familiar, the intermingling of genuine elements of protest with the crude exploiting of sensation. W. T. Stead's well-known series of articles on juvenile prostitution for the *Pall Mall Gazette* in 1885 is an exemplary case. In Jack London we see the contradictions at their sharpest. As a piece of journalism, *The People of the Abyss* is first-rate, full of precise observations of individuals and places, of doss-houses and work-houses and cellars. More important, he can catch an individual's way of speech with an apparent disinterestedness that the Cockney 'realists' could rarely afford in their brutal manipulation of 'colour'. Yet it is against the limits of this way of seeing that we continually lurch.

> A young sot; a premature wreck; physical inability to do a stoker's work; the gutter or the workhouse; and the end — he saw it all, as clearly as I, but it held no terrors for him. From the moment of his birth, all the forces of his environment had tended to harden him, and he viewed his wretched, inevitable future with a callousness and unconcern I could not shake.[34]

The 'seeing' is all the observer's. For he can approach so far, even achieve a matey kind of fellowship over a pint in the pub, only to cut short the potential energy or extension of the relationship by the crude, projected generalisation. 'He saw it all as clearly as I' — it is a confident appropriation of the young worker that Orwell will reproduce as he watches a young girl cleaning a drain-pipe from the train. 'She knew well enough what was happening to her — understood as well as I did . . .'[35] The object of observation, thus tamed and appropriated, can then be *used* for the desired gesture or attitude, in Orwell's case a humane, embittered compassion, in London's an embarrassingly inebriated romanticism. As he watches the 'young sot' strip down for the night, he muses mournfully on the fate of '. . . this young god doomed to rack and ruin in four or five short years, and to pass hence without posterity to receive the splendid heritage it was his to bequeath'. In fact, London is essentially as immune from real interchange with the people among whom he moves as the Cockney 'realist'. For all the trumpeted intrepidity, it is with some amusement that we read of the alarm with which he rushes off to a Turkish bath to sweat away the germs from one particularly sordid expedition.

In all these different kinds of writing, the separation between viewer and viewed is confirmed rather than questioned; the result and symptom of this is the elevation of 'style'. Even for Booth and his team, the tense emphasis on 'style' becomes a means of *resisting* identification with the human meanings of the city rather than of extending and exploring them. Of course all writers are in quest of a style — or cannot escape from one; the question is always how far and in what ways the chosen or created style reveals or conceals. In the case of Arthur Symons's *London: A Book of Aspects* (1909), the created style is concerned with revealing certain limited aesthetic impressions with extreme absorption, and with resisting any more challenging connection with the actual human beings who live in the city. London is drenched in Whistlerian images of night, mist, lights, colours. Here is a typical celebration of the 'smoky rose' of a sunset.

> At such a point as the Marble Arch you may see conflagrations of jewels, a sky of burning lavender, tossed abroad like a crumpled cloak, with broad bands of dull purple and smoky pink, slashed with bright gold and decked with grey streamers.[36]

But, as Symons himself implicitly admits, this rapturous exoticism is based on a real human desperation. The external phenomena of the city can only be enjoyed 'for their own sake'; we can never hope to penetrate beneath the surface. The fellow-creatures who pass us in the street are not unknown-but-knowable; they are absolute and permanent aliens. The cultivation of surface and spectacle becomes therefore the virtue of necessity. London becomes transmuted by Symons (as the Cockney by the slum-realist) into a finished and stylised art-object. Yet beneath it all, it is the helpless scepticism of the detached cosmopolitan observer that we feel, as he tours London, Paris, Rome, Warsaw, the connoisseur of their sights and sounds, but not their people.

What, then, can we offer in positive contrast, a style in which revelation exceeds concealment? For clearly it is not a question of simple success or failure. It would be easy at this point to extend the discussion beyond the present context to Hardy and James, or Lawrence and Joyce, but if we contain it within the limits of what was referred to as 'realism' at the time, moving only slightly away from the direct issue of 'the city' itself, we can find some instructive suggestions in a couple of less acclaimed writers at work in the eighties and nineties: George Moore and Stephen Crane. This is no place for debating the nature of Moore's 'realism', or the extent to which, as has been claimed, he 'made a significant contribution to the development of modern fiction'.[37] But a purely local point can be made about the possibilities that Moore demonstrates in the two most relevant novels of his early years, *A Mummer's Wife* (1885) and *Esther Waters* (1894). One's first impression from reading them beside most comparable English novels of the time remotely susceptible to the designation of 'realistic', is that here is a breath of fresh air. Kate Ede and Esther Waters, the two principal figures, are not *molested* by the narrative. Moore is drawing from his French models a style of observation that seems generously free from the moral or social reference to which Gissing and the others are still painfully harnessed. It is a very different sort of 'impartiality' from that claimed for the Cockney school by Keating. Graham Hough has suggested the (perhaps unexpected) existence of a fundamental 'moral integrity' in Moore the writer,[38] and one can refer this integrity to his feeling for the *responsibility* of language — to mediate and not simply appropriate Esther Waters and her experience. What he admired in the French tradition, beyond his specific and transitory enthusiasms, was this respect for language as an active agent.

One thing that cannot be denied to the realists: a constant and intense desire to write well, to write artistically. When I think of what they have done in the matter of the use of words, of the myriad verbal effects they have discovered, of the thousand forms of composition they have created, how they have remodelled and refashioned the language in their untiring striving for intensity of expression, for the very osmazome of art, I am lost in ultimate wonder and admiration.[39]

We can discount the modish 'intensity of expression' and banal 'osmazome': it is the words 'remodel' and 'refashion' that are important.

There is a passage in the original version of *A Mummer's Wife*[40] which illustrates Moore's distance from most of his English contemporaries. It is a descriptive scene in which the lonely figure of Kate Ede is set over against a panoramic landscape of the Potteries town where she lives. Moore is drawing directly on Zola here for the 'fugal' movement, from human figure to scene and back again, but this is less important than the success of the adaptation. Our feelings of close involvement with Kate are deliberately dissipated by direction away to the pure, aesthetic contemplation of 'patches of grass, hard and metallic in hue' and the silhouette of the church spire in 'the liquid sunlight'. But the diversion serves only to heighten our involvement as we swing back to her.

Kate saw with the eyes and heard with the ears of her youth, and the past became as clear as the landscape before her. She remembered the days when she came to read on this hillside.[41]

The narrative line weaves away from Kate again to the unexpected treasures of the bleak landscape, whose characteristics are represented by verbs such as 'glittered', 'flickered', 'glinted', 'speckled', and adjectives such as, 'dazzling', 'metallic', 'fluffy', 'liquid', 'jagged', 'angular', 'dancing', 'vibrating', and so on. But the painterly interest in light and shade and line is charged with human intention. The passage ends by returning to Kate.

She had not been where she now stood for months, and under the influence of all her new-found emotions she wondered why she had never thought before of revisiting these old places. Now, sudden as the splash of a stone dropped into a well, the knowledge came to her that she was no longer happy, that her life was no more than a burden, a misery.[42]

This is the *motive* of the whole scene — the simple statement that 'she was no longer happy'. Yet how rich those words have become by the time we reach them, after our guilty loitering over the seductive landscape. Whatever the ostensible allegiance to a theory of determinism owed by the narrative as a whole, the particular resources revealed here make impossible a simple equation between character and environment, emotion and landscape, language and reality.

Stephen Crane offers a more solid display of confidence in language in a short story called *Maggie: A Girl of the Streets* (1893). It is based on the same urban myth as Maugham's *Liza*, in its tracing of the fall of the innocent girl, but otherwise there is a world of difference. For in Crane there is a genuine attempt to create a *new* language through which to articulate the experience of characters themselves remote from the author's or reader's capacities of expression. The language has to be 'new' — neither merely the author's own, nor merely the character's own, for it has to bridge and transform the distance rather than confirm and stabilise it. Crane's story does little more than suggest the way in which this can be done, but the language he finds shows creative resources of a radically different calibre from those of Kipling, for example.

Jimmie's occupation for a long time was to stand at street corners and watch the world go by, dreaming blood-red dreams at the passing of pretty women. He menaced mankind at the intersections of streets.

At the corners he was in life and of life. The world was going on and he was there to perceive it.[43]

Crane's language consistently expands rather than reduces the inarticulate energies of characters such as Jimmie (Maggie's brother). His 'blood-red dreams' are not objects of irony or detached contemplation. Instead we are drawn into the dreams and imaginings of Jimmie the truck-driver, his belief

> ... that he and his team had the inalienable right to stand in the proper path of the sun chariot, and if they so minded, obstruct its mission or take a wheel off.
>
> And if the god-driver had had a desire to step down, put up his flame-coloured fists and manfully dispute the right of way, he would probably have been immediately opposed by a scowling mortal with two sets of hard knuckles.[44]

In any English 'realist' of the eighties and nineties, including Gissing, such an imaginative leap would have had the effect of depreciating the 'objective' reality. Gissing uses classical allusion to exactly that effect in the Crystal Palace scenes in *The Nether World*, for example, and there is a hideously cheap chapter in Maugham's *Liza*, in which he mockingly describes a bank-holiday outing in the idiom of Phyllis and Corydon. But Crane's comic idiom belongs to the same vein as Dickens's; it unites and expands, rather than dividing and depreciating. The strategic hypothesis has the effect of *transforming* the 'reality', so that we actually see Jimmie scrapping with Apollo — just as we see that Megalosaurus 'waddling like an elephantine lizard up Holborn Hill' at the magnificent opening of *Bleak House*.

Clearly, Crane's style has its own limits. It works at its best, symptomatically, within the confines of the short story or short novel. But it is on this sort of confidence in the creative and transforming, rather than the defensive, power of language, that in their different ways, Wells, Lawrence and Joyce were soon to base their fictional writing. Gissing's great value, as we shall see, is in the clarity and intensity with which he stares across the lines of separation, but neither he nor the 'realists' of the nineties, satisfied with their comfortable strategies of evasion, achieve the same extension of perception and feeling as Crane.

2 Gissing's Early Social Novels, 1880-1887

i. WORKERS IN THE DAWN (1880)

Gissing's first novel displays the rift between a set of theoretical allegiances and more immediately felt experience that will be a continuing feature of his work. Yet it is precisely the implications and energy inherent in this rift that enliven the novel's otherwise intolerable length and gaucheness.

The opening scene is of market night in Whitecross Street. It is an extended description of the 'weary toilers of our great city' in attitudes of 'relaxation'. The degradation of the setting and the human beings in it is virtually total. Such slender compensations for the drudgery of their daily work as are provided by the weekly release may lead to even deeper misery and subjection. The fancy ornament that the young lad buys for the consumptive girl may tempt her 'to seek in the brothel a relief from the slow death of the factory or the work room'. Yet, if the idiom of generalised indignation and repulsion seems easily inherited, there is at the same time an urgency of narrative involvement that belies the traditional *security* from which the movement of protest proceeds. 'Walk with me, reader, into Whitecross Street . . .' That is familiar enough, the idiom of courteous invitation — let 'us' prepare to go and observe 'them'. But it is not long before this 'we' is suffering anxieties not normally associated with the magical immunity of the descending spectator.

> Now back into the street, for already we have become observed of a little group of evil-looking fellows gathered round the entrance.[1]

The observers observed; at first glance it may seem a trite, rhetorical trick. Yet it proceeds from Gissing's deepest feelings

and produces his observer-narrator's most positive characteristic, the ability to question the assumptions governing
conventional literary and social versions of poverty.

At an explicit level the narrative offers to expose the
fallacy of orthodox religious and humanitarian responses to
this scene of misery. Bill Blatherwick is a drunk and bestial
professional beggar who puts on an expert act as a one-
armed, blind widower, with Arthur Golding (the central
character) as his child accomplice. 'Charity' in such circumstances is a well-worn system of mutual exploitation between
'society' and 'the poor', according to which the poor act out
gestures of minimal moral probity (Arthur sings hymns), and
society responds with equally ritualised gestures of assuage-
ment. The leaders of the Charity Organization Society
certainly recognised that this sort of abuse was widespread,
but their attempts to deploy society's philanthropic resources
failed to convince Beatrice Webb that 'charity' was anything
other than 'twice cursed, it curseth him that gives and him
that takes'.[2]

Yet the extent to which philanthropy was still assumed to
be a natural attitude is suggested by one of the first
intelligent appraisals of Gissing's work, an essay by Edith
Sichel entitled, 'Two Philanthropic Novelists: Mr. Walter
Besant and Mr. George Gissing' (1888).[3] For all her
impartiality, Miss Sichel is in essential agreement with the
confident attitude of condescension implied by Besant's
benign advice to the would-be novelist: 'let him remember
that in story-telling, as in almsgiving, a cheerful countenance
works wonders'.[4] The idioms of 'sympathy' that had
dominated the works of Mrs Gaskell and George Eliot had
corresponded to some of the most imaginative elements in
the consciousness of the time. George Eliot was especially
articulate about the power of art to extend experience by
surprising 'even the trivial and selfish into that attention to
what is apart from themselves, which may be called the raw
material of moral sentiment'.[5] 'What is *apart* from themselves' — that is the crux. The motion of sympathy, whether
at a facile or profound level, proceeds from an initial
certainty about the distance between and relative positions of
Self and Other. It is exactly this certainty that Gissing no
longer possesses.

The deeper interest of the novel lies in Arthur Golding's continuing and eventually unresolved attempts to live in actual relationship with the working class. Edith Sichel quite rightly noted that Gissing seemed to write 'rather to make himself clear to himself and as a personal relief, than for any altruistic purpose'.[6] Arthur is the first of many Gissing protagonists to be plunged into the city and its apparently arbitrary situations of connection and exclusion, and through Arthur Gissing dramatises many of the contradictions in his own feelings of indignation and compassion. The crucial limitation of Arthur's social concern is that for all his proximity to the suffering poor as they pass him in the street, they remain essentially Other. 'Oh, Arthur, I could die of pity for them all!' cries old Tollady, as they watch the flow of wretched humanity.

Yet Gissing knew at a deep level the implications of this sort of intense, helpless compassion. They are acted out in the novel through Arthur's marriage to the 'fallen' working-girl, Carrie Mitchell, a marriage that is of course closely based on Gissing's own to Nell Harrison. He had already used the raw material of his emotional entanglement with her in the first of his Chicago stories, 'The Sins of the Fathers'.[7] For all its crudity, the story opens with a scene that is authentic Gissing — night in a great industrial town, a lonely girl weeping in a murky archway under a shattered gas-lamp. As Leonard Vincent, a student, hurries past, he is brought to a sudden halt, attracted by a face which 'held him for a moment as immovable as though he had been gazing upon the head of Medusa'. It is difficult to dismiss as cliché an image so deeply appropriate during these late-Victorian years for a familiar kind of arrest, compact of horror and attraction. The weeping girl, as Carrie Mitchell in the novel and Nell Harrison in real life, can throw a spell of the profoundest compassion over the helpless observer. Yet just as the narrator in Whitecross Street is bereft of the protective veil for his compassion, so does Arthur's sympathy carry an involvement and vulnerability remote from the conventional idioms of philanthropy. Significantly, the bond is formed between Arthur and Carrie as they wander the lonely streets together, repelled from the Christmas scenes of grotesque communal festivity at the lodging-house they share.

It is in his further exposure of the psychological workings of sympathy in their marriage together that Gissing shows his greatest perception. For Arthur, possessed of a cultural if not class superiority to Carrie, reproduces, even at the most humane and generous extreme of compassion, exactly the same patterns of division and dependence as dominate society in general. In his attempts to educate Carrie, we recognise the issues of control inherent in a situation in which one partner gives and the other is expected passively to receive. 'Why don't you let me speak as I'm used to?' is Carrie's affecting cry. For all the obvious identification of Gissing with Arthur, the honesty of the portrayed relationship exposes the possessiveness implicit in his attempts to 'raise' his wife, to shape her personality, language and habits to his own. No wonder that Carrie goes back to her drink — though for Arthur and Gissing, this is seen as confirming her innate hopelessness. All the scene of grim, grating squabbling carry an authenticity out of the range of most of the novel.

It is the failure of this concept of Charity and of social change as directed *by* one class or one individual *for* another, that provides the clue to the novel's central ambiguity. For Gissing, although he shows with a deep instinctive knowledge the fallacy of any notion of moral or social improvement that relies solely on an external shaping or teaching, still *wants* to believe in it. The desire, formed obviously enough by the immediate relation with Nell Harrison, is transferred to the most available general theory which is Positivism. Yet the superiority of the model prescribed in this novel by the idealised Helen Norman over that implied by middle-class Charity is far from obvious. For Octavia Hill's model of at least admirably specific virtues such as diligence, thrift, efficiency, cleanliness and sobriety, Helen Norman offers only a more elevated but incorrigibly abstract model of universal brotherhood. Though this novel led Gissing into association with Frederic Harrison and other Positivists, it is clear already to what a strain the willed allegiance to the religion of Humanity was being put. It required a blindness to or immunity from the hard, immediate experiences of social and personal disconnection, with which Gissing was fortunately not blessed, to be able to make the sort of grand emotional appeal that Harrison gloried in, to the 'sure and visible advent of a future of Peace and Industry, of common brotherhood, and human feeling'.[8]

ii. THE UNCLÁSSED (1884)

Gissing's next published novel goes on to examine in more detail the condition of exile and disalignment that was the submerged core of *Workers in the Dawn*. But at the centre of this novel, there is a discrepancy similar to that in the previous one between an extended intellectual debate and a close study of specific human relationships. The thinning of the debate and almost total excision of the Schopenhauerian element for the revised edition of 1895 make for a measurably sharper narrative without altering the essential conflict. By 1883, when the novel was mostly written, Gissing's intellectual development had been marked by a decisive rejection of Positivism and a temporarily im- passioned devotion to Schopenhauerian Pessimism. Schopenhauer provided a useful collocation of theoretical notions to support that urge to perfect separation from entanglement with 'the world' that is the novel's central motive. But as in *Workers in the Dawn*, the authenticity with which 'the world' is at times recorded puts in serious jeopardy the plausibility of *any* offered theoretical solutions.

In his central character, Osmond Waymark, Gissing tries to work out the possibility of a 'life apart' that stops short of an extreme philosophical pessimism. For though Waymark aspires towards a perfect autonomy of Self, he still retains the vestigial stigmata of social concern. With what will become a familiar emphasis, his disillusionment with actual political commitment is represented as having taken place in the past. Waymark defines in a tone of characteristically acrid self-exposure the falsity of Gissing's own early political commitment, a falsity for which Raymond Williams has offered the useful term, 'negative identification'.[9]

> That zeal on behalf of the suffering masses was nothing more nor less than disguised zeal on behalf of my own starved passions . . . I identified myself with the poor and ignorant; I did not make their cause my own, but my own

cause theirs. I raved for freedom because I was myself in the bondage of unsatisfiable longing.[10]

The 'starved passions' and the 'unsatisfiable longing', however, continue with an intensity for which Gissing has not been given credit when labelled as the 'poet of despair'. A letter from Gissing to Frederic Harrison shortly after the publication of this novel shows the sort of confused and violent energies with which he was struggling at this time.

> Surely, there is a sense wanting in me ... I feel the irresistible impulse to strive after my ideal of artistic excellence. It is true, as you said, that I have a quarrel with society, and that I suppose explains the instinct. But the quarrel is life-long; ever since I can remember I have known this passionate tendency of revolt ... I write these social passages in a fury; but I scribbled in precisely the same temper when I was ten years old.[11]

Much of the novel is concerned with this sort of debate in Gissing himself, between the exigencies of this 'passionate tendency of revolt' and the available modes of expression. In Waymark (who himself writes a novel), Gissing works out the terms of a fierce aestheticism, to which he can at least temporarily pin his colours. Though Gissing denied that Waymark's opinions were anything other than a dramatised point of view, it is clear that they draw on some of his own deepest feelings. In July 1883 he wrote to his brother: 'My attitude henceforth is that of the artist pure and simple. The world is for me a collection of phenomena, which are to be studied and reproduced artistically',[12] and a year later, after the publication of the novel: 'Human life has little interest for me, on the whole — save as material for artistic presentation'.[13] The artist hammers out an impregnable armour of Self by reducing the outside world to 'a collection of phenomena', devoid of significance, appeal or threat. But the imperious gestures are as hollow as the preceding naïve social enthusiasm, and Gissing's deeper allegiances to observed and felt reality would show him this.

In Gissing's first novel, Whitecross Street had provided an initial image of human degradation against which all the

subsequent energy of the narrative and characters sought to
define itself. Similarly, in this novel the slums of Litany Lane
and Jubilee Court provide the Hell-on-Earth from which
Waymark and his friend Casti seek to escape in the lonely
watch-tower of their *culture à deux*. That theirs is at best an
ambiguous response is made clear by the course of events in
which Waymark, who has squandered a small legacy, finds
himself employed as rent-collector for these slums by an old
friend of his father, Abraham Woodstock. Waymark, and
Gissing, are painfully aware that 'culture' of any definition
does not float serenely above the exigencies of everyday
material needs, and into Waymark's mouth Gissing puts one
of his bitterest conclusions, that 'Money means virtue; the
lack of it is vice'. Yet in keeping with his self-proclaimed
egotism, Waymark takes on the job that will bring him into
the closest possible confrontation with human misery, almost
in order to *prove* the immunity of his inner 'culture'. Money,
whether as wages or legacies, is conceived only as liberating
the inner Self from material exigencies. According to
Waymark's theory and conduct, it is only a positive agent of
release. The payment that he receives from his rent-collecting
has an autonomous power, absolutely separable from the
human connections and conditions under which it is earned.

In fact the human power of the slums *does* strike back at
the detached rent-collector and his master. First, the monster
Slimy, the incarnation of the slums' bestiality, attacks and
emprisons Waymark at a crucial point in the narrative.
Secondly, the landlord Woodstock is struck down by the
smallpox that emanates from a poisonous cellar, where a
dead child's body rots. The contrast with Dickens is more
striking than the connection. For instead of the inter-
connections of a whole society implied by the disease that
reaches out from Tom-all-Alone's even to the innocent Esther
Summerson, the disease of Gissing's slum strikes with
supreme tact and selectiveness only at the guilty landlord. Ida
Starr (and Waymark) escape miraculously untouched.

The effect, therefore, appears to be one of *concession* to
Gissing's sense of necessary interdependence, between the
world of the slums and the world of 'culture', between
money and freedom; but the stronger emphasis is on proving

that these worlds are separable. This brings us to the central problem of the novel, the 'heroine' Ida Starr. In the course of the novel she fills two of the most conventional fictional roles, that of the good-hearted or well-intentioned 'fallen woman', and that of the benevolent 'angel of mercy', yet it is at least part of Gissing's iconoclastic purpose to bring these roles together in one person. The novel opens with Ida, still a child, clasping in her arms a schoolmate, Harriet Smales. She has just split Harriet's head open with a slate for taunting her with her mother's prostitution. The embrace is compounded of tenderness and remorse, a painful knot of emotion in which fear, hatred and potential violence compete with compassion, guilt and responsibility. It is an image that draws on Gissing's own equivocal feelings towards the working class in general and his wife Nell in particular. Ida draws further on Gissing's own emotional disposition in her sense of un-deserved stigma. Like Arthur Golding, she is the child of a 'fallen' parent; her mother will turn out to be the daughter of the successful capitalist Woodstock. The central energy of the narrative will be devoted towards an escape from the intolerable conditions of stigma and bondage in which Ida finds herself, the 'fallen' world of her mother and Harriet Smales, and at its lowest extreme, the inhabitants of Litany Lane.

When Waymark and Ida first meet, it is his rejection of the economic definition of their possible relationship that draws her to him. Driven by a familiar restlessness into the city streets, Waymark is accosted by a prostitute. He rejects her services, but realising the extremity of her need, gives her all the little money he has. Ida is watching from close by, and expresses admiration for Waymark's rare generosity. The bond between them is thus formed by his refusal to accept society's moral and economic definition of the prostitute. Unfortunately, the major failing of this central relationship is that instead of asserting with Waymark that Ida's inner Self can *break* free from the repressive conditioning of the outer role, Gissing makes the more extravagant claim that this inner Self has never in fact been touched at all. Significantly, the nearest that Gissing comes to an admission that Ida *needs* purification of any sort is in the symbolic scene of her

midnight baptism in the sea. The admirable emphasis on
human resistance to the tyranny of circumstance shades over
into the less plausible assertion of a perfect, incorruptible
inner integrity.

The conclusion of the novel is therefore guided by the
most blatant sort of wish-fulfilment. After her purgation of
social guilt in prison, Ida is accepted back by her grandfather
Woodstock; he is uneasily tottering towards the role of the
benevolent rich old man. But the vital contradictions
between material contingency and personality are finally
scythed down by Ida's fairy-tale transformation into the
Angel of Mercy. With a transparency that amounts almost,
but unfortunately not quite, to irony, Ida sets out to atone
for the guilt of her release by energetic philanthropy towards
the Litany Lane tenants. In a scene that is one of the most
'ignoble' he ever wrote (to use one of his own favourite
words), Gissing shows us Ida dispensing cakes and soap in her
fairy-tale garden to the delighted urchins from the slums.
'Good, gentle, noble-hearted Ida!' It is a pity that, apart from
the few flashes of early vitality, she has rarely been allowed
to be anything else. When she clinches her etherealisation
(Ida *Starr*) by forgiving Harriet Smales, the girl who plotted
her arrest, we recognise that part of Gissing's interest in her
has been the separation out into perfect polarity of the two
aspects of his own relation to Nell Harrison, the desire and
the reality. Harriet Smales is perhaps the most authentic
character in the whole novel, in the infinite scrupulosity of
her hate. She represents that aspect of Nell that convinced
Gissing of her irreversible degradation. Ida, on the other
hand, represents his forlorn desire for the existence of an
ideal, graceful 'culture' beneath the unpromising exterior.
But the real significance, in both cases, is that 'character' is
assumed to be an unchangeable attribute whether, in
Harriet's case, it is in perfect concord with her conditioning
context or, in Ida's case, in perfect opposition.

The most important line of Gissing's subsequent development lies in his deepening scrutiny of the relationship
between personality, 'culture' and freedom on one side, and
economic and social needs and conditions on the other. But
in this novel, the naked intensity of the characters' 'starved

passions' and 'unsatisfiable longings' finally obscures all other issues, questions and solutions. What we remember is the quality of *desire* that drives all the main characters, the desperate need for affection, love or connection of any kind.

iii. DEMOS: A STORY OF ENGLISH SOCIALISM (1886)

Though written after *Isabel Clarendon* (1886) and *A Life's Morning* (1888), *Demos* was Gissing's third novel to be published. It remains one of his five most important novels (though not one of his five best), by virtue of its ambitious scope as the dramatisation of a total cultural and social crisis. In this respect it is the closest of his novels to the justly better-known and considerably more persuasive *New Grub Street*.

From the writing of the two intervening novels, Gissing took an increased awareness of the claim of a particular class to the maintenance of that 'culture' that had previously been the lonely consolation of his exiled intellectuals, Waymark and Casti. Since writing *The Unclassed*, he had himself experienced for the first time, through his connection with the Frederic Harrisons, the world of leisure and 'culture' enshrined in the English country house. That he had been something less than comfortable in such surroundings is suggested by Austin Harrison's account of a garden party to which his family took Gissing.

> Gissing sat on a chair in a corner of the room, mute and dejected. The cackle and scream of idiot mirth rendered him speechless. He sat for an hour for all the world like the figure of a wet bird, amid the rustle of silk and chiffon, and never smiled till we left the house.[14]

If Gissing showed his distaste for the 'cackle and scream of idiot mirth' in parts of *Isabel Clarendon*, he also revealed his own attraction to the virtues of social poise and charm embodied in the 'Lady of Knightswell' herself. But it is nevertheless something of a shock to find this attraction apparently transformed in *Demos* into a less equivocal identification of the world of the country house as the only general social refuge for 'culture'.

Demos is Gissing's most exasperating novel. It represents real advances on his previous novels about large-scale social tensions, in the local authenticity of the Mutimers' home life, for example, and in many fine details of characterisation. But it is impossible to dissociate these evident gains from the most ambitious aspect of the novel, its controlling thesis as a version of social crisis. In an important controversy over the novel between John Goode and Alan Lelchuk,[15] it is precisely this dissociation that Lelchuk attempts in his otherwise sensitive concentration on the novel's internal workings and effects. Goode's discussion of the novel's external relations to history and ideas, it must be admitted, appears at times to reduce the novel to its ideological components with somewhat cavalier alacrity. Yet he is surely right to argue that the novel's status, if not value, lies in its crude but potent stylisation of contemporary political attitudes.

The novel offers itself as an overt parable about the moral and cultural incapacity of the working class to use power for anything other than selfish ends. The plot is based on the inheritance by a socialist working-man, Dick Mutimer, of a country house and its wealth from his capitalist great-uncle — and his consequent, inevitable degeneration. Mutimer's betrayal of his original high ideals under the pressure of attraction to a life of individual status and leisure is close enough to the central action of a later novel, *Born in Exile*, to bring home to us the comparative shallowness of its dramatisation here. Gissing deliberately withholds himself from any closer scrutiny of the complex motivations attributable to the problematic traitor, than is consistent with the thesis of the socialist's inherent egoism. The critical limitation of Gissing's case, and one that we shall see conditioning his other version of cultural crisis in *New Grub Street*, is his direct equation between the value of an ideal and the personal and moral qualities of the individuals involved in its propagation. There was good reason for Gissing's scepticism about the personal qualities of many of the leading socialists in the eighties. Yet even if Gissing's portrayal of his individual socialists had been considerably more penetrating than it is, it would still have been difficult to do justice to the variety and complexity of such historical figures as Morris,

Hyndman, Aveling or Burns. Nor would that have been the point. Engels was just as critical of most of these figures as Gissing, yet he never made the mistake of measuring the possible value of their actions and ideals solely by their personal limitations.

Part of the novel's fascination lies in the peculiar insistence of the thesis that Gissing outlined when he wrote to his brother that it would be 'a savage satire on working-class aims and capacities'.[16] We can see in a small instance the rigidity with which Gissing applies his thesis. To substantiate his claim that 'the fatal defect in working people is absence of imagination', Gissing shows us that Mutimer's literary interests are confined to matters of 'social, political, religious' interest. The nearest any of his books come to what Gissing would call literature is Voltaire. The conclusion at which the ironic tour of Dick's library is aimed is the exposure of 'the incompleteness of his education and the deficiency of his instincts'. What, one wonders, would an aggressively literal look at the reading habits of one of the actual socialist leaders of the time reveal? Ben Tillett, one of the organisers of the 1889 Dock Strike, recorded that *his* desire for self-education, amid the least encouraging circumstances possible, brought him to enjoy Lamb, Hazlitt, Wordsworth and Johnson, as well as Haeckel, Huxley, Spencer and Darwin.[17] What would Gissing have said if he heard that Tillett used to spend his evenings after a gruelling day's work at the docks, struggling to learn Latin — and even Greek! It is a simplistic juxtaposition of fact with fiction, but it serves to illustrate the weight of the mill-stone that Gissing ties round his victim's neck.

In its general plan, the most crucial falsification in the novel is the crude contrast set up between on the one hand Mutimer, the socialist, the world of slums, machines and 'vulgarity', and on the other Hubert Eldon, the well-born individualist, the world of the country house, and 'culture'. To make the country house fit for the habitation of the 'individualist' couple, Hubert and Adela, it must be disinfected of its contamination by bourgeois money and morals. To do this, Gissing resorts to the astonishing subterfuge of ascribing to Mutimer and the Demos he represents, the prime

responsibility for industrialising the beautiful Wanley Valley.
At the end, the reinstated squire, Hubert, stems the tide of
Progress by restoring the valley to its pristine purity.

> A deep breath of country air. It is springtime, and the
> valley of Wanley is bursting into green and flowery life,
> peacefully glad as if the foot of Demos had never come
> that way.[18]

It is a confusion to which the weakest part of Gissing was
always prone, the naïve identification of the working-men
with the machines that they work and the industrial system
that they serve. By thus carefully eliding out the key figure in
the real economic and social process, Dick's capitalist
great-uncle, Gissing succeeds in fabricating a wholly false
opposition between the rural peace and 'culture' of the
valley, and the urban unrest and vulgarity of the intruding
proletariat. The complex process of social change, involving
economic, social, cultural and personal factors in a whole
matrix of forces, is distorted into a starkly stylised confrontation between Culture and Vulgarity, between an 'inner
world' of devotion to beauty, art and personal relations, and
an 'outer world' of work, struggle and progress.

It is characteristic that Gissing should dramatise this
confrontation most successfully at a personal level, in the
marriage between Mutimer and Adela Waltham. Adela, the
well-bred girl, is in a sense an analogue for the inherent
'culture' of the valley, and of Nature itself. She will be
returned at the end, along with the valley, to her true owner,
the dissident squire. Gissing's evidently deep identification
with her and other women in the novel creates an emotional
centre to the narrative that rivals the overt social thesis for
the reader's attention. One critic has gone so far as to see the
marriage theme 'often usurping . . . the primacy of what is
conventionally regarded as the main subject of the novel —
socialism'.[19] But Gissing's interest in the women of this
novel, as of many of his others, grows out of the *same* nexus
of desires and anxieties as the presiding thesis. As the novel
progresses, it becomes increasingly apparent that the most
deeply felt human bonds are those between the victims of an
aggressive, brutal, masculine world. There is Emma Vine, the

pathetic working-girl cruelly deserted by Mutimer. There is Dick's sister, Alice, abandoned by her rascally husband, Rodman. There is Adela, the genteel and sensitive lady, violated by her coarse husband. Then there are the three mothers, Dick's, Hubert's and Adela's, accorded an importance not often to be found in Gissing's work. Mrs Mutimer, as John Goode notes, is a moving embodiment of the instinctive, stubborn rectitude that her son so signally lacks. All three mothers find their children drifting or wrested away from them. The sense of a community of the oppressed is the most powerful emotion in the novel, and it is logical that Adela should be drawn more closely to Stella Westlake than she ever is to either of her hard, selfish male lovers. Goode is surely ungenerous in dismissing this natural diversion of Adela's emotional needs into a Lesbian relationship as a deliberately sensational contrivance designed to ginger up the narrative.

This sense of a concealed community of suffering goes to the heart of a 'thesis' that lies deeper than the explicit political attitudes. For it is through the women, and Adela in particular, that Gissing seeks to express one of his most persistent aspirations towards proving the separability of the inner life from the outer world. It is this aspiration that lies beneath the sense of a totally divided world in the novel, the almost uniformly aggressive and brutal men, and the almost uniformly oppressed women. For Gissing sets out to prove the permanence of certain kinds of difference and separation: at the most obvious level, the separation of classes, and at a deeper, the separation of the worlds of inner culture and outer circumstance.

It is here that we should see the significance of the whole bias of these early novels' observation towards the open underlining of class difference, as manifested in the minutiae of language, dress, deportment, table-manners and so on. Yet the painstaking elaboration with which Gissing insists on absolute difference convinces us of the willed factitiousness.

At dinner he found himself behaving circumspectly . . . But . . . it had never occurred to him, for instance, that civilisation demands the breaking of bread, that in the

absence of silver, a fork must suffice for the dissection of a
fish, that a napkin is a graceful auxiliary in the process of a
meal and not rather an embarrassing superfluity of furtive
application.[20]

The elaborate preciosity rebounds on the narrator, just as it
does in the anecdote recorded in an essay, 'On Battersea
Bridge',[21] where the cultured spectator's rarefied delight in a
beautiful sunset is deflated with splendid comic timing by
the banal comment of a passing workman. It is not Dick's
simple ignorance of social niceties that is exposed, so much as
the vulnerability and paucity of a 'civilisation' (Gissing's
word) that relies on such trivial shibboleths. If that is
'culture', Dick is well off without it! The insistence reveals
Gissing's own extreme unease about the immanence of the
inner culture to which his allegiance is pledged, in the
particular routines and rituals of the country house.

The climactic recognition of absolute difference occurs in
a notorious passage in which Adela surveys Dick's face, as he
lies asleep in the railway carriage:

It was the face of a man by birth and breeding altogether
beneath her . . . He was not of her class, not of her world;
only by violent wrenching of the laws of nature had they
come together . . .[22]

The most blatant aspect of this confrontation is that whereas
Dick is supposed to be perfectly conditioned by his external
circumstances, Adela is supposed to demonstrate an exactly
antithetical inner autonomy. Here we realise Adela's centrality, for Gissing; for it is indeed from her point of view
that their relationship is studied at every stage. There are,
according to this perspective, only one set of sensitivities to
be outraged. It is always Adela's delicacy that is desecrated,
her innocence that is mauled, her courage that is confirmed.
Dick can ape the table-manners of the 'cultured' (unsuccess-
fully), and sincerely envy their social graces, but he can never
himself possess the hidden, buried treasure, the secret of this
'inner life'. He can possess Adela's body, but cannot touch
the incorruptible chastity of her inner Self.

Without defence against indignities which were bitter as
death, by law his chattel, as likely as not to feel the weight

of his hand if she again roused his anger, what remained
but to surrender all outward things to unthinking habit,
and to keep her soul apart, nourishing in silence the fire of
its revolt?[23]

In *The Egoist*, Meredith had returned a different verdict on
the possibility of 'an inner life apart' in such circumstances,
when Clara Middleton meditates to herself:

Can a woman have an inner life apart from him she is
yoked to? She tried to nestle deep away in herself . . . It
was a vain effort.[24]

Demos represents Gissing's most frantic rear-guard action,
to stave off the invasive forces of an outer world of work,
money and politics from the fragile asylum of the inner life.
It derives from that nadir of scepticism plumbed in his
well-known comment on Morris's appearance in court after a
fracas with the police in the East End:

Keep apart, keep apart, and preserve one's soul alive — that
is the teaching of the day. It is ill to have been born in
these times, but one can make a world within the world.[25]

But Gissing's best work is devoted, in spite of himself, to
showing that one cannot.

iv. THYRZA (1887)

Gissing's fourth novel centred on problems of class relationship and the experience of the city, presents a paradox that
will come to dominate most of his later work, from 1894 or
1895 until his death. For it shows a superiority in literary
terms to all his previous work (save perhaps *Isabel Clarendon*)
in the delicacy and variety of characterisation and setting, the
fluency and generosity of the narrative idiom — and yet, this
superiority seems to be in distressingly precise relation to an
overall diminution of power.

The novel can be read in close conjunction with *Demos*,
since it repeats the central stylised opposition between
Culture and Vulgarity, though from a considerably less
urgent perspective. Moreover the idealistic energy is here
represented in a figure belonging to the opposite camp to
Dick Mutimer, the 'cultured' Walter Egremont. Thus the

desire for change in the 'fallen' condition of the inhabitants of Lambeth does not spring from within as in *Demos*, but is directed from the outside. Gissing is deliberately drawing on the efforts of institutions such as the Working Men's College founded by F. D. Maurice in 1854, and the university extension courses that started in 1873.

The novel sets out to show the inevitable failure of Egremont's well-meaning attempt to bring some humanising 'culture' into the lives of Lambeth working-men through his evening lectures. His real opponent in the novel, however, is not a Mutimer-like working man, but the M.P. for Vauxhall, Dalmaine — a name that chimes with Milvain.

> Dalmaine embodied those forces of philistinism, that essence of the vulgar creed, which Egremont had undertaken to attack, and which, as he already felt, were likely to yield as little before his efforts as a stone wall under the blow of a naked hand.[26]

We see here an important change in the nature of Gissing's indictment of contemporary society. It is a shift in emphasis, that will be carried through *New Grub Street* and *In the Year of Jubilee*. For the focus is now on a total cultural degradation that includes but is no longer to be located primarily in the physical conditions of society's lowest stratum. Gissing is thus carrying through the perceptions gained from the country-house setting of *Isabel Clarendon* more honestly than he had done in *Demos*, for it becomes clear that the country houses, the locations of social and cultural power, cannot be arbitrarily willed to the deserving individuals of true 'culture', such as Waymark and Eldon. They are dominated by a class, represented at its best by the genial and gracious Isabel Clarendon and the cousin she finally marries, Robert Asquith, but at its worst, by the vulgar, philistine politician Dalmaine. It is he who represents the real controlling 'vulgarity' at the heart of society, a vulgarity to which the Isabel Clarendons and in this novel the Tyrrell family can offer no contrary principle of cultural health, but only a casual and complacent acquiescence. It is significant that the novel opens in the rural retreat of the

intellectual Mr Newthorpe, the Tyrrells' relation and Egremont's friend. For his withdrawal is symptomatic of the
diaspora of the truly cultured, to which Reardon will
contribute an elegiac lament in *New Grub Street*. The futility
of Egremont's attempts to engage battle with the impalpable,
monolithic forces of materialism now in control of society, is
only too poignantly marked by the image of the naked hand
hammering against the brute stone wall.

Yet Egremont's naïveté is proved less by the explicit
failure of his scheme, than by the implicit resilience of a
working-class way of life to which such schemes are
irrelevant. Here, as several readers have pointed out, is the
real and unexpected strength of the novel, in its generous
appreciation for some of the positive aspects of working-class
life, the sense of human beings at home with each other and
their environment, in the Saturday night market and the
'friendly lead' at the pub. The difference between the
Whitecross Street market that opened *Workers in the Dawn*
and the description of the Lambeth street-market here could
hardly be more pronounced. P. J. Keating claims with much
plausibility:

> . . . here the activity of the streets is no longer a public
> exhibition of a sub-human race, but the genuine expression
> of a way of life.[27]

It is certainly a side of Gissing that deserves to be better
known.

And yet — 'the genuine expression of a way of life'? In
what sense 'genuine'? Gissing himself claimed that he was
setting out to capture 'the very spirit of London working-
class life'.[28] But we still need to ask, in what spirit is that
spirit captured? There is a revealing moment in the fine
description of the 'friendly lead', a communal sing-song for
the benefit of a local barber who has broken his leg. Gissing
had researched this novel diligently, and the sheer precision
and wealth of detail in scenes of this kind clearly reflect it. It
is when we move from the neutrally recorded décor, the
tables, the smoke and so on, to the human beings, that we
receive the quiet but crucial check.

If they lacked refinement, natural or acquired, it was not their fault: toil was behind them and before, the hours of rest were few, suffering and lack of bread might at any moment come upon them . . .[29]

For this idiom of observation, extended and diversified as it is here, is still critically defined by the controlling generalisation. In its positive aspect, this generalisation is based on the diagnosis of a shared condition, of communal subjection to economic necessity, *within* which subjection the forms of relative release and consolation, such as we see in this fine scene, can be richly characterised. But the richness, the colour and variety, are decisively enclosed by the idiom of observation, of a generalised and distancing compassion. What is then to be looked for is the offer of something other than the subjection of the observed and the tolerance of the observer — the sense of challenge or threat.

For the evident gains, so well described by Keating, are in the end outweighed by the corresponding losses. 'The very spirit of working-class life' — where are the energies that are *not* satisfied by the quotidian consolations, the assuaging, caressing familiarity of friends and places and events that satisfies the attractive young girl, Totty Nancarrow? The two individuals who posses such energies are Thyrza Trent and Gilbert Grail. Both of them are attracted across the barriers of class to the intruding Egremont, as to an emotional and intellectual partner respectively. The disastrous triangle that constitutes the novel's main plot is closed by Grail's own emotional attachment to Thyrza. In Thyrza's case, her emotional and spiritual capacities are hinted at in her miraculous singing voice. She hushes the 'friendly lead' into awed silence when she is persuaded to sing there. And yet, though Gissing can *gesture* towards an emotional force that transcends class and social difference, it is the abysmal inadequacy of his language for articulating such disruptive energies that is most obvious. The comparison with Hardy or Lawrence is painfully damaging. Here, for example, is Thyrza at a point of crisis:

She went to the end of the bridge, and there crept into a dark place whither no eye could follow her. Her strength was at an end. She fell to her knees; her head lay against something hard and cold; a sob convulsed her, and then in the very anguish of desolation she wept. The darkness folded her; she could lie here on the ground and abandon herself to misery. She wept her soul from her eyes.[30]

Just as in the generalised scene at the pub, the language is arrested at the limits of compassion. It is almost symptomatic that Thyrza creeps into 'a dark place whither no eye could follow her' — but it is precisely the eye alone that *can* follow her in the narrative idiom, the external language of the eye, as the spectator hovers around in helpless compassion. Thyrza's misery, and corresponding desire, can only be translated into the most generalised and conventional of terms, 'the very anguish of desolation'.

In Gilbert Grail, the limits of the available means of expression are even more obvious. For the 'culture' that temporarily unites him and Egremont does not, as Thyrza's passion does, represent an authentic *challenge* to the physical context, so much as a means of transcendence, or in less elevated terms, simply escape. There is an extended passage dealing with Gilbert's reaction to the 'golden prospect' offered by Egremont, the post of librarian at the proposed library. Just prior to his receipt of this wonderful promise of release, we have seen the normal conditions of Grail's pitiful subjection to material and economic circumstance. It is a familiar image of the lonely individual walking through the city streets.

The next morning he went to his work through a fog so dense that it was with difficulty he followed the familiar way. Lamps were mere lurid blotches in the foul air, perceptible only when close at hand; the footfall of invisible men and women hurrying to factories made a muffled, ghastly sound; harsh bells summoned through the darkness, the voice of pitiless taskmasters to whom all was indifferent save the hour of toil. Gilbert was racked with headache. Bodily suffering made him as void of intellectual desire as the meanest labourer then going forth to earn bread; he longed for nothing more than to lie down and lose consciousness of the burden of life.[31]

It is a powerful and typical translation of the signs of everyday urban life into their human meanings. The fog, the lamps, the footfalls, the bells — this landscape speaks only of the tyranny of economic circumstance, the bitter routine of daily labour that drains the individual of all other talents and capacities. It is, therefore, from *this* that Egremont offers to release Gilbert. After receiving the letter, Gilbert with a natural movement retires first to the privacy of his bedroom, the single room that is the scene of all the most intense emotion in Gissing. Though this emotion is, for once, one of painful exhilaration rather than of painful depression, the movement that then follows is also familiar — out from the lonely room, down into the streets. Gilbert takes a long and detailed walk through the city, down Lambeth Walk on to Lambeth Bridge. All this time, the physical phenomena are noted with comparative neutrality, the smell of fried fish, the presence of the crowd, and then the view from the bridge, the river and the buildings. It is a long while before there is any reference to Gilbert's feelings, for the narrative is in effect *imitating* the function of the walk for Gilbert himself, which is to dissipate and control the overpowering emotion. But when reference *is* made, it is significantly expressed in negative terms. Gilbert has often stood at this point on the bridge (as Egremont will do later), prepared to jump over in the depth of misery.

> His mood was far other now; some power he did not understand had brought him here as to the place where he could best realise this great joy that had befallen him.[32]

The significance is not only the arbitrariness and externality of the 'power he did not understand', but in the fact that the only physical location and circumstances for the celebration of this 'great joy' are exactly the same as they were for the expression of his deepest misery. This is the point of the exceptionally detailed description of the external scene, the Houses of Parliament, St Thomas's Hospital, Lambeth Palace. The external, physical scene has not changed, indeed cannot be changed. What Gilbert's 'joy' can achieve is not a transformation or challenge, but only a temporary defiance of the implacable circumscribing landscape. The 'culture' to which he lays claim can only be enjoyed in the inner space made possible by some form of external economic release. This is what the curiously affecting scene on the bridge signifies, and the more permanent opportunity in the public library promises, a relative and local emancipation within a general condition of subjection. It is always towards such outposts and enclaves that Gissing's cultured minority gravitates, but Gissing is becoming severer on the possibility of a 'great good place' such as the Wanley valley provided for Hubert and Adela and the country cottage will provide for Ryecroft.

Though we are not given explicit indication of Gilbert's feelings till near the end of the passage quoted, there is nevertheless a crucial paragraph at the heart of the passage, in which plenty of feeling is expressed — by the narrator. Gilbert is passing a street-organ, to which some children are preparing to dance. With a movement that shares but goes beyond the emotions of the watching Gilbert, the narrator speaks directly to us.

Do you know that music of the obscure ways, to which children dance? Not if you have only heard it ground to your ears' affliction beneath your windows in the square. To hear it aright you must stand in the darkness of such a by-street as this, and for the moment be at one with those who dwell around, in the blear-eyed houses, in the dim burrows of poverty, in the unmapped haunts of the semi-human. Then you will know the significance of that vulgar clanging of melody; a pathos of which you did not dream will touch you, and therein the secret of hidden London will be half revealed. The life of men who toil without hope, yet with the hunger of an unshaped desire: of women in whom the sweetness of their sex is perishing under labour and misery; the laugh, the song of the girl who strives to enjoy her year or two of youthful vigour, knowing the darkness of the years to come; the careless defiance of the youth who feels his blood and revolts against the lot which would tame it; all that is purely human in these darkened multitudes speaks to you as you listen. It is the half-conscious striving of a nature which

knows not what it would attain, which deforms a true
thought by gross expression, which clutches at the
beautiful and soils it with foul hands.[33]

It is, in many ways, noble, moving and sincere: the lonely
watcher, standing in the shadows, feeling the difference and
distance, yet wanting desperately to understand and interpret
the 'unshaped desire' and half-conscious voice of 'all that is
purely human'. It is a passage that goes deep to the
contradictions in Gissing, the revulsion from the grossness of
the 'semi-human' chafing against the imaginative identification with the sense of 'the darkness'. The music that we
hear is therefore emblematic of the energy and possibility in
the general mass of working people, that can only attain
expression in such oblique ways. Thus the intellectual and
emotional desire of Gilbert and Thyrza is related to a more
general condition of desire and deprivation. And yet,
affecting and deeply felt as the declaration is, we cannot feel
that it is made, in the narrative as a whole, much more than a
declaration. For against this assertion of Gilbert's and Thyrza's
representativeness is the whole instinctive bias of the narrative towards the assertion of their *uniqueness*. Early on, we
are told of Thyrza's sense of 'life-weariness': 'it was the
penalty she paid for her birthright of heart and mind'. The
'birthright' sets her and Gilbert radically apart from the mass
of working people. They belong with Egremont to what is by
now a familiar community of the chosen, the few who are
cursed with the gift of 'passionate imagination'. It is no
coincidence that the central plot of the love complications
between Gilbert, Thyrza and Egremont becomes increasingly
detached from the dense physical context of Lambeth.
Symptomatically, the crisis of the relationship between
Egremont and Thyrza takes place in a country house.

We can return finally to the central irony surrounding the
'culture' that offers Grail and Egremont an inner haven. For
in the long passage quoted above, there is surely an anomaly
in the observer's translation of the street-organs' music into a
symbol of 'the secret of hidden London'. For these street-
organs are *actual* organs, to which the children dance and
play, and which, like the many other everyday phenomena of

working-class life, provide human beings with direct familiar pleasures. Can Gilbert's 'culture' in fact offer anything significantly different from the temporary and relative release that such ordinary phenomena provide, and that, as has been noted, it is the novel's strength to describe with such detail and affection? With typical ambidexterity, this irony constitutes the novel's strength and weakness. The 'culture' of Egremont and Grail is simply *irrelevant* to a way of life that is already provided with its indigenous means of consolation and relief from the rigours of economic necessity. Gissing knows and shows this, while still retaining an equally admirable desire to express something beyond the limits of compassion and acquiescence, the desire to break the limits of economic and social conditioning. Yet the desire to break, given the idiom and perspective of this novel, is etiolated into a desire to escape. We are left with the lively but unresolved contradictions of the street-organ passage. But they are checked at the limits of a generalised compassion — 'a pathos of which you did not dream' — for a general condition of frustration, within which we can identify, at the crisis, only with special individuals, and in special, limited ways.

3 The Nether World

The Nether World (1889) is the last and most successful of Gissing's early attempts to dramatise on a large scale the problems of energy, need and relationship in the context of extreme urban deprivation. Gissing did some careful research in Clerkenwell for this novel. His Diary shows him going over 'a die-sinker's place', for example, and getting 'useful ideas'.[1] Yet these rarely emerge in physical details in the novel, as they had done to a great extent in *Thyrza*, and would certainly have done in Zola. The value and stature of this novel is to be found in its articulation of the *quality* of human desire and suffering beneath the differences of class and individual personality. In this it is more successful than any strictly 'documentary' approach could be; Booth's investigations offer a sharp and pertinent comparison.

In the latter part of the nineteenth century, the peculiar nature of London's industrial structure dictated patterns of economic, social and political relationship very different from those of a northern industrial centre. As Asa Briggs has shown, London took on the symbolic centrality that Manchester had had earlier in the century.[2] But instead of the images of overt crisis and class-confrontation with which Manchester bristled in the thirties and forties, the images that become associated with London in the eighties are those of unseen, unexpected helplessness and destitution. In contrast to the initial motivation for Mayhew's investigations (middle-class fear of disease), Booth's work took its impetus from his realisation of the sheer ignorance of what lay beneath the 'vast smug surface' (James's phrase). What lay there could not, as yet, make its presence felt, at least in the urgent way of the Chartist forties. The absence of large-scale factory production in London, and the increasing trend towards the casualisation of a large proportion of the labour force, obstructed the possibility of the cohesive group consciousness developed by miners or textile workers, and reinforced sharp distinctions of skill between workers. It was the East End that attracted particular attention in the eighties, for it seemed to offer the most striking images of absolute human subjection. Engels concluded a well-known letter to Margaret Harkness by admitting '. . . that nowhere in the civilised world are the working people less actively resistant, more passively submitting to fate, more hébétés than in the East End of London . . .'[3] A modern historian shows that the process of withdrawal, whereby merchants and employers were no longer resident on their place of work, had created huge areas of working-class housing 'virtually bereft of any contact with authority except in the form of the policeman or bailiff'.[4] The by now conventional image of the 'two nations' acquired a new absoluteness. Arnold White, in a book that Gissing read in preparation for this novel, wrote in 1886: 'Between Dives and Lazarus the great gulf fixed becomes deeper, wider and blacker month by month and year by year.'[5]

Gissing exploited neither the so-called 'romance' of the East End, as Besant had done, nor the so-called 'realism' of the nineties, with its brawls, booze and *bonhomie*. The claim for *his* realism is not in terms of external detail, but in his identification with the suffering poor at a level that reproduces a shared human sense of physical and emotional deprivation, through some central images of frustration, helplessness and want. The images of traps, immobility, reified space and time, articulate the human quality of suffering, caused by quite specific external conditions such as the structure of the casual labour market. The casual labourer was physically trapped by the need to remain close to the irregular source of labour. The work offered was insufficient for a regular livelihood, yet enough to prevent his straying permanently into another occupation. The pattern of arbitrary and irregular employment and payment thus created a vicious circle:

> . . . the casual labour market entailed a vicious circle. On the one hand, the offer of 'inefficient' labour created a demand for it, and on the other hand, the demand for

casual labour promoted and perpetuated the supply of
'inefficient' labour.[6]

It could be pointed out that Gissing himself knew, from his
own experiences as a writer of long, cumbersome three-
volume novels, the feelings of insecurity induced by the
uncertainty of regular employment and payment. Similarly,
the terms in which Gareth Stedman Jones analyses the
exclusion of the metropolitan poor from participation in any
genuine political tradition (the Chartists had found little
support in London) are corroborated by Gissing's identification with the *sense* of exclusion, beneath class and personal
difference.

> Their aims and needs had always been short-term. Their
> past seemed eternally to have been the same — the
> interminable struggle to get enough to eat, the precarious
> hold upon a marginal employment, the dreaded antici-
> pation of hard winters, sickness and old age, the final and
> inevitable assumption into the workhouse. This was not
> history in any cumulative or purposive sense.[7]

This feeling of being trapped in time as well as in space is at
the heart of *The Nether World*.

Since the argument is that the creative core of the novel
lies in its images rather than the components of 'character'
and 'plot', it is with the images that we shall start. The
opening scene offers some key points of reference. The very
first words set the typical temporal location: 'In the troubled
twilight of a March evening . . .' — trapped already between
day and night. The figure of the traveller moves across an
urban landscape, figurative and specific. He is himself
unidentified so far; like a Hardy traveller, he represents a
human movement beyond that of the specific individual, a
basic energy not yet refracted into its 'humanised' aspects,
sexual, social, psychological, economic — it is a brief reprieve.
From a drab, factual recording of his clothes, we move to a
description of his face, that intimates the characteristic
elements of human desire that will dominate the narrative.

> To say that his aspect was venerable would serve to present
> him in a measure, yet would not be wholly accurate, for

there was too much of past struggle and present anxiety in his countenance to permit full expression of the natural dignity of the features. It was a fine face and might have been distinctly noble, but circumstances had marred the purpose of Nature; you perceived that his cares had too often been of the kind which are created by ignoble necessities, such as leave to most men of his standing a bare humanity of visage.[8]

The conflict between desire and necessity is seen from a *retrospective* vantage point. This is an old man, whose major crises are past — unlike Hardy's travellers. They will later on be recapitulated for us from that perspective, as will be many other important experiences: the growth of Sidney Kirkwood's love for Clara and his youthful radicalism, John Hewett's fluctuating career, and Clara's bitter taste of the theatrical world. In a larger sense, the whole tyrannical social structure will be viewed backwards. Relationships, social and personal, are not, as they were in Dickens, *being* made, broken, created, rediscovered — they *are* already. Past and future virtually dissolve under the weight of the present. And yet, as we can see from the passage above, although the 'struggle' may be past, 'anxiety' is still alive, for desire continues even at the edge of obliteration. The temporal location of 'twilight' is caught up and confirmed as the narrow strip that separates the high noon of critical engagement, and the darkness of resolutions and conclusions. Gissing is a connoisseur of the penultimate.

Then, in a memorable and characteristic passage, this slow, grim, but still human movement is checked against the circumscribing landscape.

The burial-ground by which he had paused was as little restful to the eye as are most of those discoverable in the by-ways of London. The small trees that grew about it shivered in their leaflessness; the rank grass was wan under the failing day; most of the stones leaned this way or that, emblems of neglect (they were very white at the top, and darkened downwards till the damp soil made them black), and certain cats and dogs were prowling or sporting among the graves. At this corner the east wind blew with

malice such as it never puts forth save where there are
poorly clad people to be pierced; it swept before it thin
clouds of unsavoury dust, mingled with the light refuse of
the streets. Above the shapeless houses night was signalling
a murky approach; the sky — if sky it could be called —
gave threatening of sleet, perchance of snow. And on every
side was the rumble of traffic, the voiceful evidence of toil
and of poverty; hawkers were crying their goods; the
inevitable organ was clanging before a public-house hard by;
the crumpet-man was hastening along, with monotonous
ringing of his bell and hoarse rhythmic wail.[9]

Here is Gissing's urban setting in all its studied, inexorable
depression. The adjectives grind on the nerves — 'rank',
'failing', 'unsavoury', 'murky', 'hoarse'. The prevailing
conditions are at best those of absence or negation (death,
leafless trees, neglected tombstones), at worst those of
monotonous anguish. For the most positive force in the
whole passage is that of the east wind, maliciously confirming
the human meanings of poverty. The cats and dogs with their
'prowling' and 'sporting' (ironically, the liveliest verbs in the
passage) alone escape the all-encompassing conditions of 'toil'
and 'poverty'. We note the way the limp syntax and
meticulous assonances of 'the rank grass was wan under the
failing day' enact the sense of energy draining away, the spirit
shrinking and sinking. It is a landscape the polar antithesis of
anything in Dickens, totally devoid of human animation, of
mysterious and exhilarating solicitation. Compare the grave-
yard that opens *Great Expectations*! And yet — even as we
register the grim, numbing paucity of that parenthesis, 'they
were very white . . .', we are caught in our downward
movement by the modest dignity of the phrase that precedes
it, 'emblems of neglect'. There is, we realise, a human voice
still present, noting and judging, as yet quietly but stub-
bornly. It is this voice that redeems the passage from total
oppressiveness. Just as 'twilight' is all the more precious for
its trembling on the edge of total darkness, so is this voice
that survives tenuously on the brink of extinction. By the
end of the novel, it can be put more positively than this, as
an *active*, defiant grasp on a basic human desire for

survival.[10] But at this point, we are only beginning to gauge the quality of the voice and its claims, — especially, perhaps, in a phrase such as 'the *voiceful* evidence of toil and of poverty'. The city is still 'readable'; it still presents evidence to be interpreted, it still *speaks* to the observer.

From the cemetery we move on to the other key opening image, the prison. How different again in its irreducibly material appearance and yet abstract oppressiveness from the discoverably human prisons of *Little Dorrit*. This one, so palpably there in front of us, has seemingly no origins, no human builders or controllers, but only a reified and reifying autonomy. It is towards the sculpture over the gates that we are specifically directed.

> It was the sculptured counterfeit of a human face, that of a man distraught with agony. The eyes stared wildly from their sockets, the hair struggled in maniac disorder, the forehead was wrung with torture, the cheeks sunken, the throat fearsomely wasted, and from the wide lips there seemed to be issuing a horrible cry. Above this hideous effigy was carved the legend: 'MIDDLESEX HOUSE OF DETENTION.'[11]

Death and suffering, the grave and the sculpture: these are the two ultimate states of reification towards which man is driven by 'Fate' and 'Society'. They represent the permanent and the temporary aspects of death against which all the energy within and without the narrative will be directed. Again, the vision is continuous with that original temporal image, of the enormous back-log, the burden of the pre-existing. It is in this larger context of their referential relation to the narrative as a whole that we should see these images, rather than their function in the merely local 'depression' to which John Goode points in his fine discussion of the opening scene.

The same critic makes an instructive misreading, when he talks about this sculpture. He points out the ambiguity of what he reads as 'the hair struggled *with* maniac disorder', and comments, 'i.e. both against and in a state of'.[12] The misreading derives from his correct perception of the implications, since the original 'in' conveys even more

blatantly than 'with', the absence of a genuine object for the
verb 'struggle'. Here, at a level so humble as to be easily
overlooked, is a good example of the consistency with which
we are referred to a central and coherent vision. For the
grammatical absence of an object in this sentence echoes the
central problem of all the energy at large in the nether
world — its absence of 'objects'. The central characters, in
whom are embodied the most positive energies, Sidney
Kirkwood, Clara Hewett and her father John, all find
themselves incarcerated in a world of inadequate signs, that
bear minimal connection with their distant, hidden objects of
aspiration. Sidney's work as a jeweller is a cruel parodic
substitute for his real desire and talent to be an artist. For
Clara, the theatrical world she manages to penetrate reveals
itself as merely a new version of the old forms of savage
competition. And in the absence of adequate 'objects', there
is a hectic urge to cling on to the little one has — hence John
Hewett's passionate, jealous love for his daughter Clara. But
when one's very last possession is taken away, whether it be
another person, a job, a room, an ideal, then — and *this* is the
meaning of 'poverty' in the 'nether world' — desire and
energy have nowhere to turn: except back, in, round. For it
is not even possible to identify an Enemy. John Hewett,
losing his beloved Clara, vents his frustration on to Sidney, as
the 'sign' of her loss — unfairly and fruitlessly. On a larger
scale, the whole employment structure of casual labour
reinforces this pattern of deflected and poisoned desire. John
Hewett finds five hundred other men queuing for the single
job he has heard rumoured. 'I wanted to fight, I tell you — to
fight till the life was kicked an' throttled out of me!' But
fight *whom*? His fellow workers are as inadequate 'signs' of
the lost job, as Sidney is of the lost Clara. Like the hair of the
sculpture, there is simply 'struggle'; only one fighter in the
ring, the other invisible, watching from the stalls.

Of course, the Enemy, the definable Other, is clearly the
'upper world', the capitalists and exploiters; their maintenance is the nether world's sole apparent reason for
existence. Yet just as the obvious oppressiveness of the prison
walls is endowed with the force of an autonomous abstraction, so is the upper world apparently not susceptible to

resolution into palpable and specific human forms. Sidney labours daily to produce jewellery for fashionable women, whom he and we never see. They are not even described as women: he shapes 'bright ornaments for the *necks* and *arms* of such as are born to the joy of life' (my italics). Similarly, we never see the landlord or bailiff who comes to take away the Candy family's furniture. There is no human confrontation, even with a Pancks, let alone a Casby. The contrast with Dickens makes one consider the way in which all his great villains from Gradgrind to Podsnap are capable of sustaining the burden of typicality. Even when in *Our Mutual Friend* the world that emanates from the cancerous spirit of Podsnap is becoming hermetically sealed off from the 'nether world', physical and symbolic, of the river, the naming of that upper world as it congregates round the Veneerings' dinner-table lays down a periphery for confrontation. To name the Other, to identify him by a shape, a quirk, a visible clue, is to tame the horror of irreducible, depersonalised abstraction; but that is exactly what Gissing's nether world cannot do for itself, and what the narrator can only do in limited ways. For he too is engaged in the struggle to reduce the abstract to the human, as he tries to see beyond the numbing generalities of the mass, the mob, the working class, and penetrate to the living and human. These are generalities that, with part of himself, he wants to confirm, and this is the intended function of the Crystal Palace scenes.

This opening scene, then, presents us with the images of deadlock, of traps and divisions, that will proliferate through the novel. The notion of time itself being trapped is particularly insistent. The child Jane Snowdon, sent on an errand to fetch Sidney, exposes the conventionality of his comforting remark, with a naïveté akin to the narrator's scepticism. 'Keep a good heart, Jane. Things'll be better some day, no doubt.' 'Do you think so, sir?' Hope is an almost unknown commodity in this world for the girl who is introduced to us as the 'thrall of thralls'. The conventional phrase, whereby the future is assumed to be at least *different* from the present, simply does not obtain. For Jane, the future has no special quality, it is simply an extension of the present. In the same way, the working day in Clerkenwell is described as an unvarying, identical today. There are no 'expectations' in this world, let alone 'great'.

To be trapped in space and time is hell, but the hell within a hell at the heart of the nether world is a slum called Shooter's Gardens. The choric figure, Mad Jack, attains his full oracular status when he makes explicit the threatened ultimate metaphor, as the narrative follows the despondent Pennyloaf after her husband into this slum. The vile, suffocating smoke and lurid fires of the baked-potato ovens do not prepare the image of Hell; this is a hell itself.[13] Metaphor in fact ceases to exist; just as the temporal differentiation between past and present and future is dissolved, so is the distance between sign and signified. The dream that Mad Jack proceeds to recount of the Angel's descent, seems to reflect the peculiar circularity of the condition in which Time is dead.

> You are passing through a state of punishment . . . Because you made an ill use of your wealth . . . therefore after death you received the reward of wickedness. This life you are now leading is that of the damned; this place to which you are confined is Hell! There is no escape for you. From poor you shall become poorer; the older you grow the lower you shall sink in want and misery; at the end there is waiting for you, one and all, a death in abandonment and despair. This is Hell — Hell — Hell![14]

This is already a posthumous state ('after death you received . . .'), yet another death still awaits them. It is a confusion that grows naturally out of the sense of trapped Time, unredeemed by normal linear expectations of death as release. Every exit is closed. Only desire and hope can create a future, and these emotions are stifled in Shooter's Gardens.

As for the possibilities of *escape*, these are viewed with bitter scepticism. There is the blessed immunity of Mr Eagles's harmless lunacy and Mrs Candy's alcoholic stupor — on the level of the cats and dogs in the cemetery. Otherwise, escape in any form, physical, emotional, intellectual, whether in dream, religion, hope or aspiration, is ruthlessly rebuffed. The bells of St James's, Clerkenwell, for example, that open Volume II, sing out a hymn of derisory significance for the inhabitants of the nearby prison: 'There is a happy land, far, far away'. Instead of the conventional offer of solace in the hope of a future state, the hymn 'makes too great a demand upon the imagination to soothe amid instant miseries'. The future, any future, is literally inconceivable as offering anything different from the 'instant miseries' of the present. We note Gissing's typically archaic, Latinate use of the word 'instant' here, as 'pressing', 'urgent' — in other words, drained of its usual *temporal* implications. Thus is the general threat of time becoming spatialised enacted within the confines of a single word.

It is to this coherent imaginative vision that the elements of 'plot' and 'character' are subordinate. With typically acrid irony, Gissing employs the most traditional of plot conventions — the will of the Benevolent Rich Old Man. Gissing's use of the will convention is nearly always precise and intelligent. For his wills are never simply agents of release (except perhaps in *The Unclassed*); in *Demos*, *The Nether World*, and *New Grub Street*, the legacies set more problems than they solve. The convention is exposed and critically examined. From his first entrance into human society, Michael Snowdon is identified by everyone as the rich old man returned from abroad, bringing great expectations for some young person. The publican whom Snowdon first accosts has no difficulty in recognising him; he knows his Victorian novels. The scene in which Clem Peckover's mother first meets him and tries to discover his financial rating, is an epitome of the continual process of economic 'reading' that goes on. The jackals who congregate round Snowdon's wealth only carry to an extreme the same translation of all human action and potential into its economic value as *everyone* is forced to in a world of chronic want. At the end of the novel, when Sidney comes home to discover that a window has been broken in the squabbles of the insufferably whining Hewett children, it is immediately into its economic significance that he instinctively translates it; it will make a disastrous hole in the weekly budget. Detail after detail reinforces the grim consistency of this vision — the sound of a lodger hobbling up the stairs in the Peckovers' lodging-house, for example. This is not just Mr Marple, the cab-driver (who, incidentally, never appears on any other occasion). This is Mr Marple, the cab-driver, whose legs are paralysed by sitting sixteen hours a day on his cab in pursuit of the pittance that earns him the dubious privilege of keeping his room at the Peckovers'.

One of the most penetrating disclosures of the ubiquity of economic 'translation', practised by narrator and characters alike with various degrees of irony, disgust and cunning, is in the portrayal of the Byasses. They are friends of Sidney's, with whom old Snowdon and his granddaughter Jane take lodgings. On their introduction to us, Gissing indulges in a brilliant, dead-pan parody of Dickensian jollity. Sam Byass, a clerk in a stationer's office, goes through an appallingly facetious routine of tomfoolery with a poker, slashing and shooting at the visiting Sidney.

> Finally, assuming the attitude of a juggler, he made an attempt to balance the poker perpendicularly upon his nose, until it fell with a crash, just missing the ornaments on the mantel-piece. All this time Mrs Byass shrieked with laughter, with difficulty keeping her chair.[15]

The narrator's silent disdain is chilling. These people can apparently turn everything into banter in a recognisably Dickensian idiom.

> Let's send to the High Street for three cold roast fowls and a beef-steak pie! Let's get custards and cheese-cakes and French pastry! Let's have a pineapple and preserved ginger! Who says, Go it for once?[16]

Nobody in this world — Dickens is a happy land, far, far away. The Byasses do *not* represent some form of comic resilience to the contamination of economic pressures, as it might first appear. When Bessie Byass hears of Jane's proposal to refuse her father's allowance, her first thought is that Jane will not be able to pay for her rooms. Her geniality, for what it is worth, is seen to be buoyed up by the shrewdness of the business woman. She and her husband mark the highest limit of the nether world and Mrs Candy the lowest, but the element of economic necessity pervades every nook and cranny; nothing and nobody is immune.

Gissing's characters are engaged in reading each other in

economic terms as compulsively as Hardy's are in sexual terms, or James's in psychological. The quality of competition, of internecine struggle for the few spars of survival, is identical. One of the finest scenes in the novel is that in which Clara, returned from her disastrous theatrical career with her face scarred for life, plays her supreme performance to persuade Sidney of the survival of a genuine emotional bond corroborating his theoretical obligation to marry her.[17] The combination of authenticity and artifice in the scene she plays is irreducible. Her horror of the life of penury and solitude that now faces her, drives her to appeal to Sidney in a way that she knows he will find irresistible. The point is that no matter what the degree of genuine emotion she may in fact retain for him, his economic meaning to her, as representing a minimum of physical security, can never be effectively dissociated. Sidney's dilemma is not helped by the fact that the girl he really loves, Jane Snowdon, is similarly dyed deep with economic significance for him, as he is for Clara. Though he immediately realises that the price put on Jane's head as a prospective heiress complicates his proposal of marriage, it is only gradually brought home to him the extent to which he is and will continue to be envied as a man on the make. The dream of 'pure' relationship, of soul speaking to soul, remains a nostalgic, impossible idyll: 'I can imagine no bliss so perfect as to marry Jane Snowdon and go off to live with her amid fields and trees, where no echo of the suffering world should ever reach us'. But there is no evading the mediation of the external, public roles shaped, projected, imposed by the pressures of communal existence, no concession to an ideal of the autonomous, pure communion of the 'inner life'.

This, therefore, is the context for the study of desire within the narrative, as it follows the twists and turns of several individuals. They are differentiated by the varying quality of protest or acquiescence with which they respond to the shared sense of oppression. At one extreme is the Hewett family. John the father, Clara and Bob the elder children, embody the most passionate, and at times deeply moving, resolution to fight every inch of the way. John Hewett is not only Gissing's finest single portrait of a

working-man (miraculously untainted by the ruinous prejudices shackling Dick Mutimer in *Demos*), but one of the
finest in any Victorian novel. What is more important is that
he does not come across at all as the product of a deliberate
intention to 'portray a working-man', but grows naturally,
effortlessly out of the general experiences of want and
exclusion that animate the whole narrative. At the end of the
novel, his continuing will to work sustains an innate, moving
dignity. The few shillings he manages to bring home afford
him 'a sort of angry joy that it would have made your heart
ache to witness'.

Yet it is perhaps in Hewett's passionate but helpless revolt
that we can recognise some of the limits of Gissing's vision. It
is something of an irony that this novel appeared in the same
year (1889) as the Great Dock Strike, for it is precisely the
impossibility of Hewett's frustration being directed toward
any more valuable form of action than individual survival
that the novel so powerfully demonstrates. If we look at the
version provided by one of the leaders of the dock strike, Ben
Tillett, we find that seen from the inside, the conditions of
labour that produced such bitterness and despair were indeed
very similar to those portrayed by Gissing. Every day at the
docks, the 'struggling mass fought desperately and tigerishly,
elbowing each other, punching each other, using their last
remnants of strength to get work for an hour or half-hour for
a few pence'.[18] And yet, striking as is the corroboration, it is
the *next* feeling that Tillett records that marks such a
contrast.

> It was then that the seeds were sown in my mind which
> made me an agitator and a fanatical evangelist of
> Labour.[19]

Hewett has lived through this phase — it is now discredited.
Tillett's whole story of the attempt to organise the workers'
resistance certainly confirms Gissing's images of apparent
hopelessness. Yet it is against this that the belief in
communal action gradually gathers strength. Tillett can
convey the sense of excitement in corporate action, in the
making of a trade union, such as Gissing could not
understand, or would have attributed to a 'mob' instinct.

These are the possibilities that Gissing refuses to contemplate, even as they were happening around him in the London of the late eighties, so dogmatic is his insistence on a psychology of inevitable egotism.

It is John's daughter, Clara, who most flagrantly demonstrates the necessary egotism of revolt. She is less scrupulous than her father, more self-conscious, and even more intense. When she gets the leading role at which she has aimed, she offers no apology to the actress she has supplanted (though typically she relents and feels compassion afterwards): 'We have to fight, to fight for everything, and the weak get beaten. That's what life has taught me'. But in the context of survival, 'strength' and 'weakness' have less to do with moral or personal qualities than with the economic security she glares at nightly across the footlights. Clara's philosophy is offered as representative of 'what is seething in the brains of thousands who fight and perish in the obscure depths'. Clara's escape from the nether world is only temporary (and, as has been noted, we cannot follow her paltry ascent; it is only described to us in retrospect later). She finds herself circulating round the periphery of society in a context no whit preferable to the one she has left behind, for its superficial proximity to the wished for state of 'belonging'. As she peers into the darkness on the other side of the footlights, the chasm between the two worlds is as absolute as ever.

The novel is rich in the variety of desire, its qualities and conditions, from the Hewetts' tortured frustration to Clem Peckover's gross physical satiety. There is Bob Hewett, Clara's brother, who is apparently at home in the nether world, but possesses a natural craftsman's skill that fails to find fulfilment in his purposeless daily labour; he turns by a casual inevitability to crime. There is Scawthorne, the lawyer's clerk, the only character in the novel to make real progress in social terms; but his success has been soured by the degradations he has suffered in its desperate pursuit. Clem Peckover is the exact reverse of Clara in her perfect animal satisfaction with the delights of the nether world. The 'strong odour and . . . hissing sound' that greet Jane Snowdon as she opens the door seem to emanate as much from this

monstrous Amazon as from the sausages she is about to
devour. Yet Clem is endowed with something of Clara's
potentially anarchic energy, and it is, as so often, a pity that
Gissing does not explore this potentiality with more open-
mindedness. At one moment, he compares Clem's 'brutality'
to that of the 'noble savage running wild in the woods', only
to follow this by suggesting that 'this lust of hers for
sanguinary domination' may be 'the natural enough issue of
the brutalizing serfdom of her predecessors'. But Gissing is no
more interested in examining where Clem's barbaric energy
may lead to than where it has come from, and (unlike Hardy
with the analogous ambiguity of Tess as 'natural' or
'man-made' victim) leaves the issues unfocused.

If Clara and Clem both embody positive energy of
different sorts, they are united in opposition to Jane
Snowdon and Pennyloaf Candy, the passive victims. Pennyloaf is drawn with exquisite accuracy, in all her pathetic,
infuriating dolefulness. Even the narrator snarls at the way
the 'good little slavey' cringes ingratiatingly before her
husband, Bob Hewett. In this world of minimums, she
represents desire attenuated to the microscopic satisfactions
of retaining a husband to bully and thrash her. Any more
positive desire seems to have been exhausted in the capture
of that husband, and it is no surprise to find him returning to
the more robust charms of Clem Peckover. Pennyloaf is as
drugged into vacuousness by poverty, as her mother by
alcohol. The absence of sentimentality only sharpens and
hardens the human tragedy beneath the paralysed surface.

With Jane Snowdon, we come also to a consideration of
Sidney Kirkwood, for these two stand, ostensibly at least, at
the centre of the novel. Sidney is uneasily stirred by the
embers of a revolt more fully embodied in the Hewett family,
while Jane offers a variation of Pennyloaf's acquiescence,
sweetened by a natural gentility and the odd glint of
buoyant, fragile humour. But she has been permanently
tainted by her early years of drudgery; her gentility can only
really ever be gentleness. Neither Sidney nor Jane are satis-
factory as *central* characters, though in themselves they are
unexceptionable. There are moments when Sidney becomes
human, as when he experiences 'a kind of brutal pleasure' at

Clara's misery in her job at Mrs Trubb's — he had hated her taking it in the first place. But for the most part, the self-control, the 'sad clearness of his vision', to which he has *already* attained when we first see him, preclude the possibility of our identifying with the progessive flow, check, transformation and reconciliation of desire with possibility. His stoical resignation offers minimal room for manoeuvre, and we are thrown back on the narrator for the articulation of the 'spirit of revolt' which he is so competent at repressing.

If this sort of discrepancy between the excessive passivity of the two central characters and the energy of the narrator puts us in mind of *Little Dorrit*, it must be to register first that Jane Snowdon is not vitalised by incorporation in a set of dynamic metaphors as Amy Dorrit is, and secondly, that this is deliberate on Gissing's part. Indeed, Jane is as near as possible to being a deliberate *exposure* of the fictional 'Angel of Mercy' image, for it is precisely in this role that her idealistic grandfather casts her. She is a consciously de-theologised version of such conventional figures as Walter Besant's embarrassingly explicit Angela Messenger in *All Sorts and Conditions of Men*. But however well Gissing's exposure of literary conventions works in other areas of the novel, the narrative desperately needs some more positive embodiment of energy than either she or Sidney can offer. In the critical scene in which she rejects her grandfather's role, she refuses only out of weakness. For all her rejection of the heroine's role, she settles for a conventional option of personal charity, the relief of Pennyloafs, the patching up of disintegrating marriages (the Byasses'). She is, in fact, and always has been, disappointingly at home in the nether world — like her former tormentor, Clem. The novel closes with the words:

> . . . at least their lives would remain a protest against those brute forces of society which fill with wreck the abysses of the nether world.[20]

That 'at least' records with justice a minimal margin for moral survival; but it narrows down precisely to *moral* terms,

energies that have ranged far wider and more freely in the
course of the narrative.

There remains to consider the force that binds these
characters to the central vision of energies and frustrations,
the voice of a consistently engaged and self-dramatising
narrator. We can gauge the problems illustrated and relative
successes achieved by this narrator, if we look at two
particular passages.

The first is the set-piece of the Bank Holiday excursion to
the Crystal Palace, made by Bob Hewett and Pennyloaf on
their wedding day. Here at least, for better or worse, is the
narrator's energy.

> Throw wide the doors of the temple of Alcohol! Behold,
> we come in our thousands, jingling the coins that shall
> purchase us this one day of tragical mirth. Before us is the
> dark and dreary autumn; it is a far cry to the foggy joys of
> Christmas. Io Saturnalia![21]

There is more than simple contempt in this, such as Jacob
Korg sees[22] — if contempt is ever simple. The narrator can
feel too clearly the naked human response to sudden,
arbitrary and temporary release from slavery, and even as he
feels it, he hates that feeling. It is by now a familiar
short-circuit. Instead of focusing protest on to the causes
lying behind the social conditions that make a Bank Holiday
the bestial carnival that it appears to him, or penetrating
more fully to an identification with the human beings
involved, the observer stops short, trapped, at hatred of the
immediate surface phenomena. Certainly he can feel the wild
exhilaration of release felt by the 'slaves of industrialism', but
instead of directing his energies towards all that is covered by
'industrialism', he gets stuck with the 'slaves'; yet he cannot
reduce *this* abstraction to specific and human terms either. If
the major achievement of the novel is its dramatisation of the
way in which, in such a set of social conditions, energy
becomes contained, frustrated and displaced on to arbitrary
and inadequate objects (such as the targets at the fun-fair —
wily Afghans and treacherous Russians), its major limitation
is the narrator's failure to recognise the workings of this
displacement in himself.

But a second passage can illustrate the grim determination of this narrator not only to show, but also, more inwardly, to *know*. It is a description of the new Model buildings that are replacing slums like Shooter's Gardens.

> Vast, sheer walls, unbroken by even an attempt at ornament; row above row of windows in the mud-coloured surface, upwards, upwards, lifeless eyes, murky openings that tell of bareness, disorder, comfortless within . . . Acres of these edifices, the tinge of grime declaring the relative dates of their erection; millions of tons of brute brick and mortar, crushing the spirit as you gaze. Barracks, in truth; housing for the army of industrialism, an army fighting with itself, rank against rank, man against man, that the survivors may have whereon to feed. Pass by in the night, and strain imagination to picture the weltering mass of human weariness, of bestiality, of unmerited dolour, of hopeless hope, of crushed surrender, tumbled together within those forbidding walls.[2 3]

Charmless, blunt, but wholly grasped, this is an achieved rhetoric. It simultaneously enacts and defies the sense of massive, overpowering oppression in the form of specific physical phenomena. Here, in the Farringdon Road buildings, is epitomised the intractability of the material external form, behind and inside which is concealed an inner reality towards which the narrator tries to penetrate. '*Strain* imagination . . .' These stones offer no help, no Dickensian anthropomorphic encouragement. Gissing's paragraph reaches its climax with a bruising, battering series of abstractions. 'Weltering mass' seems an admission of defeat, the relapse into numbed horror. And then, almost miraculously, the next paragraph effects exactly the movement the narrator seems to have despaired of achieving. 'Clara hated the place from her first hour in it . . .' The deadlock is broken, the reified vision dissolved under the pressure of this penetration. The external vision of horror has been transformed as we move *through* the stones to Clara. It is this movement that enacts the positive affirmation, that knowledge, or knowing, is possible.

This is the finest aspect of the novel, its understanding of what it feels like to be trapped 'inside' — a building, a slum, a class, a hell. For despite the restrictions of Gissing's language, his ways of recording and judging, there survives this desire to discover the human reality behind the dehumanised appearance, the discovery that can alone redeem and transform the waste land. And this struggle to survive is all the more poignant for its near impossibility on the stark, narrow, twilight edge. Desire, energy, passion *do* continue in the face of overwhelming pressures to immobilise and anaesthetise them, into acquiescence, despair or nostalgia. It is a measure of *The Nether World's* achievement that it makes Morris's *News from Nowhere* intolerably comfortable by comparison.

Part II

THE WRITER, SOCIETY AND THE LITERARY WORLD

4 Images of the Writer and the Literary World

New Grub Street (1891) owes its justified pre-eminence in Gissing's work to the coherence with which it embodies one man's version of cultural crisis. We shall need to consider the extent to which the novel's vision coincides with and deviates from changing historical actualities. But in order to understand its imaginative context, we must also look at the images of the writer most influential on Gissing himself, and most prevalent among his contemporaries.

At the start of the century the Romantic poets provide some decisive definitions of the writer and his relationship to society. On the one hand, there is the expanding vista of inner space, of dreams, visions and nightmares, glorifying and demeaning a new, problematic sense of Self; on the other, an increasing responsibility for the world outside the new palaces, temples and towers of the artist's imagination. From these contradictory pressures derive all the subsequent major antinomies, the terms persistently modulating in accordance with emotional and psychological need, and objective historical reality. What is constant is the *energy* implicit in the distance between the terms, Self and Other, Imagination and Reality, Writer and Society. The creative mind strives to control or disarm this impersonal energy by destroying or neutralising the sense of distance. This can take the form of obliterating the distinction between the terms, of recapturing or creating a paradisal or utopian unity, historical or imaginative, or it can take the form of effectively discrediting one of the terms (usually, but not always, 'the world'), so as to assert the virtual autonomy of the other.

In this respect, the notion of 'integrity' that plays such a central role in the life and work of Gissing and other late-Victorian writers, has to be seen in continuity with a preceding tradition shaped and modified throughout the century. There is one writer above all who set his massive imprint on the still fluid attitudes and images proposed by the Romantic poets: Thomas Carlyle.

So much of Carlyle was diffused throughout Victorian consciousness that there is little need to unearth signs of direct 'influence', but such evidence as there is of Gissing's admiration for him is important. This extract from a letter soon after Carlyle's death in 1881 reveals what was rapidly becoming an old-fashioned reverence for the ideals of a preceding generation, and a characteristic sense of exile in a fallen world of mediocrity.

> Does it not seem now as if all our really great men were leaving us, and, what is worse, without much prospect as yet of any to take their place ... What a frightful thing would be a living generation utterly made up of mediocrities, even though the honest and well-meaning exceeded the charlatans![1]

It was a consolation that he viewed with increasing scepticism. Carlyle's contempt for the sham and the mediocre was fuel to Gissing's own temperamental proclivities, and there is a note of affection in his references to 'old Thomas', 'the old fellow', that bespeaks his recognition of affinity. *Sartor* he considered 'one of the most *important* books of the century',[2] noting with scorn a casual remark in the *Daily Telegraph*, 4 May 1899, that it was 'a ponderous volume which few people have ever finished'.[3] Gissing included it in a list of his seven favourite books.[4]

From his admiration for Froude's *Life*, and some comments on an article on Carlyle written by his friend Bertz,[5] we may surmise that Gissing took a particular interest in the dramatic details of Carlyle's professional life, and its wider implications. The image of the writer projected by Carlyle is one of absolute integrity in the face of the debasing solicitations of the outside world, of publishers, editors, readers, money and fame. As a prototype of the artist exiled from contemporary culture, this is of extreme and seminal relevance to Gissing. For Carlyle is deeply concerned with the power of the word, the potential power of the true artist, the Hero as Man of Letters, and the actual power of the spurious literary men, the scribblers at the heart of the nation's cultural chaos. In its sharp oppositions, it is a version of cultural crisis that is close to that of *New Grub Street*. The true literary man — 'the light of the world; the world's Priest' — labours away 'in his squalid garret, in his rusty coat'. Such a note as the following in Carlyle's Journal would have won Gissing's enthusiastic approval: 'Authors are martyrs — witnesses for the truth — or else nothing. Money cannot make or unmake them . . .'[6] But 'the true Church of England' has been taken over by the scribblers. The exile of the fragmented community of true artists ('this anomaly of a disorganic Literary Class') is claimed as 'the heart of all other anomalies, at once product and parent'.[7]

Gissing's bitterness at the tyranny of publishers and editors is mild in comparison with Carlyle's pungent abusiveness. The difficulty that he had in finding a publisher for *Sartor* was only the most vicious clash in a permanent state of war between the autocratic demands of prophetic genius, and the sordid mechanical details of its mediation to the outside world. Of John Murray he wrote, 'The man behaved like a pig . . .'[8], and poor Fraser, who was in fact the one to accept *Sartor*, was dismissed as a commercial broker, and the 'infatuated Fraser, with his dog's meat tart of a magazine'.[9] It is in the absoluteness of the polarisation between the pure inner message and its 'mechanical' clothing that Carlyle adumbrates the feelings of writers at the end of the century. His first visit to London in 1824 had convinced him of the resolution never to be a mere 'literary man'.

A miserable scrub of an author, sharking and writing 'articles' about town like Hazlitt, De Quincey, and that class of living creatures, is a thing which, as our mother says, 'I canna be'.[10]

It was this achieved aloofness which Carlyle recalled in his *Reminiscences* as the spiritual state in which he returned to Scotland after his first descent into the nether world of London.

In a fine and veritable sense, I, poor, obscure, without outlook, almost without wordly hope had become independent of the world.[11]

It was the same image of serene immunity that he projected to his brother in 1835.

> So I sit and write, composed in mood; responsible to no man or to no thing; only to God and my own conscience: with publishers, reviewers, hawkers, bill-stickers, indeed on the Earth round me; but with the stars and the azure Eternities above me in the Heaven.[12]

Here is that more robust version of Marvell's 'drop of dew' ('So the world excluding round,/Yet receiving in the day'), that exercised such a fascination for Gissing. For Gissing and later writers, however, the issue of inner integrity has degenerated into a more desperate struggle for survival. In retrospect, therefore, Carlyle's image of achieved integrity, the apocalyptic confirmation of which is celebrated in the famous chapter in *Sartor,* takes on the significance of a Utopian ideal.

If Carlyle provides a useful focus for pulling together diffused attitudes that would have reached Gissing through many various voices, Gissing's relationship to Dickens is by contrast precise and direct. Indeed there is no better way of characterising his own concept of the role of the writer than by close examination of his elusive, conflicting attitudes towards Dickens. Admiration, nostalgia, distaste: Gissing was as poised between attraction to and repulsion from the image of authorship embodied in Dickens, as he was in his attitudes towards class or personal relationship.

First, there is the genuine and generous admiration. This has two main aspects, the first of uncritical nostalgia for the formative images of a particular historical epoch, associated with Gissing's own childhood and early manhood. In 'Dickens in Memory', he recounts how his first vision of London was influenced by Dickens. 'In time I came to see London with my own eyes, but how much better when I saw it with those of Dickens!'[13] The more decisive aspect of his admiration, however, was for the personal dedication, vigour and determination with which Dickens created an identity for himself as a great and popular writer. Forster's *Life* (which he himself abridged and revised — itself something of a feat) was one of his favourite books; he never tired of reading of 'that wonderful career of matchless energy, of artistic fervour and conscientiousness'. In it was to be found 'the root of the matter — how Dickens taught himself to be a writer of books, and how, one after another, those books were written'.[14] He wrote this with feeling, for many was the time when he had been sunk in despair about his own creative potential, only to turn for inspiration to Forster's *Life*. Together with Daudet's *Trente Ans de Paris*, they were the two biographies that had 'a supreme attraction' for him; but, as we would expect, the attraction was not without a mordant note, for 'they always excite me to discontent and misery . . . The happiness of those stories at once delights me and wrings my heart.'[15]

The combination of delight and misery that Gissing records points towards the contradictions in his more detached, critical evaluation of Dickens, to be found in *Charles Dickens: A Critical Study* (1898), and the prefaces written for the Rochester edition, collected in *Critical Studies of the Works of Charles Dickens* (1924). The objective value of these studies, and the historical importance of the former, have long been recognised. They are also as interesting for what they reveal to us of Gissing's own point of view, prejudices and sympathies, as for their insight into Dickens.

The dominant tone that Gissing establishes is one of *distance* from a literary achievement belonging to a cultural and historical period now definitely past. This attempt to set Dickens impartially in an historical perspective is one of his most important contributions to the history of Dickens criticism. As Pierre Coustillas has pointed out,[16] he successfully reconciled the warring claims of detractors and enthusiasts for whom up until then Dickens had been a close presence, demanding embrace or rejection. In the opening chapter of the *Study* (1898), entitled 'His Times', Gissing sets out to characterise Dickens as a struggling aspirant to, and then successful representative of, a rising middle class, sharing its most admirable qualities of energy, self-confidence and self-criticism, but not devoid of its failings. Without deprecating the importance of Dickens's severe critique of the miseries attendant on the aggressive spirit of 'progress', he is

careful to point out the limits of Dickens's 'radicalism'.
Indeed what had once appeared as 'radical' attitudes could
now often be seen as 'conservative', in their anti-democratic
bias. Gissing's own extreme ambivalence comes into play
here. For him, Dickens's ability simultaneously to share and
to criticise the central forces shaping contemporary society
represents an ideal image of the integrated, yet still independent, author. But it is an ideal no longer practically available
for Gissing himself as a creative writer — those forces and
that allegiance belonging to an era irrevocably past. Dickens
had indeed been the 'man of his time', and good luck to him.
But the 'man of the time' now was, in Gissing's version,
Jasper Milvain, the shameless entrepreneur.

The importance of this image of Dickens as the 'man of his
time' cannot be over-estimated; Gissing emphasised its
implications at every turn. In his abridgement of Forster's
Life, for example, he inserted a number of his own
judgements, and at the moment of Dickens's first major
success with *Pickwick*, he comes forward with this authoritative generalisation:

> The moment was favourable to a new writer of original
> powers . . . A new era of social and political life had just
> begun; the middle class was entering into its dominion. To
> that class Dickens belonged by birth and by sympathy, and
> throughout his career it had no more remarkable represent-
> ative.[17]

Gissing was able to appreciate the strength and weakness of
Dickens's intimacy with his readers with peculiar sharpness.
He could enviously admire the assurance on which Dickens
drew of shared needs and ideas ('During at least one
generation, Charles Dickens, in the world of literature, meant
England . . .').[18] Yet at the same time, out of the very
inviolable confidence in 'belonging', Dickens could stand
apart and criticise the conventional. Here was, for Gissing, an
ideal, miraculous reconciliation of distance and intimacy,
independence and integration.

> Among the rarest of things is this thorough understanding
> between author and public, permitting a man of genius to

say aloud with impunity that which all his hearers say within themselves dumbly, inarticulately.[19]

Now this is a very suggestive and pertinent formulation. The sort of rapport that Dickens had with his readers came, in Gissing's time, to be the sole prerogative of writers such as Marie Corelli, Mrs Humphry Ward and Grant Allen, writers who saw themselves explicitly in the great tradition of the moralising, sage-like novelist. But for them it was less a question of articulating the *hidden* views and emotions of their readers as Gissing had suggested in relation to Dickens, than of manipulating, with adequate dexterity, an already existing currency of attitudes. The problem for Carlyle's 'true writer' becomes indeed one of penetrating beneath the surface assumptions and conventions to an increasingly inaccessible secret 'reality', namely 'that which all' (or merely a satisfying proportion of) 'his hearers say within themselves dumbly, inarticulately'.

It was to exactly this issue that Hardy addressed himself in a preface to *Tess*, written in 1892 for the fifth and later editions. It was 'quite contrary to avowed conventions' that the public should have welcomed a novel in which the heroine begins with an experience 'which has usually been treated as fatal to her part of protagonist'.

> But the responsive spirit in which *Tess of the D'Urbervilles* has been received by the readers of England and America, would seem to prove that the plan of laying down a story on the lines of tacit opinion, instead of making it square with the merely vocal formulae of society, is not altogether a wrong one . . .[20]

The questions Hardy raises here are crucial: what is the relation between 'tacit opinion' and the 'vocal formulae of society'? or to put it more sharply, is the 'tacit opinion' to which it is the writer's duty to penetrate, actively embodied in the values and forms governing, albeit unobtrusively, the cultural life of the nation, or is it precisely 'tacit' as the private consolation of a privileged but helpless minority? Hardy and Gissing shared a bitter scepticism about the existence of a genuinely homogeneous and reachable 'tacit

opinion'. Gissing seems indeed to have accepted this almost
from the start; community and communication for the 'true
author' could only be with the few lonely watchers. Of his
first novel, he wrote at the time: 'it must be accepted by
intellectual people if at all'.[21] (The few were even fewer
than he expected; only 49 copies sold in three months out of
the 277 printed, at his own expense, and most of the edition
remaindered.) Hardy, on the other hand, with a real
popularity such as Gissing never achieved (*The Bookman*,
January 1892, listed him among the top twelve contemporary authors for 'selling value'), had more of a move to
make towards disillusionment. But after *Jude*, he wrote to
Edmund Gosse in terms that echo Gissing's (and James's)
acquiescence in a severely circumscribed, and even then still
hypothetical, circle of communication.

> As for the story itself, it is really sent out to those into
> whose souls the iron has entered, and entered deeply at
> some time of their lives. But one cannot choose one's
> readers.[22]

Returning to Dickens, we can recognise the fascination
that he exercised for Gissing, at the edge between objective
admiration and personal envy, the latter shading over
sometimes into positive distaste. This last element has often
been overlooked. To do Gissing justice, one has to say that in
his published comments his sense of the liabilities as well as
the virtues of Dickens's rapport with his readers is in the
main controlled. He is quick to point out the occasions on
which Dickens can be accused of pandering to his readers'
susceptibilities, such as in the revision of his original plan to
show Walter Gay's gradual degeneration in *Dombey and Son*.
He sees a similar *volte-face* in the miraculous transformation
of Boffin in *Our Mutual Friend*, concluding with a revealingly
excessive severity: 'Avoidance of the disagreeable, as a topic
uncongenial to art — this is Dickens's principle'.[23]
Though he restricts such generalised indictments to a
minimum, the evidence from his private writings suggests the
element of deliberate self-control. Any impression of *def-
erence* is quite dispelled. It is something of a shock, for
example, to read a note in his *Commonplace Book* that

starts: 'To realize the inferiority of Dickens to Thackeray . . .'[24] Coustillas has shrewdly pointed out the discrepancy between the general air of surprise that greeted the announcement of the projected study of Dickens beforehand, and the subsequent conventionality of linking their names.[25] The immediacy with which Gissing was afterwards accepted as an authority on Dickens, receiving commissions for prefaces and articles, obscured the extent of the distance between them. While admitting the obvious temperamental differences between them, readers have tended to speak of Gissing as a 'follower' of Dickens in a misleading way. Gissing wrote to Wells, for example, while he was working on the *Study* at Siena: 'I have made a good beginning with my Dickens, and long to have done it, for of course it is an alien aubject.'[26] When Gissing was asked for another volume on Thackeray for the same Victorian Era Series by the editor, John Holland Rose (a contemporary at Owens College), it was with regret that he declined, feeling the need to keep his name before the public as a novelist. He wrote at the time to Clodd: 'I should *like* to try my hand at Thackeray, who, be it said between us, appeals to me much more strongly than Dickens.'[27] It is instructive that of all the references to Dickens and Thackeray in his *Commonplace Book*, those to the former are invariably critical, those to the latter invariably appreciative. If Dickens's 'grave defect' was his solicitude for 'the murmurings of the imbecile public', it was precisely Thackeray's scorn for it that appealed to Gissing. He felt that Thackeray was prepared to challenge many of the comfortable assurances behind which Dickens was too quick to hide, particularly in the representation of working-class life; and to challenge in a way that had become a *duty* for the novelist of Gissing's own generation. In the *Study*, he talks of the 'morally mischievous' idealising of working-class girls in Dickens (though his own prostitute heroine in *The Unclassed* had been as remote from plausibility as Martha in *David Copperfield*). Fanny Bolton, on the other hand, was 'one of the truest characters in all fiction', even painfully so.

It may, after this, seem a contradiction that Gissing should have cited Thackeray's confession in the preface to *Pendennis* of accepted limits to artistic presentation,[28] as an instance of capitulation to the tyranny of convention. The occasion was a debate on the censorship of the circulating libraries, initiated by an article of George Moore's in the *Pall Mall Gazette*, 1884.

> It is a hard thing to say, but Thackeray, when he knowingly wrote below the demands of his art to conciliate Mrs. Grundy, betrayed his trust . . .[29]

But we should take Gissing seriously (as the *Punch* lampoon that subsequently excoriated him did not),[30] when he says, 'It is a *hard* thing to say', since he is citing Thackeray for the very reason that he was the writer of the previous generation who came closest to the sort of challenge to convention Gissing felt to be necessary. Hence the proportionate disappointment at his admission of defeat. Nearly all his private references to Thackeray suggest the creative encouragement to 'sincerity' that he offered. The 'flood of nauseous & lying eulogy' that erupted on the death of the publisher George Smith prompted him, so Gabrielle Fleury records, to this comment:

> The Art of Fiction has this great ethical importance that it enables one to tell the truth about human beings in a way which is impossible in actual life . . . Thackeray's moral usefulness is especially great in that respect.[31]

This is a considerably more mature attitude, incidentally, than that displayed by the belligerent antinomianism of the *Pall Mall Gazette* letter.

We must look now at the conditions of Gissing's own time that stimulated such particular interest in the images of hostility and appeasement observable in the writers of a previous generation. For the attitudes, expectations, forms and institutions that governed the literary world of the 1880s had all been established in an earlier era. The great publishing houses such as Macmillan and Bentley had been built up through two generations into well-regulated and respected business concerns. Like the even more central institutions of the two great circulating libraries, Mudie's and Smith's, they owed their success to the instinctive capacity of their founders for embodying and sustaining the values, tastes,

needs and habits of the economically and culturally ascen-
dant middle class. In her recent history of Mudie's,
Guinevere Griest has shown the immense power apparently
concentrated in the hands of this one man, Charles Edward
Mudie, as he mediated the everyday flow of cultural, moral,
emotional and political images into the homes of the Reading
Public. But by the 1880s this power and this Reading Public
had been settling for several decades into increasingly
comfortable and seemingly permanent postures. Even in
1865, James Thomson had denounced the slavish subservience
of contemporary literature as a whole to the spirit of
Bumble: 'Woe be to any one who shall have the audacity to
shock his cherished, his sacred convictions, on any social or
moral or religious matter!'[32] With Mrs Grundy in place of
Bumble, this became a familiar cry in the 1880s, when it
seemed to writers like Gissing a paramount duty to dispute
the stranglehold on free creativity exerted by Mudie and the
exemplary 'two ladies from the country' who objected to a
scene in Moore's *A Modern Lover*. In his *Pall Mall Gazette* letter
just referred to, Moore produced a startling image of Mudie
as a sort of maniacally moral surgeon.

> ... it is by this amputation that humanity becomes
> headless, trunkless, limbless, and is converted into the
> pulseless, non-vertebrate jelly-fish sort of thing which,
> securely packed in tin-cornered boxes, is sent from the
> London depot and scattered through the drawing-rooms of
> the United Kingdom.[33]

The antagonistic writer was faced, so it seemed, with an
almost impenetrable, monolithic alliance between reader,
publisher and distributor. Between writer and publisher,
writer and reader, there had grown up the same brutal
deadlocks as characterise the social confrontations of these
years. The writer, embittered by experiences such as Gissing
had with Smith and Payn, would be likely to regard the
publisher as a grasping Philistine, out to squeeze the
maximum profit out of the precious child of his imagination.
This blunt comment of Richard Bentley II to Helen Reeves,
author of *Coming through the Rye*, suggests the painful
incompatibility between author's and publisher's view of the
physical object, the book. (He was refusing her demand for

extra payment; she had sold the copyright to the publishers
twenty years previously.)

> If I sold a horse or a picture tomorrow for an agreed
> amount, I should never receive another penny even if it
> won the Derby or was discovered to be an Old Master.[34]

Not the least important change characterising the literary
world of the nineties was the diminution of friction between
writer and publisher, through the closer regulation of methods
of payment and the advent of the literary agent.

But the really crucial confrontation during the eighties,
working through that between writer and publisher, is the
one between writer and reader. Here, in the changing image
of the 'ordinary reader', we can watch the sharp shift that
takes place. In the eighties it was always in the area of the
moral restrictions imposed on the artist that controversy was
fiercest. In this explanation of Smith and Elder to Gissing for
their refusal of *Mrs. Grundy's Enemies* (1882), we can see the
key formula. The novel was 'too painful to please the
ordinary reader and treats of scenes that can never attract the
subscribers to Mr. Mudie's library'.[35] This image of the
'ordinary reader' that they invoke belongs to a period *prior*
to 1890. It is a clear, well-established image that takes in the
comfortable physical circumstances of the act of reading
(leisure, privacy, light), the social and political attitudes to
which the reader consciously or unconsciously subscribes,
and, most probably, the reader's sex. As the publishers' note
neatly demonstrates, the concept was inextricably tied to the
institution of the circulating library. It was towards the end
of the eighties that the circulating library system began at last
to founder, though the official end of its supremacy can be
dated from the effective death of the three-volume novel in
June 1894. Despite George Moore's vigorous claims for the
role of knight-errant, it was not so much the demand for
artistic sincerity that toppled the system, as the more general
economic and social pressures demanding the expansion and
diversification of readership, as well as of reading matter. The
whole idea of a 'select list' for a 'select readership' was no
longer adequate to cope with the expanding needs and
numbers of those who wanted to read. It becomes in-

creasingly difficult, therefore, to produce a single 'identikit' picture of the ordinary reader. Instead of the localised image of the cheek of the young person, criteria of tolerance or acceptability shift towards the mass and the abstract, 'the public', 'our readers'. Moreover, the image of the reader's rejection becomes no longer the blush, but the yawn. It is now boredom the publisher fears rather than moral outrage.

It is of course misleading to attribute sole culpability for the complex changes that take place at this time to the 'new journalism'. We shall look later at the way in which a new generation of publishers was instrumental in some positive liberations and realignments that Gissing ignores or distorts in *New Grub Street*. Nevertheless, it is important to recognise how far and in what way Newnes and others replaced Mudie in the symbolic as well as actual positions of power. Newnes's success, like Mudie's before him, was based as much on a correct interpretation of needs and attitudes as on a positive shaping of them. The essential qualification was the naïveté to believe in this formula of Newnes's: 'I am the average man ... I don't have to put myself in his place. I am in his place. I know what he wants.'[36] (The writer who quotes this points out the risible anomaly. Newnes would utter these words in all earnestness and humility — surrounded by the aura and trappings of the stupendously successful, *un*-average businessman.) What *was* new was the image of power, corresponding to real changes in the economic conditions of communication. The strategic phrase that has replaced 'the ordinary reader' is 'what the public wants'. Beneath the amiable cliché is the tougher image of readers out there to be *captured*. Instead of a pre-existent readership to which Mudie shaped his tactics, there now exists only a market situation, out of which the entrepreneur creates his own customers. The images of power pass from the publisher or circulating library chief to the newspaper editor and proprietor. In a diary entry in 1880, just before he became editor of the *Pall Mall Gazette*, W. T. Stead made this revealing confession of intent:

I think I see my way now to make the paper a success ... If my health keeps good, I shall in after years be the most

powerful man in England. My great newspaper will seize me
and I shall have a power for good which no one at present
possesses.[37]

The vision of power (which it was left to others to realise)
corresponds to a sense that the 'ordinary reader' is no longer
an independent entity out there, to be deferred to,
humoured, cajoled. The image of the 'ordinary' can instead
be continually reshaped and exploited to appeal to something
tractable in everyone.

Newnes's image of the 'average man' gathers importance,
therefore, as the specific phenomenon to which Mudie's
image genuinely corresponded is becoming more and more
blurred. How then does this changing image of the reader
relate to the changing image of the writer? In Gissing's own
self-images of the writer three main phases can be distinguished. The first, heavily influenced by residual notions
of an earlier age, offers the image of public moralist and
reformer; the second, the writer as heroic exile and martyr to
the cause of free, independent vision; the third, the writer as
member of a literary fraternity, still marginal to the general
culture, but assured of some sort of public status. Of these,
the second phase is easily the most important. But if
antagonism to the conventional is the most dominant single
characteristic of Gissing's image of the writer, it is vital to see
the change in the quality and orientation of this hostility
connecting with the changing image of the 'conventional'.

The phase in which Gissing felt that he had a social mission
was fortunately brief, though in 1882 he could still delude
himself into thinking that 'philosophico-social speculation'
was his real bent. But within a year, he was beginnning to
claim allegiance to a theory of 'Art for Art's sake'.[38] In
doing so, he was making use of a notion that appealed to
many very diverse writers of the time, usually as a means of
negative definition rather than positive commitment. Like
Hardy and James, Gissing was concerned to free writing from
the constrictions of intentionalist criteria by which serious
fiction was usually judged, Art *for* Social Reform, Art *for* a
Moral Purpose. The word 'sincerity' becomes particularly
important in the vocabulary of the time as a motto of

resistance, invariably in association with the word 'realism'. Gissing wrote, for example: 'Realism . . . signifies nothing more than artistic sincerity in the portrayal of contemporary life'.[39] This, we might note, suggests the major difference between British and European discussions of 'realism' during these years, that in Britain, the debate is rarely concerned with form or method, the writer's relation to his material, but primarily with the relation between the writer and his readers.

Taking a large perspective, we can see that all these stances and commitments, to 'realism', 'sincerity', 'Art for Art's sake', are more or less defensive and defiant. In the novel, the confidence to dispense authoritative judgements from the centre of a narrative diffused through multiple actions, characters and issues, is now becoming an acquirement brandished only by popular writers such as Mrs Humphry Ward and Marie Corelli — writers who see themselves as descendants of the high Victorian tradition. It is precisely from this concept of the writer's role and responsibilities that Gissing was eager to dissociate himself in the eighties. The deliberate eschewal of popularity became in itself an assurance of value. After reading *Diana of the Crossways* in 1885, Gissing noted of Meredith: 'He is great, there is no doubt of it, but too difficult for the British Public. What good thing is not?'[40]

In the 1890s the problem of the minority writer becomes complicated by the recognition that he *has* achieved his 'freedom', but at the expense of a more permanent and disastrous subjugation. For despite the fuss that could still be made by Bishop Hows and Mrs Oliphants over the moral turpitude of *Tess* and *Jude*, a radical change has taken place in the reception of antagonistic or controversial literature. A new publisher such as Heinemann could build up a profitable market in explicitly controversial subjects, such as the 'woman problem'. Novels such as Grant Allen's *The Woman Who Did* (1895) or Sarah Grand's *The Heavenly Twins* (1893) could exploit what Henry James ironically called 'the larger latitude'. There is no more remarkable instance of the apparently abrupt shift in the general climate of opinion than in the attitudes officially displayed by the British public towards Zola. As is well known, Henry Vizetelly had been imprisoned for three months in 1889 for publishing translations of Zola in England. Yet within four years, Zola himself came to England and was received with respect and acclaim. Gissing was a connoisseur of ironies such as this, and enjoyed the letter to *The Times* (27 September 1893), signed 'Inquirer', pointing out the fickleness of the high-principled British public.

But if this seems a victory for the forces of artistic freedom and sincerity, it also contains the essence of the new and possibly more insidious form of society's manipulation of the artist. For now, instead of the image of public moralist, so rapidly receding from credibility, the artist is manoeuvred into a new role as 'personality', performer, celebrity. In this respect, the fate of the antagonistic writer of the eighties is analogous to the fictional fortunes of the dangerously militant working classes. Once their serious challenge has been deflected and absorbed in the nineties, they become harmless and colourful 'characters'. Most of Henry James's superb stories of the literary world written in the 1890s are based on exactly this new image of the writer, whereby the public's recognition elevates him to the same stellar level as the brilliant financier or diplomat or hostess, without casting a second glance at the objective achievement of his work. 'That', as the exemplary journalist Mr Morrow remarks in 'The Death of the Lion', casting a disparaging glance at the great novelist's latest production, 'is not *news* — not what our readers want to hear.' This is the crux — 'our readers'.

It is worth pausing for a moment to note the cumulative effect of a real column similar to the one called 'Smatter and Chatter' to which Mr Morrow is supposed glibly to contribute. *The Bookman*, started by Robertson Nicoll in 1891, quickly established itself as a 'quality' magazine, containing some first-rate criticism. But alongside the high-level reviews and essays is a recognisably new idiom, to be found above all in the column that opens the magazines, its 'News Notes'. For the column projects exactly this image of the writer as 'personality', in its 'human interest' approach; the spirit of Newnes hovers benevolently. We read about so-and-so's plans, his health, his marriage, his travels, his death, and best of all, his offer of anecdotes. Perhaps more significantly, the column acts as a permanent gauge of writers' public status, continually noting their relative popularities, the delicate shades of reputation, the continual jostling for position. The atmosphere created is of a forum for airing writers' market- able value — and indeed for simultaneously shaping it. The names that recur most frequently during the early years are Kipling, Stevenson, Barrie. *The Bookman* also utilises that most symptomatic of journalistic innovations — the 'inter- view' (originated by W. T. Stead in the eighties). James has great fun with this in 'The Death of the Lion', but he is making a sharp point about the shift of attention that was once in Mr Deedy's decorous days accorded to a detached critical assessment of a writer's work. The new editor, Mr Pinhorn, like the editor of 'The Cynosure' in 'John Delavoy', is now solely concerned with the writer's opinions, habits and eccentricities. Gissing expressed some sardonic doubts about the appropriateness of *his* 'eccentricities' for the desired image of amiable respectability.

> When I read 'interviews' of authors, descriptions of their abodes ('He has built himself a charming house' &c) I can't help thinking how it would startle people if anyone faithfully described *my* abode & manner of life.[41]

At this point, as the reference to James suggests, we need to look more closely at the way in which Gissing's con- temporaries responded to these apparently radical changes. How far do they corroborate his version of acute cultural crisis?

It was certainly as an ally that Gissing wanted to see Hardy, even after his disillusionment with him personally. Before he had even read *Tess*, he wrote enthusiastically to Bertz:

> It is glaringly unconventional, and earns its applause in the very teeth of a great deal of puritanic prejudice. Hardy is a nobly artistic nature. I am glad and proud that he has yet a future of growth before him.[42]

Gissing's attitude to Hardy was always somewhat equivocal,

as the wording here about 'a future of growth' might suggest.
(After reading *The Woodlanders* in 1888, he noted patron-
isingly: 'Hardy cannot deal with anything above the humours
of the rustics . . .')[43] But Hardy had been fighting the
conventional expectations and definitions of the writer's
business for years. Alexander Macmillan had recognised from
the young man's first novel in 1868, *The Poor Man and the
Lady*, that he was 'in grim earnest' and 'meant mischief'.[44]
But according to Hardy himself, it was a few years later, after
the major success of *Far from the Madding Crowd* in 1874,
that he first became fully conscious of the network of
pressures impinging on the writer, both in his work and his
social personality. It was the consternation of the editor and
publishers of the *Cornhill* at the new direction he was taking
in *The Hand of Ethelberta* that prompted him to thought. He
was living at this time in London, and necessarily became
absorbed in many of the social rituals the literary man was
expected to perform. His unease with the histrionic plane on
which the literary world and London 'society' as a whole
seemed to exist, finds expression in repeated images of
somnambulism. In his *Life*, we receive a revealing account of
his doubts at this time, about his capacity and willingness to
play his expected role in this dream-world.

> One reflection about himself at this date sometimes made
> Hardy uneasy. He perceived that he was 'up against' the
> position of having to carry on his life not as an emotion,
> but as a scientific game; that he was committed by
> circumstances to novel-writing as a regular trade, as much
> as he had formerly been to architecture; and that hence he
> would, he deemed, have to look for material in manners —
> in ordinary social and fashionable life as other novelists
> did. Yet he took no interest in manners, but in the
> substance of life only.[45]

The dichotomy he describes is very close to that perceived by
Gissing, between the solitary creative activity of the 'true'
writer ('events and long habit had accustomed him to solitary
living'), and the increasingly ritualised gestures thrust upon
the professional writer ('to go about to dinners and clubs and
crushes was not much to his mind'). Leslie Stephen's
sister-in-law was shocked by the writer's heretical tendencies

into expostulating: 'a novelist must necessarily like society'. The professional image of the writer was indeed growing corpulent from more than the social round of wining and dining. Hardy was deeply anxious about retaining his independence. When Walter Besant was conducting his vociferous campaign for the award of titles and distinctions to men of letters, Hardy quietly remonstrated that the writer was *not* a respectable professional man to be bribed into upholding conventional definitions of success.

> The highest flights of the pen are often, indeed mostly, the excursions and revelations of souls unreconciled to life; while the natural tendency of government would be to encourage acquiescence in life as it is.[46]

But though in many ways close to Gissing in feeling, Hardy's own considerable public success would naturally prevent his extension of the stance into a generalised version of cultural crisis. It is Henry James who, though very far from sharing Gissing's experience of physical exclusion, comes closer than any other writer of the time to Gissing's identification of cultural crisis. Where Hardy was disturbed, James was fascinated by the dilemma of the artist, as being simultaneously committed to the most private, indeed sacred, of inner activities, and to participation in the public routines of society. As early as 1874, he had written to Mrs Wister in response to possible criticisms of *Roderick Hudson,* of this paradox of detachment and involvement:

> ... how can the artist, the painter of life, the recorder, the observer, stand on the outside of things and write about them, and throw himself at the same time into the act of living ... How become involved in life — and remain uninvolved?[47]

It is, of course, *the* question for James. He could toy with the paradox as if it were an impossible geometrical shape, turning it this way and that, assaulting it with irony and passion, from the level of extended debate in *The Tragic Muse,* to that of the absorbed lecture, 'The Lesson of Balzac', to that of the flamboyant romance, 'The Great Good Place'. And as Dickens provided for Gissing an image of transcendent

integration, so did Balzac for James; it is instructive to find
the similar blend of envy, and even condescension, in their
genuine admiration.

The majority of James's stories of the literary life belong
to the 1890s, and they dramatise very precisely the changing
conditions under which the writer finds himself more and
more deeply entangled in the accoutrements of his social
identity, as his creative inner Self suffers an increasing exile.
It is the redemption of this inner life that George Dane finds
in the the extraordinary fantasy-release of 'The Great Good
Place'.

> The inner life woke up again, and it was the inner life, for
> people of his generation, victims of the modern madness,
> mere maniacal extension and motion, that was returning
> health.[48]

The absorption of Art, the sanction of the inner life, into the
sphere of mere 'extension and motion', the frenetic interchange of a vacuous social and cultural currency — this is the
prime characteristic of the literary world of the nineties. In a
tale such as 'The Death of the Lion', James takes us beyond
the spatial limits of *New Grub Street* into the fashionable
drawing-rooms of 'society'. In contrast to Gissing, James
shows the possibility of a minority writer such as Paraday or
Vereker or Dencombe attaining a genuine public status that is
scarcely conceivable for Reardon or Biffen. But there is little
comfort to be gained from this recognition. For the quality
of society's applause is soon seen to depend on exactly those
recommendations of fashionability and news-value that
Gissing identified in *New Grub Street*. James's artists may
face a different threat from Gissing's. Instead of starvation
and the workhouse, St George, Paraday, Dane and the
others face the less immediately painful prospect of suffo-
cation in the pungent embrace of society's acclaim. But if
Gissing's artists are trapped outside on the freezing pavement
looking in at the window, James's artists meet their eyes in
fraternal suffering as they gaze out from within.

The poised ironies of James's stories show more tolerance
for the possible survival of the serious minority writer within
the oppressive web of cultural publicity; but James is,
beneath these, as committed as Gissing to the image of

disastrous schism. 'The Lesson of the Master' (1888), for all
its ironic dexterity, projects a vision of pure incompatibility
between the inner world of Art and the outer world of
material and physical fulfilment. (With characteristic precision James leaves perfectly unresolved the problem of
whether St George is indeed the redeeming knight-errant who
saves Paul Overt from the monster of wordly entanglement, or
an arch impostor who steals the maiden from under his nose.)
'The Coxon Fund' (1894) revolves around the absolute
distinction between the two spheres of activity and value: the
sphere of external judgement and respectability, the clockwork categories of Clockborough, summed up by its M.P.,
George Gravener ('The only thing that really counts for one's
estimate of a person is his conduct'), and the sphere of the
spontaneous and intuitive, in which the disreputable genius
Frank Saltram can alone be appreciated.

As Leon Edel suggests, the literary stories of the nineties
often seem to be deflections from the less manageable
experience of James's assault on the London theatre during
these years.[49] The culminating débâcle of the first night of
Guy Domville (5 January 1895) offers a symbolic confrontation cruder and more painful than anything in James's
fiction. When James was led nervously onto the stage at the
end of the performance, he was confronted by a sight that
could be taken as directly emblematic. Trapped between a
derisively howling pit below and gallery above, the instinctively sympathetic stalls clapped bravely for the shocked and
bewildered author. It was a paradigmatic confrontation
between the forces of mass vulgarity and an embattled
cultural (and social) élite. As such, it offered the justification
for James's revealing claim to his brother, at the end of the
play's otherwise uneventful run, that it had been 'A rare and
distinguished private success and scarcely anything at all of a
public one.'[50] But the more deeply felt response was
contained in an earlier letter to W. D. Howells, a letter that
echoes the bitterness James had felt at the reception of *The
Princess Casamassima* several years before.

I *have* felt, for a long time past, that I have fallen upon evil
days — every sign or symbol of one's being in the least
wanted, anywhere or by any one, having so utterly failed.

A new generation, that I know not, and mainly prize not, has taken universal possession.[5 1]

James had perhaps never been any more sanguine than Gissing about active participation in a controlling cultural élite, but they both testify to the bitterness of the minority artist at his relegation to such a deeply wounding position of *irrelevance*. The artist's aspirations are reduced to a minimal human connection, the audience of one that the dying writer Dencombe of 'The Middle Years' (1893) finds in the young doctor: 'The thing is to have made somebody care'. It is one of James's most moving stories.

Most important writers of the time, though differing over their interpretation, would have agreed about the existence of a schism. In general terms, it could be seen to have two main aspects. First the divorce, as it related to the reader, between 'mass' and 'minority' art; secondly, the separation, even within the individual, between the 'true' writer and the professional literary man. As regards the first aspect, William Morris, for example, shared Gissing's scepticism about the future of an etiolated minority culture, though for him there was the redeeming vision of a true popular art to supersede the false. Similarly, even a stalwart mediocrity such as Walter Besant corroborated, with a different stress, the dichotomy explored by James between the lonely sphere of true creativity and the importunate, pragmatic world of business. In his preface to *The Pen and the Book* (1899) Besant wrote with disarming urbanity of the moment when the writer lays down his pen: 'Here the artist ceases and the man of business begins.'

Nevertheless, it *was* possible to ignore or reinterpret the very real changes that were taking place in such a way as to perpetuate the image of a single and homogeneous Reading Public. This was naturally the interpretation most welcome to popular writers such as Marie Corelli in their eagerness to exploit the tradition of intimate rapport with the Reading Public. Besant was the sort of figure highly instrumental in fostering this interpretation, even at the same time as he was deeply involved in changing the actual conditions and rights of authorship. His 'Art of Fiction' lecture in 1884, which provoked James's justly more famous answer, offers propositions about a homogeneous and infallible Reading Public that justify the rationalisations governing the increasingly successful marketing of popular fiction. Besant is clearly aware of the contradictions between aesthetic and commercial value, but he sets out to blur these with great determination. For instance, what starts off as an apparently 'Jamesian' critique of the popular notion of the artist as entertainer, turns out to be a shrewd recognition that art that has *pretensions* to aesthetic or moral value may have a more permanent appeal than art that frankly confesses itself as entertainment. This is obviously a way of getting round the example of the popular classics of the past, Scott, Dickens, George Eliot. What they show, according to Besant, is that you are more likely to 'succeed', if you flatter the reader into thinking he is being elevated as well as entertained — exactly the rationale behind Marie Corelli's image of herself as popular moralist. But in fact, Besant is prepared to jettison even this creative orientation, by theologising the Reading Public into the ultimate (and mysterious) arbiter of all value. There is no such thing as good or bad literature — only readable literature.

> ... in Fiction, the whole of the English-speaking race are always eager to welcome a new-comer; good work is instantly recognised, and the only danger is that the universal cry for more may lead to hasty and immature production.[52]

It is not surprising that Gissing looked on Besant with something like contempt ('the most commonplace of celebrities'), blaming him for the 'extent to which novelists are becoming *mere* men of business'.[53]

Besant's image of the Reading Public as a single entity sanctioning an absolute hierarchy of 'success' would of course meet with Marie Corelli's approval. For her, the 'true' Reading Public instinctively recognises genius and righteously rejects minority decadence ('crazy old Ibsen', etc). But what is most curious is the sight of her corroborating Gissing's feelings about the villainous effect of the commercial intermediaries, publishers, reviewers, editors — from a quite different angle. Her feud with the literary world started in 1886 with the luke-warm reception of her first novel, *A Romance of Two Worlds,* and escalated to violent mutual abuse in the 1890s. There was some justification for her characterisation of the *impotence* of this literary world (as opposed to Gissing's version of its power), in its failure to prevent the phenomenal success of novels such as *Barabbas* (1894) and *The Sorrows of Satan* (1895). In the anonymously published *The Silver Domino* (1892), she put these words into the mouths of the great fraternity of critics:

> The only unfortunate thing about it is that we are losing power a little. The public read too many books and begin to know too much about us and our ways, which is very regrettable. We like to toss together our own style of literary forage and force it down the gaping throat of the public, because somehow we have always considered the public an Ass, whose best food was hay and thistles.[54]

It is surprising to find, beneath the blustering polemics, the precise indictment of the 'new generation' of cultural controllers, that what they manufacture is 'not the "voice of the people" at all; it is simply the voice of a few editors'. In fact, Marie Corelli herself is as much an exemplary product of the changing structure of the literary world as any writer. The ostensible judgements of the reviewers and editors were of minimal importance beside the value of *controversy* as a supreme marketable commodity, as she realised when she wrote: 'The more you abuse a fellow, the more his books sell . . .' The hostile, disparaging literary world collaborated with her in confirming the role of martyr, prophet and priestess, which she so desperately and pathetically desired.

All the writers so far discussed had come to creative maturity (if the word can be applied to Marie Corelli) by, at the latest, 1890. But what of the writers of a slightly younger generation, writers such as Arnold Bennett and H. G. Wells, born about ten years after Gissing? Would they too be likely to see the time as one of crisis and collapse? In the early stages of his career, Bennett offered some tentative but suggestive alternatives to Gissing's stark dichotomy between 'mass' and 'minority' art. In a collection of essays published

in 1901 as *Fame and Fiction*, he makes an attempt to come
to terms with the division between 'mass' and 'minority' that
Gissing interprets as a straightforward and disastrous schism.
Though himself upholding the high aesthetic value of writers
such as Turgenev, Moore and Gissing himself, Bennett
suggests the necessity for recognising the existence both of
multiple and variable audiences, and of variable criteria of
value. Now this welcome effort to see beyond the crude
deadlock between 'mass' and 'minority' takes in the genuine
advance towards more manoeuvrable criteria of market and
aesthetic value opened up by the changing structure of
publishing methods and reading habits in the 1890s. Bennett
rightly rejects the notion of a simple debasement of taste. The
'cultured' readers of an earlier generation had lapped up the
banalities of Martin Tupper, and their descendants were as
avid devotees of *Tit-Bits* as the hordes of the newly educated.

Yet it is pertinent to point out the limitations of Bennett's
tolerance. It was still possible for him to find positive moral
qualities in the writers he singled out as typically 'popular' — Miss Braddon, Charlotte M. Yonge, Sarah Grand,
Marie Corelli. Miss Braddon, for example, with a grasp of
objective fact which he sees as basic to any good novelist,
represents an 'ultimate decency' of average humanity (a
cardinal moral principle beneath Bennett's own novels). But
the essential decency, charity and tolerance that Bennett
wants to interpret as the basis of popular fiction is only one
possible set of ingredients in the recipe for commercial
success. Jane Helen Findlater offered a very different version
of contemporary popular literature in *Stones from a Glass
House* (1904). She points to changes in the popular image of
the heroic such as Bennett, in concentrating primarily on
writers of a previous generation (Miss Braddon's,
1837–1915), had preferred to ignore. According to Miss
Findlater, *now*

> . . . the hero is the successful man, and the successful man
> is the one who has managed to wring from Fortune's
> grudging hand — *by any means* — those things which are
> popularly named her gifts: wealth, fame, popularity.[55]

Bennett's proposition of the plurality and diversity of

possible audiences is a necessary corrective to Gissing's stark antitheses. But it is Gissing who is asking the crucial questions about cultural *value*, the disposition of cultural power and the quality of its dominant images: who is *using* the 'popular', how and for what ends? We find a word that Bennett uses about Miss Braddon's characters rebounding on his own assumptions with some force — 'comfortableness'.

But Bennett's own career offers even more illuminating perspectives on *New Grub Street*. From a distance, his progress would seem to exemplify some of Gissing's worst fears for the survival of the artist in the increasingly tentacular embrace of the communications media. Gissing would have shuddered at the prospect of a professed admirer of Turgenev descending to the writing of *How to Become an Author: A Practical Guide,* let alone *How to Live on Twenty-Four Hours a Day* and the other 'Practical Philosophies'. *How to Become an Author* is a practical manual for success in terms of the money and fame Bennett was himself soon to enjoy to a tune usually associated with the interment of artistic integrity. There is plenty of justification for Ezra Pound's acid cameo of 'Mr. Nixon'. By the time Beaverbrook offered him the job of Director of Propaganda for a few months in 1918, Bennett was able to accept it without salary, since he was making at least £300 a week from his writing. This was more than Gissing had been used to making in a *year*. Even after some comparatively successful years in the mid-nineties, a bad year such as he had in 1897 could suddenly plummet his annual income down to the starvation level of £101 13*s* 4*d*; he called it 'the year of terror'. Of course it is not simply a question of figure. In Bennett's career is enshrined (or entombed) the image of 'success' that is never entirely absent from the writer's consciousness, even or especially in the negative rationalisations of a James or a Gissing. The hard cash, the luxury yachts, the country house, the celebrity circles, all constitute one sort of successful healing of the separation between Self and the World: an audience *has* listened, even if it is not the right audience or the right listening. To achieve this, Bennett first projected an image of himself as Jasper Milvain, and then, to a large extent, became that image.

In the extraordinary autobiographical sketch *The Truth about an Author* (1903), Bennett fabricates, as John Gross has pointed out,[56] an exactly inverted image of Gissing's one of failure. Bennett's story is of unbridled, unashamed success. The first, statutory anecdote of his literary career is of the eleven-year-old's prize poem. What is characteristically different about this child prodigy is that he is the only one of the class to succeed in writing a poem at all — except one rival who turns out to have cribbed his. His subsequent progress from an unpaid column on *The Staffordshire Knot*, to freelance journalism in London, assistant, then full editorship of *Woman* magazine and beyond, is, as he relates it, a series of brilliant, unexpected *coups*. He is continually impressing people, humbling the senior partner of the lawyer's firm where he initially works, for example, by the erudite books he buys (but does not read) in the lunch-break, stunning the hosts who have just returned from visiting Browning in Venice, by remembering the name of his palace when they have forgotten it. It is, we realise, a 'success story' in a particular vein, for the tone of the title is neatly ambiguous, at the same time flippantly women's-magazinish and deliberately iconoclastic. It sets up the space in which Bennett will manoeuvre between contempt and reverence for the whole business of literature and his relation to it. In this respect he is very similar not only to Jasper Milvain, but also to Kipling's Dick Heldar in *The Light that Failed* (1891). The fascination of the book, and what saves it from total vulgarity, is the narrow edge maintained between outrageous arrogance and self-deprecating awareness. We have the un-nerving sense of watching roles, tones, attitudes being tried on, mocked and applauded at the same time — as if Bennett were simultaneously the actor and spectator of himself. It is very close to Wilde's sort of arrogance (another women's magazine editor!) — the calculated effrontery that invites and preempts the spectator's dissent or abuse.

The central quality of this projected *persona* is infinite adaptability. The terms of the oppositions with which Gissing struggles, between Art and Life, Culture and Business, simply dissolve. At one point, describing the process of bargaining with a syndicate for a serial he is writing, Bennett pauses to

muse upon the totally commercial aspect of such work, that
is bought and sold 'just like any other fancy goods'.

> I had entered into a compact with myself that I would
> never 'write down' to the public in a long fiction . . . What
> became of this high compact? I merely ignored it. I tore it
> up and it was forgotten, the instant I saw a chance of
> earning the money of shame . . .[57]

When Bennett comes up against the moral brick walls of the
artist's conscience, he simply shrugs his shoulders and walks
through. And it is the magnificent shamelessness of this
triumphant ego that is the real theme of the book. If the will
seems only to exist in Gissing in order to be crushed by the
world, the world, for Bennett here, seems only to exist in
order to dramatise the triumph of the will. Godwin Peak and
Jude Fawley had been turned away at the city gates, but
Bennett's young provincial penetrates with miraculous ease.
Indeed, instead of finding his expectations challenged and
chastened by contact with urban 'reality', he finds them
actually confirmed and magnified. London simply hands over
the keys of its citadels with abashed humility. In fact, of
course, we come away with a minimal sense of having heard
or seen anything tangible about circumstance or London at
all (which is perhaps surprising in view of the diligence with
which Bennett's own novels reproduce objective 'fact'). The
prime and only subject of the narrative is the identity of the
narrator himself; not the conquest of London and literary
fame, but the quite isolated issue of the successful integration
of a public Self. The extent to which this is a stylished image
of omnipotence can be easily gauged by comparing it with
the very different (though not necessarily more authentic)
images of malady and defeat that dominate Bennett's first,
heavily autobiographical novel, *A Man from the North*
(1898).[58] The patterns of desire frustrated have been simply
discarded in favour of the patterns of desire fulfilled.

Both the semi-fictional Self projected here and the 'actual'
personality of at least the later Bennett bear witness to the
imaginative power of the image of Jasper Milvain. But at the
same time, there are complexities in Bennett's personality
and career that expose the limitations of the image. Gissing

does not tolerate the possibility of real creative talent coexisting in Jasper Milvain with journalistic facility. Jasper could never have written a novel as fine as *The Old Wives' Tale.* And this dogmatism appears even more misguided when we look at the example of H. G. Wells.

Looking back on the early stages of his career in his *Experiment in Autobiography*, Wells wrote:

> The last decade of the nineteenth century was an extraordinarily favourable time for new writers and my individual good luck was set in the luck of a whole generation of aspirants.[59]

The contrast with Gissing could hardly be sharper. In what is in one sense his appendix to *New Grub Street, The Private Papers of Henry Ryecroft* (1903), Gissing confirms through Ryecroft his vision of the literary world as a microcosm of the world's rampant, internecine strife.

> Year after year the number of you is multiplied; you crowd the doors of publisher and editors, hustling, grappling, exchanging maledictions. Oh, sorry spectacle, grotesque and heart-breaking![60]

It is partly of course a difference of temperament, but it is also a question of generation. Wells (who enters the pages of *Ryecroft* as 'N-') felt at one with the 'new men', the new classes of people reading and thinking in new ways.

> New books were being demanded and fresh authors were in request. Below and above alike there was opportunity, more public, more publicity, more publishers and more patronage.[61]

This is the most direct challenge of all to Gissing's vision in *New Grub Street.* This is the version 'from the inside', of what it felt like to enjoy in their crude state the energies and possibilities so prudentially marshalled by Jasper Milvain. Wells is the prime example of the multi-level creativity denied to Jasper; the journalism and pot-boilers subsidised his more serious writing with a logic that makes Gissing's hauteur seem absurd. Yet Gissing seems himself to have recognised the wider significance of the contrast between them, when he makes Ryecroft say, with reference to 'N-', 'I represent to him, of course the days gone by . . .'

Returning to Gissing, we can draw some conclusions about the changing image of exile that dominated his career. His growing consciousness of the quality of the minority writer's exile in relation to the general culture reaches its culmination in the writing of *New Grub Street*. But after this, he begins to enter a new phase in which the exile accepts the company of other exiles. For a man who lived so much in the world of books, his own and others', he had been desperately deprived of actual intellectual intercourse. There is a particularly poignant example of his difference in this respect from Henry James, in their relation to a writer they both admired, Alphonse Daudet. James knew him personally, and even went on holiday with him. But Gissing could only worship from afar. When he was in Paris, he found out Daudet's address, and went to stand outside his house. He wrote in his Diary: 'Stood & looked & thought. Could Daudet know of me, assuredly I should not need to stand out in the street.'[6 2]

In the 1890s, however, as his reputation achieved a modest but genuine solidity, he won an initiation of sorts into a literary 'fraternity'. His invitation to the Omar Khayyám Club dinner in honour of Meredith on 13 July 1895 could be taken as symbolic. To his surprise and pleasure he was forced to make a short speech. The years of lonely integrity, he realised, had won him the respect of his fellow writers if not of readers at large. He tasted at least some of James's sense of fraternity, meeting James himself, enjoying friendship and correspondence with Meredith, Hardy, Wells and Conrad. The distance that Gissing traversed can be neatly measured by juxtaposing the comment about his first novel *Workers in the Dawn*, already quoted, with some words to Edward Clodd in 1902, about the work that was to become *Ryecroft*. In 1880, Gissing wrote: 'It must be accepted by intellectual people if at all.' In 1902, he wrote to Clodd:

> I shall be disappointed if you do not like it. For it is written for people like you, whom the general uproar of things does not deafen to still small voices.[6 3]

Despite his connections with people such as the Frederic

Harrisons, the 'intellectual people' remained largely an abstraction up until the mid-nineties; but by 1902 Gissing could address himself directly to one of them, as an equal. Moreover the tone has changed, from the rhetorical, public terms of 'it must be accepted by . . .', to the personal, intimate, 'I shall be disappointed if you do not like it'. The 'still small voice' is a humble, resigned note of opposition to 'the general uproar', instead of the bold challenge to more specific repressions and conventions — 'Gissing the Rod' as *Punch* had facetiously exclaimed, back in 1885. Gissing found, eventually, the consolations of a sense of 'belonging' — but at a price.

For the most valuable of Gissing's achievements depend on a more active sense of community with fellow sceptics and subversives, such as we find expressed with a rare determination in this letter of 1890:

> My part is with the men & women who are clearing the ground of systems that have had their day & are crumbling into obstructive ruin . . .[64]

It was only out of faith in the possibility of a communal act of this sort that Gissing could produce his major work. Here, therefore, is the radical ambiguity about the condition of exile from which his writing is drawn. For on the one hand, it can be conceived as solitary and fixed, conferring the dignity of achieved independence as well as the stigma of rejection. But on the other hand, it can be transformed into an image of a shared or shareable experience, through which the writer can connect with the element of 'exile' in every reader, and thereby create the more difficult and valuable imaginative community that must precede the true physical community. It was to the first notion that Gissing the man was deeply attracted, but to the second that Gissing the creative writer aspired.

5 New Grub Street

The more immediately personal context of *New Grub Street*
(1891) in Gissing's own life is as important as its wider
imaginative context. The death of his first wife in 1888, and
the closely related writing of his last novel of working-class
life (*The Nether World*), had set him free to take the
Continental holiday he had long dreamed about. On 26
September 1888 he left London for Paris.

His Diary and letters for the subsequent months spent in
Paris and Italy show him revelling in every possible aspect of
Europe's cultural feast, paintings, buildings, theatres,
lectures, landscapes. The richness of the diet was almost
unbearable for the man who had been starved of such
nourishment. On his first visit to the Vatican, the excitement
made it impossible for him to look at anything. He himself
had been quick to define the nature of the change he was
undergoing, noting in his Diary this revealing opposition
between the 'social concern' associated with London, and the
aesthetic idealism associated with Europe.

> I experience at present a profound dislike for everything
> that concerns the life of the people . . . All my interest in
> such things I have left behind in London. On crossing the
> Channel, I have become a poet pure & simple, or perhaps it
> would be better to say an idealist student of art.[1]

But the fascination of Gissing's Diary, as of his later
travel-book, *By the Ionian Sea* (1901), is exactly his failure
to fill the role of 'poet pure and simple', in which he
optimistically casts himself.

The circumstances under which Gissing aspired to a pure
communion with European 'culture' were very different from
the smoothly regulated cocoon surrounding even the moder-
ately affluent English traveller. The exigencies of hotel bills,
meals and transport were as infuriatingly insistent in Naples
as their quotidian equivalents in London. Gissing was

characteristically sensitive about this. Always meticulous in matching his reading to his situation, he naturally turned to Ruskin when he reached Venice. But Ruskin's Venice, he noted to his disgust, was seen from a physically different perspective: the view from the Grand Hotel, the angles and values of the wealthy tourist. Gissing found it 'a great fault'. One could add the comparison of a nearer contemporary, Henry James. In Italy, as in London, James moved easily in a sphere of society that represented, at least seen from the outside, the possibility of communion with socio-cultural equals, from which Gissing was excluded; instead of the gracious evenings and the rides in the Campagna, only the solitary, earnest pursuit of the joys of Art. And the loneliness is very evident, even in the midst of the cultural feast, for it was not so easy to be the 'poet pure and simple'. It was with gathering nervous frustration that he sat in a restaurant on Old Year's Night, 1888, a solitary foreigner in a throng of exuberant Florentines. Finally he could stand it no longer and 'rushed out into the streets' — a movement that is by now familiar.

For, again typically, it was not even a 'pure' loneliness. Gissing recorded an incident that took place on the ship back from his second visit to Italy and Greece (1889—90), that he recognised as symbolic of his equivocal social status. The ship's parson discovered from someone in the first class who recognised Gissing's name, that he was a 'celebrated author'. Thus was it his fate to communicate tenuously and hypothetically with the 'first class', but to associate actively only with the second. For if the condition of loneliness involved exclusion from community with his 'equals', it did not carry a complementary immunity from contagion with his inferiors. It is with almost comic predictability that the Diary entry carrying Gissing's bold declaration that he has become a 'poet pure and simple' should end with this pathetic deflation (lines that are, incidentally, omitted from the quotation in the *Letters to his Family*;[2] but it is precisely the vulnerability of the assertion that is essential to an understanding of Gissing):

> Imagine then how it jars on my nerves to be perpetually in contact with Plitt. From head to foot this man belongs to the working class.

Now this companion is a significant, indeed almost a
symbolic, figure. Plitt was a German artist ('though of very
slight attainments') whom Gissing had known in London for
a year or two before the trip to Paris. Gissing was as wilfully
perverse in his choice of travelling companion as in his choice
of wives, for it was only two days after their arrival in Paris
that they had their first clash over the style of their lodgings.
As usual, Gissing was the one to give way, venting his chagrin
only within the safe confines of his Diary: 'I have never
known intimately so stupid a man'. For the next two
months, until Plitt was finally shrugged off in Naples at the
end of November, Gissing's Diary writhed daily under the
increasingly obsessive recordings of Plitt's grossness and
Philistinism, his inability to appreciate the aesthetic treasures
of Paris before which Gissing so earnestly genuflected. Plitt
becomes, therefore, an embodiment of the cultural debasement that supersedes social and physical debasement as the
central concern of Gissing's work in the nineties. For he
represents in a distressingly intimate form all those forces of
'vulgarity' detracting from Gissing's pure communion with
Art. Plitt's is the voice of enthusiasm for a new 'mass
culture', that finds expression in the advertisements, the
posters and soap-box designs that sent him into raptures.
While Gissing worshipped at the Louvre, Plitt would revel in
the aesthetic merits of flower-posters in a grocer's shop. It is
no longer the suffering poor, the smell, the sound, the touch of
the slums, that represent the most immediate threat to the
artist-intellectual's needs and values. The great threat is now
offered by Plitt and his cronies in Philistinism, the fellow-
tourists in Rome whose banalities Gissing recorded with such
assiduity, and who prompted this cry to his friend Bertz:

> Many of them are absolute shop-boys and work-girls. How
> in heaven's name do they get enough money to come here?
> And where are the good cultured people?[3]

Where *were* the 'good cultured people' indeed? It was a cry
that rang throughout his whole life, and it is the informing
question behind *New Grub Street*.

The novel was written in the autumn of 1890, after a

typically long, but quite exceptionally painful period of gestation over the summer. On 1 March he had returned from his second European winter to a familiar London morning of fog, snow and slush: the holiday was over. He desperately needed a new impetus and direction for his work, such as *The Emancipated*, written between the two European trips, had failed to provide. Most of this long summer of false starts was spent with his mother and sisters in the family home at Agbrigg, near Wakefield — the longest period he had spent at 'home' since his settling in London in the late seventies. This was a vital factor in the unprecedented directness of the novel that slowly, painfully grew out of a reappraisal of his personal and creative prospects.

The most important single point about Gissing's portrayal of the literary world in this novel is his subtle intimation of power changing hands. The literary world itself is viewed from an entirely oblique angle, through the comment and gossip of a few figures hovering uneasily around its fringe, or in Jasper Milvain's case, aspiring to gain entrance. But the key aspects of this sense of transition are clearly marked. The newness and contemporaneity of the situation are hammered home by those recurrent words, 'now', 'new', 'modern', 'to-day'.

There is nothing especially new in itself about the centralisation of this literary world in London. But London is not just any big city now. It is at the heart of a communications industry, that with the advent of the telegraph and linotype, and the backing of increasing concentrations of capital, is expanding and co-ordinating the resources of the written word to cover the globe. London, as Jasper understands perfectly, is now a world-city, a focal point not just for world trade and finance, but for world news, fashions and cultural attitudes. The age of publicity is dawning. The possibilities of *power* are ranged on a new scale, and Gissing's narrative is patterned according to the efforts of characters either positively to grasp some of this power or at least to align themselves with its field of force. The bitter recognition to which Reardon gives voice is that the increasing power centred in London has resulted in exactly the reverse of a shining cultural capital. He has been attracted by an image of the literary life that he comes to recognise as enshrined in the past. His lament to Biffen echoes Gissing's cry: 'where are the good cultured people?'⁻

> We form our ideas of London from old literature; we think of London as if it were still one centre of intellectual life: we think and talk like Chatterton. But the truth is that intellectual men in our day do their best to keep away from London — when once they know the place. There are libraries everywhere; papers and magazines reach the north of Scotland as soon as they reach Brompton.⁴

But this is meagre consolation for the dispersed, exiled band of lonely cultural 'loyalists', the 'few awake and watching'. Their cultural capital still stands, but it has been taken over by the insurgent forces, the new men. Reardon is deliberately characterised as a mediocre, but genuine talent, to illustrate the *expectations* of such a man to find a role within a controlling cultural élite, such as was recognised to be in control of the major cultural institutions of previous generations, but which has now suffered an irreversible diaspora. At the heart of the novel is this take-over by a new generation of proprietors, businessmen, editors, publishers and writers. The emotional centre of the novel is correspondingly in the bitterness of the minority artist, not merely that he is now (as he has always been) a minority artist, but that this minority is no longer functioning at the centre but at the periphery of the general culture.

The perspective of the narrative is similar to that of *The Nether World*, in that our direct vision is confined to the sphere of the excluded and exploited, while the upper world of the controllers is only glimpsed in the distance. But now this upper world at least holds distinct names, biographies and activities. In *The Nether World*, power was fixed and permanent, but now it is in motion; the owners and controllers are at least identifiable, if not reachable. The key figures, mentioned but never seen, are Clement Fadge and Mrs Boston Wright, the new editors, Jedwood, the new publisher (seen, in fact, once very briefly) and Markland, the popular novelist. These figures are skilfully insinuated into the aspirations and envies of the characters we *do* see, struggling to survive on the sharp edge between success and failure. There are also a number of minor 'presences' that build up the panorama behind the constricted forescene. There is Ralph Warbury, for instance, the 'all-round man of letters', one of the new breed of bright young men from Oxford and Cambridge. In this respect, Warbury bears the same loose resemblance to Andrew Lang, say, as Jedwood to Heinemann, and Markland to Hall Caine: each economically represents a new phenomenon.

Jasper, as always, understands the process of the writer's socialisation, under the aegis of a Lang's elegance and a Besant's busy-ness. The 'new literary man' is a hard-working professional who hires out his labour at different levels, contributing to different grades of magazine and journal, reviews, essays, literary gossip, perhaps even a leader column for a daily paper. Jasper's model of his working day is the exact antithesis of Reardon's, the well-oiled clockwork regularity and the morose, frantic stuttering. Besant and Arnold Bennett both reproduce with the same relish this image of the respectable and industrious worker, polishing off a series of daily assignments with the professional dexterity of the doctor or lawyer.[5]

The genial athleticism of the freelance is made possible by the blurring of the lines of cultural demarcation that ensued on the breakdown of an earlier truce between quality and popular periodicals. During the middle years of the century, there was little competition between the quality journals of ideas, criticism and reviews, the popular (in this sense, 'middle-class') magazines with their staple diet of sentimental fiction, and the cheap penny magazines. The various markets were well defined and could be served with little conflict. But the 1880s mark a transition from truce to active hostility.

> The new mass magazines, like the urban newspapers, were tailored for all classes and all levels of intellect — at least they levelled all into one homogeneous 'market' — while the magazines once dominant took a secondary place, in the periphery of culture, where they inevitably fell into decadence.[6]

One of the results of this shift in the balance of power is

that a new distinction is made, by men like Jasper, between 'Literature' as the transcendental creation of other-wordly men of 'genius', and the work of the professional literary man, prepared to write intelligently on any subject put before him, from cookery to Greek mythology. Andrew Lang took pride in exactly this sort of 'beautiful thin facility', as James derisively called it. Jasper is of course all too ready to concede the perfect ephemerality of this kind of writing. Like all the manuals of advice to young aspirants that appear around this time, he reiterates the absolute distinction between the genius and literary man, the aesthetic and commercial value of a book. But this was precisely the distinction that Gissing had himself made, from the *other* side of the fence, in a letter to Hardy in 1886, when he referred to his resolution 'to pursue literature as distinct from the profession of letters'.[7] It is one thing, however, for a Milvain to concede this division, while paying lip-service to the notion of Great Literature that exists in a transcendent sphere outside the exigencies of getting published and finding readers, let alone enough to eat. It is another for a Gissing to make the desperate rationalisation that 'in literature my interests begin and end'. Beneath both attitudes is the sense that it is the Milvains who have won control of some of the key mediating positions of cultural power, without access to which the idealistic artist, let alone the genius, cannot survive.

The central indictment of the contemporary literary world made by Gissing, is that it has achieved a total industrialisation of writing, and reduction of the world to the status of a thing. Remote from our view are the owners, employers and managers, whose ranks Jasper is determined to join. Close before our eyes are the factory hands, differentiated only by their capacity and willingness to regulate their intellectual energies to the production of so many words per minute, so many articles per day. No wonder that for Marian Yule in the Britain Museum reading-room, the prospect of an actual 'Literary Machine' is a dream of release. For the machine is the only workable image; the 'old hack horse', the image associated with Alfred Yule, is hopelessly outmoded.

The reading-room itself stands physically at the centre of

the novel, as the literal store-house of literary culture. The main characters are differentiated by their attitudes towards and use of it. Alfred Yule is the one most closely associated with it, so totally has his life become determined by the sheer mechanics of scholarship. Gissing makes a quiet but effective distinction between his 'dead' pedantry and his daughter's 'live' use of literary culture, when they are on holiday together at the beginning of the book. Though Marian is so city-bred that she cannot recognise an ash on her country walk, she can use her literary knowledge (two lines from Tennyson) to enrich the physical object before her. Her father is also made to quote two lines of poetry, but for him the country landscape is only the excuse for a sardonic, introverted joke at the expense of the unfortunate poet Cottle. Not only has he lost all capacity to recognise the minimal value of the Shadwells and Settles, he has lost all instinctive response to the world outside him, natural and human. With his 'peculiar croaking' laugh and 'seamed visage', he inhabits an angular, desiccated world of his own, in which a complimentary footnote from a friend is worth more than his daughter's love.

As for the three other main characters, Marian loathes the reading-room; in her is concentrated all the instinctive revolt against the mechanisation of the intellect. Jasper raids the reading-room for smatterings of knowledge to flavour his facile concoctions. But Reardon, like Yule, is at home there; indeed he would gladly curl up into a snug corner, were it not for the all-embracing constraints of earning money. Though he is close to Yule in his proclivity to make literature a substitute for life, Tibullus and Diogenes Laertius are still 'live' literature for him, even if they are as remote from the present as Shadwell and Cyriac Skinner. The classical past to which Reardon and Biffen pay homage offers the image of a genuine ideal, as well as the indulgence of simple escape. Homer, like the Athenian sunset glorified by Reardon, belongs to an ideal world of free creativity (*'that* was not written at so many pages a day') and natural beauty, that stands in polar contrast to the time-bound city of dreadful fog and murk. But the dream, as usual in Gissing, is so distant from the reality that it cannot inter-act or transform; it can

only offer temporary consolation. Biffen and Reardon bend
passionately over their Greek metres — 'as if they lived in a
world where the only hunger known could be satisfied by
grand or sweet cadences'. Literal hunger always returns. The
ideal past is only a dream world, from which the privileged
fool is jerked back into reality. As he lies dying, Reardon
wakes from his vision of the Greek dawn: 'The glory
vanished. He lay once more a sick man in a hired chamber,
longing for the dull English dawn.'[8] It is quintessential
Gissing, down to the crushing detail of the 'hired chamber';
the narrator's generosity in giving Reardon a 'chamber' rather
than a mundane 'room' is painfully undercut by the fact of
its being 'hired'.

Both the strengths and the limitations of the vision of the
literary world put forward by Gissing can be located in the
rigour with which the alternatives are posed; on the one hand
Art, on the other Business; success, failure; inclusion,
exclusion. It is worth picking up some of the aspects of the
objective historical situation already touched upon, in order
to define the limits of Gissing's vision of total cultural
disaster. For the innovations in publishing that took place in
the 1890s, for example, were in fact very far from simply
directed towards the exploiting of a new mass market.
Gissing was himself soon to benefit from the changing
literary scene in several ways. He would discover that a new
publisher such as A. H. Bullen could take a much broader
view of the 'value' of a writer like Gissing to his firm, than
Gissing would have dreamed possible. We can place Gissing's
own version of the new publisher, Jedwood, beside one of
the actual new publishers, Heinemann. Both are shrewd
enough to harness the earning potential of one of the new
popular novelists, Jedwood by a literal and Heinemann by a
figurative marriage — Heinemann's first published book was
Hall Caine's *The Bondman* (1890), which made them both
thousands. But Gissing is misguided as well as ungenerous in
attributing to his fictional publisher only the pragmatic
flair for 'ventures which should appeal to the democratic
generation just maturing'.

Besides giving unprecedented encouragement to new and
young writers, the new publishers were mounting an assault

on the assumptions and practices of the established houses, which made it possible for the minority writer to find his particular audience more directly than was possible under the old conditions.[9] For these new publishers were willing to recognise the existence of different levels and types of market, and to organise their resources accordingly. Heinemann had over ten years' practical apprenticeship to another publisher, Nicholas Trübner, before he set up on his own in 1890. He could use his enthusiastic technical knowledge to regulate the relation between the type of book, its possible audience and its cost. But it was not just a new sort of business acumen that Heinemann provided. His first list in 1890 shows the fallacy of any simple categorisation of his energies. The two crucial successes were Hall Caine's *The Bondman* and Whistler's *The Gentle Art of Making Enemies*. Certainly neither of these discredit Gissing's thesis; of the latter, we are told, by a friend of Heinemann's, 'The volume created just the kind of sensation aimed at.'[10] But if these two books gave him financial security and sensational publicity, one of the other features of this last was genuinely ambitious, and at first far from directly rewarding. The 'International Library' series of translations of foreign fiction (at 2s 6d for paper cover and 3s 6d for limp cloth) did not start very auspiciously, though Maupassant's *Pierre et Jean* did retrieve some of the debt incurred by the translations of Bjørnson (Norwegian), Emil Franzós (Polish), and Mathilde Serao (Italian). Yet Heinemann perservered, and by the end of 1892 the series was well established. He continued to experiment, introducing Maeterlinck to Britain, for example, as well as supporting the more solid reputation of Ibsen. Thus while continuing to 'exploit' the vein of the unabashedly popular or controversial (though even here one cannot relegate Sarah Grand's *The Heavenly Twins* (1893) or Max Nordau's *Degeneration* (1895), say, to such simply dismissive categories), he could actively encourage the 'minority' writer such as James or Conrad and the distinctly 'minority' venture such as the first English edition of Adolf Furtwängler's masterpiece on Greek art, *Meisterwerke der Griechischen Plastik*. The image of a unified, homogeneous Reading Public, tied to the centralising institution of the circulating library, was disintegrating into more encouraging fragments than Gissing's version of anarchic competition for the pockets of the 'new generation' suggests.

The major limitation of Gissing's view of the literary world in *New Grub Street* can be stated thus: whatever one's judgements about the personal moral qualities of a figure such as Heinemann, the 'new men' of which he is representative can never be simple evidence of cultural decline in themselves. For the conditions which they are instrumental in shaping can contain possibilities and release energies not necessarily related to the virtues and vices of the individuals apparently 'in control'. The oblique perspective of the novel is, therefore, an evasion of the complexity of historical change, since the narrow angle is based on a crude generalisation about the depravity of the 'new men'. This insistence on proving a case is, from the point of view of historical accuracy, the novel's greatest flaw. Yet it is precisely the single-mindedness with which Gissing carries through this vision of an absolute dichotomy between Art and Trade, 'culture' and 'progress', that is responsible for its creative urgency. There is a strong evolutionary thesis underlying the narrative, according to which physical victory and moral degeneration are interconnected. It is nevertheless part of the novel's strength that it resists the correlative equation of physical defeat with moral nobility.

The action revolves around the problem of who will get the money and the mate. For every winner, there is a complementary loser: Jasper and Reardon, Amy and Marian, Whelpdale and Biffen, Fadge and Alfred Yule. It is characteristic of the neatness of this pattern that Fadge's moment of triumph, the appearance of his illustrated portrait, should coincide with Alfred Yule's ignominious departure from London. It is a similar neatness that balances the opening scene of the Milvains' family breakfast in provincial straits and longings, with the closing scene of Jasper and Amy's dinner, in metropolitan comfort and fulfilment. Through the narrative drives an undeviating current of power, with which words such as 'progress' and 'the future' are associated, and all the important characters are seen decisively to succeed or to fail in adaptation to this force. This is the point made by the scene in which Jasper and Marian watch the express train thunder beneath the bridge towards London. It is less a question of the train's 'symbolic' function as representing 'both his driving ambition and the disconcerting sexual attraction Marian possesses for him' (as one critic has said),[11] than of the literal effect it has on the two characters. Whereas Jasper is thrilled by the 'dread force and speed' of this 'symbol' of technological progress, Marian is depressed. There are only two ways of reacting to progress, either enthusiasm or revulsion, determination or apathy.

Even a transitory figure such as Mr Baker, Biffen's ambitious student, is carefully aligned according to his capacity to 'succeed'. He will pass the exam for which he is studying, and rise from the status of docker or bargeman to work in the Customs. But he is also the occasion for one of the instructive loopholes in the strait-jacket of the general thesis of cultural degeneration. Along with Jasper's sisters and Amy Reardon, Mr Baker prompts Gissing to a moment of unexpected tolerance for the possibility of *individual* improvement, maturity or expansion, within the overall picture. P. J. Keating lumps him together with the other working-class figures in the novel (Mrs Goby and the furniture-dealer), in order to convict Gissing of a class generalisation of which he is, unexpectedly perhaps, *not* guilty in this novel, at least at this point. 'They are totally insensitive and thus inferior to the people with whom they come in contact.'[12] Gissing in fact goes out of his way to emphasise the innate and moving tact that prompts Mr Baker to pay Biffen for his instruction out of Reardon's hearing. He does indeed belong to the breed of the 'survivors', with his 'robust figure' and 'clenched fist', but his 'intelligent' look, his 'modesty' and 'delicacy' in effect elevate him morally beyond any of the other 'survivors' in the book, except perhaps Dora Milvain. The irony of the wry interchange he has with Reardon over the difficulties of 'compersition' is directed at least equally at the helplessness of the man who can pronounce the word 'properly', as at the uncouthness of the man who cannot.

But such moments as this, or the admission of 'a noticeable maturing of intellect' in Amy after she leaves Reardon, only momentarily disturb the main pattern of the action. The disruptive complexity suggested by Amy's intellectual expansion is swiftly neutralised by reference to the *ersatz* intellectuality of contemporary periodicals. The prevailing thesis dictates that personal qualities such as 'sensitivity' or even 'maturity' are mere nuances beside the biological capacity for 'success' or 'failure'. One belongs either with the 'stronger' or the 'weaker'. In an early scene, Reardon returns home from a dismal trudge round the park, to find Jasper and Amy sitting together. Coming in from the dark, he enters with 'dazzled eyes'; it is as though he were the intruder instead of Jasper, the stranger who blunders in with his burden of gloom to disturb the charmed circle of light and vitality.

It is natural that, given this peremptory schism between the lost and the saved, the key scenes of the novel should be ones of *confrontation* between individuals. These scenes reflect the single most important movement in all Gissing's work towards states of extreme opposition, both within the narrative in thematic terms of class, cultural and personal crisis, and at the level of narrative structure itself. This novel is as concerned with the disintegration of individual human unions as with the disintegration of general cultural unity — the relation between the two is a blunt assumption. There are three central relationships between a man and a woman: between a husband and wife, Reardon and Amy; between a father and daughter, Alfred Yule and Marian; and between potential lovers, Jasper and Marian. Each of these culminates in a scene of crisis.

All the important male characters are afflicted with sexual desire: not even Jasper and Biffen are immune. Yet, as in all other spheres, Jasper is the one who can most successfully adapt to this dangerous force. In exact contrast to Jasper's pragmatism is Reardon's sentimental idealism. The wry, perfunctory tone of the narrator, as he describes Reardon's attraction to Amy, suggests the fatality and irresistibility of sexual desire.

> As for the poor author himself, well, he merely fell in love with Miss Yule at first sight, and there was an end of the matter.[13]

It is of more than passing interest to note that this phrasing is echoed in a Diary entry of Gissing's for 11 August 1890.

While staying with his family, he met a girl named Connie Ash a couple of times. His Diary could hardly be more laconic: 'I am in love with her, & there's an end of it.' The relationship came to nothing, as Gissing seems to have expected. Reardon is again drawing on an attitude with which Gissing was closely familiar, when he expresses an extreme Schopenhauerian devotion to the purity of aesthetic contemplation, as an antidote to the embroilments of the will-to-live. The sight of beauty such as his Athenian sunset is 'infinitely preferable to sexual emotion'.

> I have lived in an ideal world that was not deceitful, a world which seems to me, when I recall it, beyond the human sphere, bathed in diviner light.[14]

Yet whatever the degree of Gissing's identification with such an attitude, it is, like all the motions towards escape, checked and placed within the context of *this* human sphere, here and now. Reardon's ideal love, like his ideal literature, can exist only in imagination or memory; the two ideals fuse together when he reads to Amy from Homer the passage of Odysseus's awed admiration of Nausicaa.

Reardon's sentimental idealisation of women has disastrous consequences, for he rapidly regresses towards a male despotism that aligns him closely with Alfred Yule and the appalling Widdowson of *The Odd Women*. The refusal of both Marian and Amy to conform to their defined roles as ministering angel or acolyte undoubtedly wins our sympathy, though we understand simultaneously the validity of Reardon's complaint at Amy's frigidity. The two central scenes of confrontation between Amy and Reardon reflect the total breakdown of mutual definition, in which the expectations embodied in the Other are decisively discredited. Reardon is not going to be the successful author Amy imagined; Amy is not going to be the devoted helpmeet, soldiering bravely on through thick and thin. When Reardon tells her that he has arranged to return to a job as a hospital clerk, this is the last straw for Amy: 'I am certainly not the wife of a clerk who is paid so much a week.' In the second scene, at Amy's house, we register how well Gissing understands the almost arbitrary physical obstacles preventing two people conversing directly and freely. Amy is instinctively repelled by Reardon's shabby appearance, Reardon by Amy's studied elegance. This is no casual misunderstanding; it grows out of one of Gissing's deepest beliefs, that experience is ruled tyrannically by masks and images of the presented Self, against which the hidden emotions struggle vainly for expression.

This fierce repression of inner emotion is certainly the key to Alfred Yule's household, the emotional locus that in some ways stands at the centre of the novel. Gissing takes pains to draw the parallels between Yule and Reardon in their increasingly desperate possessiveness of their women. Both project their frustration on to the image of a rival — Jasper. Yule aims the same wild accusation of Jasper's evil influence on Marian as Reardon had with regard to Amy. But in his daughter Marian are concentrated most of the positive virtues denied to Reardon, in some ways her natural counterpart in failure and deprivation. For all the evident proximity of Reardon to many aspects of Gissing's own personality and experience, it is unnecessary to see him, as Jacob Korg does, as the 'tragic central character'[15] in the novel. Marian certainly has more right to the first adjective, and, as will be argued, almost as much right to the second.

Marian's refusal to submit to her father's intolerable dictatorship is genuinely moving, where Amy's comparable rebellion only commands acquiescence in its logic, for we feel the extent to which Marian's bid for self-fulfilment makes unexpected demands on her instinctive compassion and gentleness towards others. It is rare indeed for a character in Gissing to transcend his or her innate passivity in this way. The two climactic scenes of confrontation with her father parallel those between Amy and Reardon, and culminate in those typical moments of total opposition, the polarisation of Self and Other: 'Their eyes met, and the look of each seemed to fascinate the other.' These scenes seem inevitably to gravitate towards such exposures of the naked ego, of brute desire and denial, when Reardon seems silently to cry, 'I want sympathy', Amy, 'I want clean sheets', Marian, 'I want love', and Alfred Yule, 'I want to be an editor again'. One of the most moving moments in the novel occurs when

Marian hears that she has lost the modest legacy that, as she
knows quite well, has persuaded Jasper into offering
marriage. When she summons her father to her bedside, the
roles are for once reversed between them, she haughtily
summoning and curtly dismissing, in the same way in which
he has been used to treating her. The unexpected but
perfectly plausible outburst of bitterness only confirms her
humanity and reveals the depth of her desire, at the same
time as it retrospectively illuminates the process by which
deprivation has soured her father — for it is exactly her
father's tone that she uses:

> 'This of course happens to me,' Marian said, with intense
> bitterness. 'None of the other legatees will suffer, I
> suppose?'[16]

But it is not only on behalf of herself that Marian
challenges her father. Cursed by marriage with a social
inferior, Alfred Yule has tried desperately to 'save' Marian
from infection by her mother's defects of speech and
manner. The resultant tragedy of dissociation between
mother and child is conveyed with a delicacy for which
Gissing is not often given credit. The mother wears a
permanently puzzled look on her face, for she desperately
wants to understand her daughter, and share her feelings. The
situation is closely similar to one in a tale by Hardy, written
almost contemporaneously with this novel.[17] In 'The Son's
Veto', the clergyman father turns his son into an educated
prig rather than allow him to be sullied by his working-class
mother, once a servant at the vicarage. Hardy's tale,
deliberately a parable in intent, differs from Gissing's
treatment of the situation in focus as well as in the extent of
the generalisation. For Gissing, it is the 'educated' child who
is the centre of attention; for Hardy, it is the mother,
uprooted from her native ties and oppressed by a 'culture'
from which she is excluded. Mrs Alfred Yule too has been
torn away from her native surroundings and ties in the
''Olloway Road', and Gissing is well able to suggest the
minutiae of class tensions between herself and her envious
relatives, who always suspect her of the condescension she
tries so hard to avoid. But the differences from Hardy are as

instructive as the similarities. For Gissing sees no intrinsic
value in Mrs Yule's 'natural ties' as Hardy does in Sophy
Twycott's. There is nothing equivalent in Gissing to the
suggestion of sexual attractiveness in Sophy's nut-brown hair,
and the emotional attachment between her and her old lover
Sam Hobson. Mrs Yule has only the redeeming qualities of
kindness and gentleness. But, most important of all, the focus
of the relationship is not on her at all; it is on her daughter
Marian, who is as much the victim of the oppressive
education her father has forced on her, as the mother.

It is rare indeed for Gissing to question his deeply-rooted
sense of educated 'culture' as an essential good. On his one
visit to Max Gate in 1895, it was exactly the inferiority of
Hardy's 'culture' to Meredith's that he used to distinguish
between the two.[18] (He had recently visited Meredith at Box
Hill also.) Yet in this aspect of this novel, at least, he does
seem to come nearer than anywhere else to Hardy's
questioning of the intrinsic value of an educated 'culture'
that produces only at best the pathetic consolations of Greek
metrical effects (and, though we know that Gissing revelled
in such pedantry himself, in the context of the novel they are
meant to be pathetic), and at worst the nightmare sterility of
the Yule family. The questioning does indeed stop short of
the extreme generalisation, because it is always rigorously
conducted under the terms of *this* set of conditions, with
those men in control. But Marian's vision of hell in the
reading-room, and her sense of 'all literature as a morbid
excrescence on life' serve the same function as an extreme
generalisation against which the specific circumstances are
measured, as the metaphor of the 'nether world' in the earlier
novel.

It seems more than likely that Gissing was drawing directly
on his own family relationships in depicting some of the
tensions in Alfred Yule's household. As has been noted, the
long summer before the writing of the novel had been spent
with his mother and two sisters in their home near Wakefield.
This extended period of frustration, of false starts and
repeated abandonments, suggests a crisis in his creative life,
that could only be solved by a direct confrontation with the
problems of the writer's life, as shaped by his personal vision

of the sharp oppositions between success and failure, the ideal and the practical. But though he sketched one self-image into Reardon, the self-image of depressive failure centred on the nightmare summer months of 1890, it was into Marian Yule that he projected his deepest desires for emotional fulfilment, and his deepest fears about the value of the education and 'culture' that had taken him so far away from the insular world of his Yorkshire home. Into one sentence in the novel, he puts directly the feelings that he often recorded as the dominant impression whenever he returned home. Of Marian and her mother, we are told:

> The English fault of domestic reticence could scarcely go further than it did in their case; its exaggeration is, of course, one of the characteristics of those unhappy families severed by differences of education between the old and young.[19]

Reardon represents one vital aspect of Gissing's response to the struggle, the Ryecroftian regression towards the safe nooks of scholarly quibbles and the self-indulgent serenity of Athenian sunsets. But Marian's response is true to the best in Gissing, the deep and passionate cry: 'what use are books and learning? I want love'. In Reardon, and even more scathingly in Alfred Yule, Gissing depicts phases of himself: in Alfred, the portrait of the man who knows he is unloved and unlovable, and in Reardon, the man who *fears* he is so. But Marian represents another aspect of desire, the aspect that is not yet inured to loneliness, but still expects, hopes, wants love.

If the novel is as concerned with the tyranny of desire as the pollution of literary culture, it is even more pervasively concerned with the tyranny of money. There is a deep anomaly, however, in the role that money plays in the narrative, an anomaly that links up with the cracks in the version of cultural crisis. According to the encompassing moral vision, it is necessary to endorse a traditional judgement on the degrading effects of the pursuit of money, to which Jasper and his fellow 'new men' are committed. As Robert Selig has pointed out,[20] it is the direct equation between the word and the coin that is this 'new generation's' ultimate blasphemy. But at the same time, there is a quite different thesis offered about the role of money, that applies more narrowly to the *individual's* moral and emotional well-being. For if the pursuit of money degrades, it is even more certain that the lack of money will degrade even further. If it were only Jasper who claimed the inter-dependence of economic security and fine feelings, we would be rightly suspicious; but the narrative insists at almost every turn that everyday human decency, generosity, tolerance, and love, are only possible, or at least much more likely to be sustained, on the basis of a minimal material security. For Amy's mother, for example, 'life was a battle. She must either crush or be crushed. With sufficient means, she would have defrauded no one, and would have behaved generously to many . . .' The effect that their legacies have on Amy and Marian is, at least initially, to soften and expand the former's attitude to Reardon, and to increase the latter's self-confidence immeasurably. The narrative continually supports Jasper's contention that as a prerequisite for tolerable human relationships as well as individual fulfilment, money is indispensable.

The difficulty is that the generalisation is seen only from the perspective of 'lack', creating, as in the case of the other sharp dichotomies, a dangerously radical opposition between absolute states of poverty and sufficiency. All the characters would agree with Amy that poverty is 'a misery that colours every thought', and with Reardon, that 'this world might be a sufficing paradise to him if only he could clutch a poor little share of current coin'. But in Jasper's case (and to a lesser extent, Amy's), we *do* see a character who succeeds in clutching his little share of current coin, and contrary to the provocative theory put forward that money can ennoble, we see the disappointingly traditional sight of its degradation. This is the reason for the increasing dissatisfaction with which we view Jasper's portrayal, and it points to the underlying discrepancy, suggested in the comments on Mr Baker, between the governing thesis of general cultural and moral decay, and the possibility, indeed positive likelihood, of individual benefit and progress.

In the final scene, we see Jasper and Amy firmly ensconced within the camp of the 'victors'. We recognise that certain virtues are possible within this charmed circle that were impossible outside, but the remarks they make about the now permanently exiled Marian ('only a clever school-girl' with 'ink-stains on her fingers') indicate the extent to which these virtues are rigorously referred to membership of the group. The remarks about Marian strike us as peculiarly vicious; but Jasper and Amy must confirm their absolute distance from her. It is not possible, however, for us fully to share in the progress of an individual across the sharp frontier between success and failure. This final scene, so neat, so glib, is not the one demanded by the novel's internal logic. Gissing's deep, humane identification with those who are left outside, requires that the final scene should belong to Marian, and her lonely, loveless vigil in the provincial library.

This, then, is the paradox about money, that the *pursuit* of it must degrade, but the *possession* of it is necessary for the sustenance of all moral and personal good. Although in this novel the paradox is uncontrolled and disruptive, it becomes focused as the central theme of Gissing's next novel, *Born in Exile*. And there it is significant that Gissing concentrates narrowly on the single individual figure trying to cross the boundary between want and security, at the expense of any more general attempt at a coherent social or cultural vision.

If we return to the achievement of *New Grub Street* as a whole, we can reach the following conclusions. The novel represents a partial vision of cultural crisis, conditioned by a personal structuring vision of incompatible dualities. It leaves out of account both the complexity of historical change in the actual conditions of writing, publishing, distributing and reading, and the personal complexity in a Jasper Milvain that might allow him to produce a novel as good as, for example, *The Old Wives' Tale*. Yet despite the qualifications, the core of Gissing's vision seems indisputable, both in fact and in feeling. A radical change *did* take place in the status of 'quality' art and the minority artist, that can fairly be characterised as an unprecedented exclusion from the central positions of cultural power. In our own century, we have

seen, on one hand, the further exploration of this exile, and
on the other, an increased flexibility and possible interaction
between the opposing terms 'minority' and 'mass'. All these
developments may seem to place Gissing's sceptical, dogmatic
vision of cultural disaster in a distant perspective. But the
questions he asks, about quality and value, remain close.

Part III

DESIRE, AUTONOMY AND WOMEN

6 The Exile and the Country House

i. ISABEL CLARENDON (1886)

The significance of *Isabel Clarendon* (written 1884, but published 1886) in terms of Gissing's development, has already been mentioned in relation to *Demos*. It represents Gissing's first major break from the insistent urban context and fierce class tensions of his first two published novels. Yet for all its evident technical advances, Meredith was surely right in advising Gissing to get back from the country house to his proper setting. *Isabel Clarendon* is perhaps the best representative of a whole set of Gissing's novels, that betray a fundamental rift between the ostensible theme and setting, and the animating emotions of desire and need. *A Life's Morning* (1888), *The Emancipated* (1890), *Denzil Quarrier* (1892), *The Crown of Life* (1899), *Our Friend the Charlatan* (1901), *Veranilda* (1904), *Will Warburton* (1905) — all these novels offer some intelligent insights and moments of characterisation, without ever approaching the concentrated power that distinguishes the major novels. The most valuable aspect of these secondary novels lies in fact in the unexpected disruption of the apparently primary narrative action (the political elections of *Denzil Quarrier*, the complicated religious wars of fifth-century Italy in *Veranilda*), by the revelation of intense individual need. Characters such as Dagworthy in *A Life's Morning* and Marcian in *Veranilda* obtrude a tortured emotional ferocity that the main current of the narrative is simply incapable of sustaining.

Yet *Isabel Clarendon*, at least, draws directly on some of Gissing's deepest preoccupations. It is only an apparent escape that the 'exponent' character, Bernard Kingcote, makes away from the city to the idealised rural retreat, the ascetic white-washed cottage. Gissing can identify closely

with this actual migration that Kingcote optimistically
defines as a search for 'freedom':

> From sights and sounds which disgust me, from the
> contiguity of mean and hateful people, from suggestions
> which make life hideous; free to live with my fancies, and
> in the thoughts of men I love.[1]

But the literal escape, as Gissing proceeds to expose with
some rigour, is only a naïve enactment of the real internal
migration, that is continually qualified by inescapable human
and social connections and needs — and specifically by the
twin exigencies of money and desire.

Against Kingcote's Ryecroftian dream of resigned rural
solitude is set the actual and active world of the country
house. Gissing is clearly drawing on his own experience of
this world with the Harrison and Gaussen families in the
summer of 1884. Critics have also pointed to the evident
influences of Meredith and Turgenev on the setting and
certain elements of characterisation. But the central dramatic
tension remains Gissing's own, between the marginal, isolated
intellectual and a desperately ambivalent social group,
offering in its uncomfortable contiguity a general denial but
individual invitations. Isabel Clarendon, the gracious and
beneficent Lady of Knightswell, stands in a relation to the
intellectual recluse Kingcote analogous to Ida Starr's relation
to Osmond Waymark. Isabel and Ida both appear to belong in
a deeply representative way to a social group from which the
man is detached, and yet at the same time to transcend this
conditioning so as to offer the possibility of 'pure' relationship. But if there *is* one genuine advance in this novel, it is in
the way Gissing exposes the processes of self-deception,
whereby such a miraculous severance of existence and
essence is supposed to be achieved in Ida Starr.

As the two worlds of the country house and the
white-washed cottage come into contact, with their different
expectations, values and tastes (*Queen* magazine versus Sir
Thomas Browne, hunting versus reading), we appear to be
watching a conventional movement towards mutual adaptation, the end in sight being the declaration of love between
Isabel and Kingcote. This declaration does indeed take place

with conventionally felicitous timing, at the end of Volume I, when Kingcote comes to visit her as she is convalescing after a serious fall. But it is very far from representing a *rapprochement* between the two worlds. The effect is sharper and more unexpected. Up until this point, Isabel has been characterised almost exclusively in deliberately conventional terms of the charm, grace and beneficence of the country-house lady and society hostess. And it is in terms of exactly this fictional idealisation that Kingcote's desire for her is formulated. He 'worships' her with embarrassing Ruskinian humility as his 'pure-browed Lady', his queen. But at the same time he wants to divorce this idealised image from its supporting social context, to relate to her as the medievalised 'Lady of Knightswell', rather than the lady of an actual country house, with guests, wards, dependents and suitors.

Yet Kingcote is not totally mistaken in this false connection. There *is* a real bond between them, though he fails to recognise and develop it. For beneath the oppressive weight of the fictional paradigm under which she labours, there is another, 'real' Isabel Clarendon, who reveals herself with startling intensity when she has 'fallen', literally and emblematically. It is only at this point that we realise the full human meanings of the will around which the action revolves, the actual disposition of money and power on which Isabel's 'grace', like that of so many country-house heroines, has seemed so effortlessly to float. Gissing has prepared for this moment of disintegration with character-istic precision. The country house, when we first see it, is explained as being very far from an ancient family seat. Despite their resounding name, the Clarendon family won it only a generation back through adroit speculation. Isabel herself, though we only hear the full meaning of this at the end of Volume I, has been elevated to the level of a society hostess by virtue of her good looks. The penniless daughter of a country solicitor, she faced a dismal future as a governess until 'saved' by marriage to the wealthy, elderly Clarendon. As the details of the will he left are revealed, it becomes clear that Isabel has been cruelly punished for her desperate desire for security and status; she is being forced to act as guardian for his illegitimate child, who will in fact be the one to inherit the wealth. It is only when we hear this story from Isabel herself that we register the full depths of her feelings of bitterness and exploitation, and that it is precisely in her role as *victim* (like Ida Starr) that she offers the possibility of connection with the lonely alien Kingcote.

Kingcote too is as far from secure in his world of solitary intellectuality as she is in hers of fashionable society. It is not long before he writes to his energetic friend Gabriel that his solitude is intolerable. For money and desire intrude, the interconnected compulsions over body and soul. The desire directed towards Isabel is balanced by the inherited connection of reponsibility for his impoverished sister in London. His return to London draws on Gissing's most powerful feelings, the shrinking, raw revulsion felt at the nerve ends. Here, in the city, are the responsibilities and ties that measure Kingcote's dream of sweet rural retreat, or, as it has been ironically modified, the dream of country-house grace in the white-washed cottage. No wonder he sits listening to the street noises of Camden Town, and begins to question the relativity of the dream and the reality.

> At this moment Isabel was sitting alone and thinking of him, sitting amid the graceful luxury of her refined home. Was *that* a dream of joy, or *this* a hideous vision?[2]

It is his failure to distinguish the real relationship between the idealised and separated image of desire (Isabel sitting alone), and its supporting social and economic context (the 'graceful luxury'), that constitutes the crux of their relationship. For Isabel, as her history makes plain to us, cannot float above this surrounding context. She is as much the unconscious victim of the tastes and values of the society to which her longing for security has habituated her, as the explicit and conscious victim of the cruel will. Kingcote makes, in effect, an ironically inverted 'negative identification' with her exploitation, analogous to Gissing's own temporary 'negative identification' with the oppressed working class.

The second volume traces Kingcote's progressive disenchantment with the fallacious connection. Gissing is nowhere better than in the details of such a process of painful disentanglement, as Kingcote is torn by the ambiguity of his desire for an imagined and a literal connection. The turn towards the true relationship is simultaneously hinted at, with a 'Jamesian' obliqueness to which contemporary readers took righteous exception.[3] For his true counter part in dissociation is Ada Warren, Clarendon's illegitimate child, now an aggressive, rebellious intellectual. There are certainly echoes of Turgenev here, if only in the situation and the movement. We remember, for example, the transference of Arkady's emotional attachment from Anna Sergeyevna to her patronised ward Katya in *Fathers and Sons*. The comparative shallowness of the attraction between Bazarov himself and Anna Sergeyevna could similarly be seen reflected in the essential egoism of that between Isabel and Kingcote, each projecting their own dissatisfaction on to an available other, a mutuality of frustration within the containing, undisturbed context of the country house. The resemblances are not without interest, but, as we shall see in *Born in Exile*, it is what Gissing *makes* of the various elements, of challenge and frustration and acquiescence, that is important. There is certainly little but their piano playing shared by the two wards Katya and Ada Warren. It is Ada, in fact, who comes nearest to the real energy of disruptive challenge concentrated in Bazarov or Godwin Peak. For she alone sees through the fictions of the country house. Indeed it is with a quite exceptional bitterness that she exposes the emptiness of the role that Isabel acts out, as the Angel of Mercy, the dispenser of Charity. As the illegitimate child forced into an ambiguous situation in her dead father's house, Ada nurses a wholly intelligible resentment at the dutiful tolerance, compassion and restraint acted out by Isabel. The memory of her arrival in this alien world of luxury is the most striking moment in the novel. The graceless, ugly, aggressive child with her 'detestable London-working-class accent' sees through the kindness of the gracious lady to her instinctive revulsion. 'That night she had gone to bed hating the beautiful lady with a precocious hatred.' Throughout the novel, Ada's fierce, barely repressed aggression remains the most positive challenge to the apparently settled world of the country house. In her potentiality for revolt, Ada belongs with some of Gissing's most memorable women, especially Clara Hewett and Rhoda Nunn. Yet, disappointingly, it remains only a potential in this novel, for the only external means that Gissing can find to express it is in her renunciation of the willed wealth, the deliberate but limited gesture of independence.

It is thus of great significance that Gissing should turn again to the issues dramatised, or perhaps only played with, in this novel. For in *Born in Exile*, the triangular relaionship between Godwin Peak, Sidwell Warricombe (the gracious lady) and Marcella Maxey (the passionate but repressed intellectual) repeats that between Kingcote, Isabel and Ada, but with a radical reorientation. Peak pursues with an energy of which Kingcote is incapable his 'type of perfectly sweet womanhood', but it is under the pressure of social, economic and psychological forces from which Kingcote is disappointingly immune. Peak's 'true' partner, Marcella, performs a crucial act of renunciation similar to Ada Warren's, but instead of thereby heroically confirming their shared aloofness from the shallow world of bourgeois security, she smashes Peak's last chance of *joining* it. The energy of frustration, the sharp opposition between need and security, the interconnection of material and emotional deprivation and exclusion — all these receive a precise focus and direct dramatisation through the central figure of Godwin Peak. For all its local intensities, *Isabel Clarendon* fails to translate these forces and issues into a consistently powerful action.

ii. BORN IN EXILE (1892)

Born in Exile holds a special place in Gissing's work, in so far as it anatomises with an unprecedented concentration those paradoxes of the simultaneous desire for connection and autonomy that are usually more deeply submerged or widely diffused. For in Godwin Peak's efforts to 'knit himself into the social fabric', we do at last *follow* the exiled individual's desperate assault on society's ramparts. In this sense, Peak rewrites the barely glimpsed histories of Clara Hewett's failure and Jasper Milvain's success with a new directness and detail.

As is well known to students of Gissing, the opening sections of the novel set at Whitelaw College draw indirectly on Gissing's own experiences at Owens College. Gissing admitted that Peak was 'one phase of myself',[4] while denying that the novel as a whole endorsed his single viewpoint uncritically. It was the 'study of a savagely aristocratic temperament',[5] many of whose fierce prejudices Gissing recognised in himself. But he was justly insistent on the representative aspect of such a personality. He made the virtue of this typicality the main emphasis of a letter to his friend Morley Roberts in 1895.

> The most characteristic, the most important part of my work is that which deals with a class . . . distinctive of our time — well-educated, fairly bred, *but without money*.[6]

This is the paradox of connection and separation that Gissing himself lived through and that he explored in Godwin Peak: *connection* through education and temperament to the world of Edith Sichel, Mrs Gaussen and the Frederic Harrisons, in his own case, and to that of the Warricombe family in Peak's — a world of material security, ordered relationships, accessible 'culture'; but *separation* by brute economic facts. Gissing felt with particular acuteness his kinship with women like Edith Sichel, whose acquaintance he made through her interest in his work. She belonged 'to a circle of wealthy and cultivated people, who have personal acquaintance with all the leaders in literature and art', and was herself 'distinctly intellectual'. No wonder the remoteness of such personal and social charms as she symbolised inspired him to the savage confession: *'I cannot stand obscurity'*.[7] And yet, obscurity was exactly what he chose by his marriage to Edith Underwood, and a letter to his sister Ellen from Exeter just prior to the marriage shows him under no illusions about this:

> Of course I shall have no society here. My ambition now is to make my name known, whilst personally I remain unseen and unheard of . . . We shall have to see whether I can keep my mind active without the help of congenial minds. I have the feeling of being deserted by all who ought to be my companions; but then these miseries are useful in giving a peculiar originality to my work.[8]

The novel was begun very soon after the marriage, so that the dramatisation of Peak's desperate desire to possess all that is represented by the Warricombes' home coincides with the nadir of Gissing's own sense of exclusion. The previous summer (1890), he had written haughtily in his Diary: 'English Society is no more for me.'[9] Now he was beginning to examine the depths and the attendant psychology of this extremity of exile.

We first see Godwin Peak as a gauche, solemn, intense student at the Whitelaw College prize-giving. He walks off with many of the prizes, though he is beaten into second place for most of them by the golden boy, Bruno Chilvers. This initial set-piece presents us with the image of institution-alised competition that conditions Peak's outlook on life. Peak desperately wants to win society's prizes, though he is under no illusion as to their intrinsic value. It is the evidence they carry of an achieved 'belonging' to which he aspires. Whitelaw College itself is endowed with the typical character-istics of 'health, spirits, and comfort' that Peak sees enshrined in the rampant self-assurance of the English middle class. The contradictions of his fastidious, humourless hyper-sensitivity, are related at the start to the discrepancy between his sense of uniqueness and his longing to belong.

> Like all proud natures condemned to solitude, he tried to convince himself that he had no need of society, that he despised its attractions, and could be self-sufficing. So far was this from the truth that he often regarded with bitter envy those of his fellow-students who had the social air, who conversed freely among their equals, and showed that the pursuits of the College were only a part of their existence.[10]

Bruno Chilvers is the exact antithesis of Peak, in his total absorption of inner Self in outer role. Mabel Donnelly describes him as a 'mellifluous hypocrite',[11] but this surely misses the point. Chilvers bears the same relation to Peak as Farfrae to Henchard in *The Mayor of Casterbridge;* both are born winners, who carelessly snatch all the prizes from under the loser's nose. But Chilvers is no more the villain than Farfrae. 'Hypocrisy' implies the consciousness of discrepancy between word and thought, a consciousness that Peak has, but Chilvers has not. For Chilvers, like Jasper Milvain or any of Conrad's 'world-proof' characters, is simply oblivious of a discontinuity between action and imagination. Godwin is exiled in a world dominated by the naïve, the sincere, the extroverted, and the closed circuit of mutual corroboration that characterises the College prize-giving: 'every student who achieved distinction ... was felt to bestow a share of his honour upon each spectator who applauded him'.

The second main context in which we see Peak is his home. He is grotesquely sensitive about his dependence on patronage for his place at the College, and about the 'vulgarity' with which sister, brother, uncle and nephew are all tainted. But it is not the class constrictions that have crippled Peak, so much as a more general deprivation — and Gissing is undoubtedly drawing on his own experience here. For it has been the absence of particular Others in the context of childhood and growing up, that has conditioned Peak's inability to conceive of Others except in generalised, abstract and understandably hostile terms. His parents had no intimates who could provide the corroborating images of adult Otherness, against which the developing child might test his consolidating identity. How different, say, from Pip's childhood in *Great Expectations*, with its educative, nourishing variety of adult kindness, cruelty, strength, mystery and eccentricity. For Peak, Others represent little but threat to his fierce desire to be separate and unique. The occasion of his brother Oliver's acquisition of a fashionable new hat sparks off a typically acrid exchange.

> 'Have you no *self*? Are you made, like this hat, on a pattern with a hundred thousand others?'
>
> 'You and I are different,' said Oliver impatiently. 'I am content to be like other people.'
>
> 'And I would poison myself with vermin-killer if I felt any risk of such contentment!'[1] [2]

Part of the hysteria of Godwin's outburst is caused by his own secret longing for conformity, though certainly not at this lowly level. The desire for inner uniqueness and the desire for outward acceptance into conventional society are travelling in diametrically different directions, producing the effect of grinding, neurotic frustration.

Peak's ambition is to 'knit himself into the social fabric'.

But in order to do this, he must cultivate a perfect double consciousness, a perfect split between private feeling and public gesture. His one great terror is *exposure*. His dependence on patronage and his lowly social origins are not in themselves particularly appalling secrets. When an irredeemably vulgar but enterprising Cockney uncle proposes to blazon the family name over a new restaurant opposite the College gates, a young man of normal resilience would be able to shrug off the embarrassment of this 'secret sharer'. It is not the secret itself, so much as the *act* of being exposed, that is Peak's nightmare; for this would destroy the illusion of perfect inner chastity, the illusion on which his fraudulent assault on the world is based.

The nature and implications of this desire for inner 'freedom' are the novel's central theme. When this freedom is threatened, Peak gives up his scholarship, and sets off, like many a provincial aspirant before him, to the big city. But before this, on his long walk home from College after an uncharacteristic night of dissipation (uncharacteristic because it debases him to the level of the 'vulgar masses'), he undergoes a critical experience. He starts to survey his future with frankness and determination.

> All he had to fight the world with was his brain; and only by incessant strenuousness in its exercise had he achieved the moderate prominence declared in yesterday's ceremony . . . Was he in any respect extraordinary? were his powers noteworthy? It was the first time that he had deliberately posed this question to himself, and for answer came a rush of confident blood, pulsing through all the mechanism of his being.[13]

It is directly subsequent to this moment of a heightened, indeed unprecedented, sense of Selfhood, that he experiences an exactly contradictory sense of self-dissolution. He has been interested in geology from childhood (his intellectual bent is stressed to be scientific rather than 'artistic'),[14] so he turns aside to study a small quarry. As he sits holding a fragment of rock in his hand

... a strange fit of brooding came over him. Escaping from
the influences of personality, his imagination wrought
back through eras of geologic time, held him in a vision
of the infinitely remote, shrivelled into insignificance all
but the one fact of inconceivable duration. Often as he had
lost himself in such reveries, never yet had he passed so
wholly under the dominion of that awe which attends a
sudden triumph of the pure intellect.[15]

The juxtaposition of these two experiences, the 'rush of
confident blood', and the 'triumph of the pure intellect'
suggests the key paradoxes of Godwin's desire for 'freedom':
can it be a freedom *of* the self, or only a freedom *from* the
self? can it be autonomy or only escape? The triumph of the
intellect here annihilates the confirmation of identity that
the 'rush of confident blood' just signalled. The desire of the
blood torments, but only through and in the blood can the
Self be confirmed; the intellect releases but also dissolves. It
is a familiar impasse in writers of the time, that often finds
expression in relation to such images of dissolving time:
Gissing's geological strata here perform the same function as
the stars in Hardy. The Self is trapped but sustained by the
constituent dimensions of Time and Space, and released but
annihilated by their transcendence. It is the consolation and
temptation of this latter experience, against which Peak's
struggle to hammer out a positive confirmation of identity
will be measured.

At the end of Part I, Godwin leaves home with a flourish,
setting out on 'a voyage of discovery'. But when Part II
opens, ten years have already passed since his arrival in
London. He has achieved nothing. Like Jude Fawley at
Christminster, he meets a blank wall of exclusion from any
form of social advancement. Gissing had himself experienced
very similar feelings after ten years of his own life in London.
On Sunday, 17 June 1888, he had made this melancholy
entry in his Diary:

I have lived in London ten years, and now, on a day like
this when I am very lonely and depressed, there is not one

single house in which I should be welcome if I presented myself, not one family — nay, not one person — who would certainly receive me with good-will.

Godwin and Jude are bluntly rebuffed, forced away to try their assault by new, oblique paths. Godwin's chance appears when he arrives on holiday in Exeter. He is preparing to indulge his geological enthusiasms when he catches sight of the Warricombe family, whom he had met ten years previously through his college friend Buckland Warricombe. In them and their country house he sees enshrined the ideal of material security that he is determined to grasp.

This English home, was it not surely the best result of civilisation, in an age devoted to material progress? Here was peace, here was scope for the kindliest emotions . . .[16]

Peak is particularly attracted by Buckland's sister, Sidwell. The association of his geological studies with an escape from Self is again set against the painful but stimulating specificities of the 'blood' and its desires.

What to him were the bygone millions of ages, the hoary records of unimaginable time? One touch of a girl's hand, one syllable of musical speech, — was it not that whereof his life had truly need?[17]

But the desire to possess Sidwell is less sexual than theoretical. She represents for him a type of feminine refinement and gentility — 'the lady as England has perfected her towards the close of this nineteenth century'. His first visit to her home is the scene of his critical test. In order to be admitted and accepted, he finds himself forced into the assumption of an outward pose of religious conformity, and even — ludicrously — of the intention of ordination. This social identity that he suddenly finds himself landed with is in flat contradiction to his real inner beliefs, which he has recently expressed in a virulent, but fortunately anonymous, attack on religious orthodoxy in a review. No wonder that in the course of the subsequent masquerade, he experiences a treacherous, hysterical hilarity in conversation with the decent, solemn Mr Warricombe. He even has to grasp his own wrist, like Dickens's Merdle, 'with involuntary attempt to recover his familiar self'.

From this point on, Peak leads a double life, in which his public performance and inner feelings are at total variance. It is the eventual impossibility of sustaining this absolute separation that is dramatised with progressive complexity. As his motto, Peak takes a phrase expressive of this impossible ideal, which Gissing had noted in his *Commonplace Book* as the motto of 'the liberals of the late Renaissance': 'Foris ut moris; intus ut libet' (outward conformity; inner freedom).[18] Initially, he gives a perfect performance, but in retrospect it takes on the aspect of 'a mad dream'. Some disembodied automaton has played his part for him; now he must live the nightmare through. Gissing had himself been only too aware of the farcical anomaly of his own 'double life' during the early years of his marriage to Nell. On one hand the 'inner reality' of the hell-on-earth he shared with her privately; on the other, the elegant, fashionable drawing-rooms in which he figured as tutor and guest through his connection with the Harrisons.

Jacob Korg has pointed to Peak's connection with Dostoevsky's Raskolnikov (amongst others),[19] in his attempt to assert the complete independence of identity from context, and morality from conditions. One does not have to go so far afield, however, to recognise his connection with certain well-known types. For in a quite obvious sense he is the traditional hypocrite, intent on sustaining an often ludicrous abyss between being and seeming, for which he will eventually be punished. Yet there is no more blatant way of marking the difference between Dickens and Gissing than by contrasting the Dickensian hypocrite with Gissing's Peak. For Gissing, as for Conrad, it is not hypocrisy so much as *charlatanism*, since the duplicity is now seen from the inside, as the index to a privileged, if guilty, vision. The 'charlatans' such as Peak or Razumov, adopt or have forced on them external roles that are totally incompatible with their innate dispositions. In precise contrast to them are set the characters who are apparently able to identify themselves totally with their outward roles, the Captain MacWhirrs and Jasper Milvains. Instead of the Dickensian hypocrite, seen with uniform objectivity from the outside, we have now on one hand the charlatan, and on the other the chameleon. Peak, like Razumov, is richly aware of the treachery he is practising on his inmost sense of Self, the sense of uniqueness out of which he has written his scathing denunciation of contemporary Christianity. This article is in fact the evidence of his true inner Self, that will eventually betray the factitious public Self he tries to sustain.

There are two main reasons for Peak's failure to see the duplicity through. The first is the impossibility of escaping the traces of his own past social identity. These are enshrined in actions and attitudes that live on in the relationships he has contracted in London, above all the relationship with Marcella Moxey, the intellectual 'new woman', who is in love with him. He cannot possess himself entirely, since he is the object of her desire and of his other friends' memories. Peak's error is to conceive of himself as an autonomous subject, the sole originator of desire. He leaves out of account the constraints to which the individual submits as soon as he becomes the *object* of another's desire. This leads on to the second related reason for his failure. Godwin is the involuntary object of his London friends' perceptions, speculations, and in Marcella's case, desires, that prevent him from controlling and concealing his 'real' identity. The secret of his authorship of the controversial article eventually and inevitably leaks out. But he is also the object of the intellectual and emotional responses of the individual with whom he deliberately engages himself, Sidwell Warricombe. His attempt to exercise total control over his image in Sidwell's heart and mind, fails not only because of the external discrediting, but also because the image of himself he creates in her eyes becomes unnecessary and a positive obstruction, as soon as she falls in love with him. For Sidwell's love is based both on the image he has created for her, *and* on her intuitive perception of an inner Self hiding behind the outer mask. The crisis comes when the created, outer image is proved to be false, and her love is seen to be neither so shallow that it immediately dissolves, nor so strong that it can adhere simply to the 'inner' being.

The novel ends with the defeat, but not the destruction, of the glimpsed connection. Godwin dies, as he was born, in exile. Gissing has managed to suggest that the autonomy of the inner Self is at the same time a fiction doomed to exposure, but also a permanent potentiality, capable of transformation through the redemptive intervention of another into a new, *mutual* freedom. Peak imagines that the Self can be set free, or confirm its freedom, by possession of the object of desire; but only by becoming the object of another's desire can a new and paradoxical freedom be achieved. Peak in fact confuses 'autonomy' and 'freedom', thinking that freedom can be won, while autonomy is retained. It is in the revelation of such confusions and illusions that Gissing's great value lies.

This reading of the novel sees it primarily as an anatomy of the psychology of exile. Jacob Korg has argued the case for its relation to a number of European novels of spiritual crisis, Turgenev's *Fathers and Sons*, Jacobsen's *Niels Lyhne* and Dostoevsky's *Crime and Punishment*.[20] Gissing was certainly a great admirer of these three novels, and had re-read the first two the spring previous to the writing of *Born in Exile*. One cannot help feeling, however, that it is misleading to yoke these novels together as forcefully as Korg does, and then to extrapolate a 'real theme' in the following way:

> This attack of science on metaphysical tradition, which Comte termed the central intellectual conflict of the nineteenth century, is the real theme of *Born in Exile*.[21]

Gissing certainly *uses* this 'intellectual conflict', but it is hard to accept that this is the novel's 'real theme', since it so conspicuously fails to explore the 'ideological dimension' in the way in which Dostoevsky does (and to a lesser extent the other two also). For Peak's conflicts are not primarily 'intellectual'. The 'ideological dimension' that Korg singles out may align Peak with other 'young heroes intoxicated by the moral freedom offered by materialism, as he [Gissing] himself had once been', but this cannot surely be claimed as the *centre* of the novel. And 'intoxicated'? Surely an inappropriate word for Peak or Niels Lyhne, or even Bazarov.

Peak's 'enlightened scientific views' are in themselves rationalisations of his antagonism to society. His deception is not
undertaken out of 'uncompromising intellectual honesty'.[22]
He finds himself swept into the deception before he has time
to think — 'without premeditation, almost without consciousness'.[23] It is 'under the marvelling regard of his
conscious self' that he displays his new-found piety.

Clearly there *are* some suggestive affinities between Peak
and Turgenev's Bazarov, but the divergences are equally
instructive. Though Bazarov feels strongly his difference from
the genteel, ordered world into which he blunders, he is not
tormented by bitterness at his exclusion from it, by any sense
of class stigma. The crucial difference from Peak is that
Bazarov is not seen to *suffer* from any feeling of exclusion.
He is for the most part amused, ironical, or irritated by the
genteel world and its rituals, but quite devoid of Peak's
desperate, bitter desire to be included. The central conflict or
confrontation could indeed be said to be similar, between the
freed, lonely Self, and the world of belonging, but the
reaction and treatment are very different. In place of the
self-confident, articulate Bazarov, the hyper-sensitive,
anxious Peak; instead of Turgenev's poised and sweeping
narrative idiom, extending from the sharply ironic to the
freely lyrical, Gissing's angular, intense absorption.

In the case of Jacobsen's fine novel, the affinity is more
diffused. As in Gissing's novel, we do not feel that the
protagonist's rejection of conventional religion is the motive
cause of his subsequent crises of identity, but rather one of
the symptoms. What is indeed very close to Gissing is the
sense of the implacable chasm between desire and reality —
desire as the vain, dream-nourished product of the imagination battering against an intractable 'reality'.

> . . . life takes no account of dreams. There isn't a single
> obstacle that can be dreamed out of the world, and in the
> end we lie there crying at the edge of the chasm, which
> hasn't changed and is just where it always was . . .[24]

Thus one of Jacobsen's characters in a vein of fierce
scepticism that would have appealed to Gissing. Face to face
with the bankruptcy of the new creed of atheism, Niels

expresses at the end a stoical resignation with which Gissing must also have identified: '. . . to bear life as it was! To bear life as it was and allow life to shape itself according to its own laws.'

One can hardly argue with Korg's generalisation about the links between Russian nihilism, French Positivism, and English agnosticism: that, in the broadest terms, they are all manifestations of a general spiritual crisis. Nevertheless, if *Born in Exile* succeeds in contributing to an understanding of this general crisis, it is by virtue of its dramatising the very *specific* currents and idioms of desire and need, that precede their articulation in the 'ideological dimension'.

7 Women and Marriage

i. MARRIAGE AND THE VICTORIAN NOVEL

Gissing's work presents a rich variety of women, for which he has been justly admired; from the neurotic Maud Enderby to the carefree Totty Nancarrow, the self-effacing Mrs Alfred Yule to the horrendous Ada Peachey, the sensible Lydia Trent to the giddy Alma Rolfe, and so on. One can say, nevertheless, that in the broadest sense, their interest for Gissing has two main, related aspects. On the one hand, there are the victims, trapped in many and various ways, by class, by sex and by money: Carrie Mitchell, Ida Starr, Jane Snowdon, Marian Yule, Monica Madden and many others. On the other hand, there are the rebels, actively engaged in passionate and sometimes desperate revolt against their limiting circumstances: Ada Warren, Clara Hewett, Rhoda Nunn and Nancy Tarrant being the most memorable. Gissing was able to engage with the frustrated energies of an identifiable group when he could see beyond the class issues, and in so far as the primary, though certainly not exclusive, obstacles to which they bear witness are those of sex and its cultural definitions, women were ideally qualified. In a more general sense, the discrepancy between women's inner feelings, needs and desires, and their available or prescribed social roles, offers a focus for the dramatisation of Gissing's own deepest preoccupation, the interpretation of this discrepancy into the terms of an active desire for the 'inner' to become incarnate in the 'outer', or of a regressive desire for the maintained purity of the inner life in the face of an irretrievably hostile outer world.

The second half of the nineteenth century saw a general increase in theories and activities that can be loosely associated under the title of sexual radicalism, and a specific questioning of women's social and personal roles. In the external sphere, there was the slow progress of legal reform

176

through the different stages of the Married Woman's Property Act, from its introduction in 1856 to its consolidation in 1882. There were the reforms in education, with the founding of Queen's College (1848), Bedford College (1849) and Girton (1872). There was the campaign to open the professions to women, with especial controversy over the medical profession.

It is instructive, however, that the main attention of the official feminist movement in this country, that started in the 1850s with the Society for Promoting the Employment of Women, was directed not towards marriage and the married woman, but towards the position of the single woman. There simply were not enough men to go round, and between 1851 and 1871 in particular there was a sharp increase in the number of single women, fated never to marry. For marriage was, of course, according to the entrenched ethos, the prescribed social role.

> Married life is a woman's profession; and to this life her training — that of dependence — is modelled. Of course by not getting a husband, or by losing him, she may find that she is without resources. All that can be said of her is, she has failed in business, and no social reform can prevent such failures.[1]

Thus the voice of the most implacable orthodoxy. Attempts to challenge this orthodoxy met with scorn, abuse and hysteria. Eliza Lynn Linton, in an exemplary article entitled 'Woman's Place in Nature and Society'[2] (the two being synonymous), unmasked the horror of 'a third sex', the alien 'men-women', unnatural 'hybrids'. It was hard luck on the 'odd women' who failed in the marriage stakes but — 'How much of this desire to share in the lives of men is simple weariness at the uneventful calm of celibacy?' Women of course are not cursed with sexual desire like men. Mrs Linton comforts herself with one of those many ingenious adaptations of Darwinian theory, the thought that the 'hybrids' will not survive the rigours of natural selection, as unfit and degenerate types.

If the feminist movement was not itself particularly concerned with the issue of marriage and the married woman, its enemies certainly were. *The Saturday Review*, and the hard orthodox opinion it represented, saw the movement as a direct threat to the institution of marriage. And rightly so, for no true effort to redefine the relations between the sexes could stop short of interrogating the basis of contemporary marriage. This was what Mill and Engels set themselves to do, in the two most important theoretical contributions to the questioning of sexual relationship, Mill's *On the Subjection of Women* (1869) and Engels's *The Origin of the Family, Private Property and the State* (1884).

Both writers attempt to identify the deeper social implications beneath contemporary opinion and practice. Both see in the issue of the marriage relationship wider issues of power and subjection. Kate Millett has made excellent use of the opposition between Mill and Ruskin in the representation of attitudes towards women in Victorian society,[3] particularly in relation to what she defines as 'the doctrine of manly guardianship'. Mill exposes the actual repressions cloaked beneath the ideal of male Chivalry, that finds its nauseating apogee in 'Of Queens' Gardens'.[4] (Though Ruskin surely cannot deserve Kate Millett's cruel 'senile eroticism', when he was so manifestly and appallingly a *victim* himself.) The chivalric ideal may have replaced a previous ethos of force, but the subjection of women is only more deeply engrained through their complaisance — as Mrs Linton amply demonstrates. Nothing, according to Mill, could be more insidious than 'the silly deprecation of the intellectual, and silly panegyrics on the moral, nature of women'.[5] We can recognise now the bland poison in the propaganda disseminated by such extraordinary documents as *The English Wife: A Manual of Home Duties*, where the role of Angel in the House is laid out with unctuous care:

> From the tumultuous scenes which agitate many of his hours, he [the husband] returns to the calm scene where peace awaits him, and happiness is sure to await him, because she is there waiting, whose smile is peace, and whose presence is more than happiness to his heart.[6]

Mill's achievement was to meet the claims of these fictions to be the 'laws of nature' ('everything which is usual appears natural'), and expose them as man-made, the product of a particular era and society.

Engels also, though from a sharper and more historical perspective, inveighed against the actual injustices behind the fictions of tolerant Chivalry. In the light of Lewis Morgan's anthropological research (the ignoring of which in this country Engels was quick to interpret in terms of 'conspiracy'), the historical and economic basis of contemporary bourgeois marriage could be examined in some detail. Engels's conclusions were characteristically aggressive. Monogamous marriage represented 'the subjugation of one sex by the other'.

It is the cellular form of civilised society, in which the nature of the oppositions and contradictions fully active in society can be already studied.[7]

Engels pushes a long way beyond Mill's impassioned humanism in his identification of the economic basis of personal relationship. 'Within the family he [the husband] is the bourgeois and the wife represents the proletariat.'[8] It is a stark and extreme proposition, and certainly the organised feminist movement in this country at that time would not have known what to make of it. But it is indeed these issues of power and dominance in the relationship between man and wife that the imaginative writers of the time are concerned to dramatise.

It is important to recognise the way in which the controversy about sex attracted many different voices, differing in motivation and expression. There was after all a certain amount of justification for orthodox opinion's sometimes hysterical confusion of sexual and political radicalism. William Morris was certainly not afraid to work out the implications of the total change of experience embodied in a socialist future.

... will ... the family of the times when monopoly is dead be still as it is now in the middle classes, framed on the model of that of an affectionate and moral tiger to whom all is prey a few yards from the sanctity of the domestic hearth? Will the body of the woman we love be but an appendage to her property?[9]

The sexual heretics who gathered around Edward Carpenter, for example, brought a wide range of interests together, different shades of social, political, psychological dissatisfaction, that were again expressed in very varying ways.[10]

And yet, in Carpenter's circle and beyond, the underlying imaginative patterns are clear. On one hand, the desperate fear and rejection of an identity that is imposed from without; on the other, the horror of an inner Self that threatens, by its failure to reach expression, to rend the individual apart. In Olive Schreiner's novel *The Story of an African Farm* (1883), the central character Lyndall expresses the first sort of terror, of the individual's fluidity and spontaneity being reduced to prescribed definitions.

> We all enter the world little plastic beings, with so much natural force, perhaps, but for the rest — blank; and the world tells us what we are to be, and shapes us by the ends it sets before us.[11]

It is in these terms that Hardy's Sue Bridehead challenges the 'social moulds' that await women, and it is naturally to Mill that she turns for support (though in so doing she seems temporarily to rival Phillotson in pedagoguery).

On the other side, there is the complementary terror of being unable to express, and thus to control, a hidden, compulsive inner Self. This is where the experience of the homosexual connects with that of women in general, and it is for this reason that homosexuality becomes with comparative suddenness a crucial and widespread issue. John Addington Symonds wrote to Edmund Gosse about the pioneer study of *Sexual Inversion*, on which he collaborated with Havelock Ellis:

> ... the position of a young person so tormented is really that of a man buried alive & conscious, but deprived of speech. He is doomed by his own timidity and ignorance to a repression which amounts to death ... This corpse, however, is obliged to bustle around and make an appearance every time the feast of life is spread.[12]

These are indeed powerful images, reverberating beyond the

particular sufferings of the homosexual, images of death-in-
life, of a total divorce between being and seeming, that reach
down to some of the deepest feelings of the age. One
recognises in this context the significance of Wilde's *The
Picture of Dorian Gray* as a parable of this nightmare divorce.
Symonds's own personal history presents us with an even
more direct confessional intensity. Sitting at respectable
dinner-tables with famous men such as Gladstone and
Tennyson, while underneath he struggled with unbearable
turmoil, he saw himself as one of the 'hollow men':

> How I loathe myself. At a great London dinner party last
> night I was among Marshalls Monteagles Myerses & Spring
> Rices, & they all talked & seemed to think that I had
> something to say too. It was all I cd. do to withhold
> myself from falling flat upon the floor & crying out to
> them: Behold I am a scare crow a thread paper a
> hypocrite, I am not what I look, tear off the clothes &
> flesh & find the death & hell inside: if anyone of you have
> got a God let him first search me, let him scatter me to the
> winds and discover my emptiness.[13]

It is clear that the progressive questioning of the nature of
'marriage' in the novel around this time reflects a deep sense
of the disconnections between appearance and reality to
which the homosexual and women in general were the most
explicit martyrs. What, then, had been the significance of the
centrality of marriage in the earlier Victorian novel, a
significance that the later writers were examining with some
scepticism? For previous writers, the importance of marriage
had been as the expression of confidence in the ideal or
possibility of consensus. Within the novel, individuals find
their separate identities confirmed and extended by mutual
definition, and through the 'external fiction' writer and
reader achieve a similar reciprocity. The Self finds in the
Other a reflection of its own desired self-image. It is extended
as well as confirmed, by recognition of the Other's autonomy
over and above the function of confirmation. Marriage
represents, therefore, an agreement about definitions, each
party exacting and submitting a required degree of hege-
mony. The desired self-image is limited, curtailed from

infinite aspiration on the one hand, but given definition, saved from chaotic formlessness on the other. But in the second half of the century we witness an increasing scepticism about the possibility of equilibrium. Relationship seems *only* possible in terms of pursuit and aggression. The other must be reduced to fixity before it reduces us.

It is with George Eliot and Meredith that the concentration of these issues in the study of marriage becomes most pointed. Before this, the English novel has been primarily concerned with courtship rather than marriage itself, with the extended prelude in which, to take *Emma* as the classic case, the young girl is allowed time to grow towards an ideal marriageable type. (What happens afterwards? but that *is* the end, or rather, as the narrative would have implied to many, indeed most, of the readers, *your* end, my dear — gently withholding the funereal ambiguity of 'end'.) In the Casaubon and Grandcourt marriages, George Eliot begins seriously to push through the imaginative barrier. It is a harsher, tougher vision of the price of enlightenment. Emma, after all, *was* lucky, though Jane Austen marvellously contrives the appearance of luck as grace. What George Eliot austerely rejects is that neat equation between the inner enlightenment and the external reward, wisdom and wedding-ring; Dorothea's education starts after the altar. (In one of her reviews, George Eliot flays the sort of emotional flabbiness rampant in most contemporary novels, that deceives the reader into thinking that 'duty looks stern, but all the while has her hand full of sugar-plums'.)[14]

As we relate her emphasis on the disciplining of imagination and the renunciation of Self to the contemporary history of women's social roles and opportunities, we can well understand the pressures to interpret the barriers in terms of a tragic impasse. The unsatisfied aspirations towards expression, independence, action of any significant kind, are dragged back to the confines of 'inward vision'. It is against this that Dorothea struggles —

> . . . the stifling oppression of that gentlewoman's world, where everything was done for her and none asked for her aid — where the sense of connection with a manifold

pregnant existence had to be kept up painfully as an inward vision, instead of coming from without in claims that would have shaped her energies.[15]

But for Meredith, renunciation and 'inward vision' were not enough. *The Egoist* (1879) is an exhaustive exposure of the fictions of courtship, beneath which the woman relinquishes command of and responsibility for her full potency, imaginative, spiritual and sexual, to the proprietor, the husband. Though it masquerades as ballet, this is pitched battle. Willoughby's energy is entirely devoted to reducing a chosen Other to his mirror image. The process of Clara's education — how different from Emma's or Dorothea's — is the process of learning the weapons and strategies of survival, no longer a question of chastening a Self, but of keeping it intact. The narrative pattern that emerges is typical of the later Victorian novel, in the apparently ceaseless flux and reflux of pursuit and resistance, and in the defiant Clara, Meredith dramatises exactly that gap between inner feeling and available expression that makes women of such central significance to the writers of this time.

> ... her prim little sketch of herself, set beside her real, ugly, earnest feelings, rang of a mincing simplicity, and was a step in falseness. How could she display what she was?[16]

Clara descends to the recognition of that horror we saw so savagely expressed by Symonds, of possessing an intolerable inner secret that cannot be expressed.

> Her horrible isolation of secrecy in a world amiable in unsuspectingness, frightened her. To fling away her secret, to conform, to be unrebellious, uncritical, submissive, became an impatient desire ...[17]

The martyrdom of submission exposes itself as a temptation, because the force and the responsibility that Clara carries are turning in a new direction. The force, shared by all Meredith's vital young women, is richer and more varied than Dorothea's, through its association with 'Nature', with physical as well as spiritual potency. It is not necessary to profess undeviating admiration for the various ways Meredith finds to give expression to this 'Nature', in order to see the difficulty and implications of this recognition, that woman now has responsibilities to herself. With Meredith's women, we begin to feel that growth or development may be for its own sake, rather than for its production of a marketable object. As we follow Clara through to the Carinthia of *The Amazing Marriage*, we sense the really major break-through, whereby the woman's identity is no longer to be confirmed exclusively, or even primarily, through a single dependent relationship.

The Meredith of the later novels, *Diana of the Crossways* (1885), *One of Our Conquerors* (1891) and *The Amazing Marriage* (1895), provides a suitable point for breaking off the present discussion. For they offer both the most subtle arraignment of the contemporary conditions governing the relations between man and woman, and the most positive suggestion as to the possibilities for creating new conditions. They show Meredith at his most genuinely acute in the analysis of the engrained psychology of marriage. For George Eliot, marriage presented only the possibility rather than the general likelihood of disaster — and personal, rather than social disaster. George Eliot's women make identifiable errors, projecting false images on to the Other, and learning through suffering a wise humility in the face of the 'real' out there. Meredith's men and women, less fortunate, are condemned to a never-ending conflict over the mutual provision, receipt and creation of each others' images. The tragic, farcical incompatibilities of May and January, or Beauty and the Beast, they are obvious enough. But what of the subtler degrees of divorce that coexist with intimacy, the changing, mingling shades of hatred and affection, brutality and tolerance, reticence and generosity? This is one of Meredith's great themes, the subject of the poems of *Modern Love*, and of his last completed novel, *The Amazing Marriage* — the theme of married divorce, or the divorce inherent in *all* contemporary marriage. It is Meredith who, through Clara Middleton, distils the most unanswerable and representative of silent screams: 'We women are nailed to our sex!'

ii. THE ODD WOMEN (1893)

In this novel, Gissing finds a focus for his continuing investigation of identity and relationship in the specific contemporary issue of female emancipation. The *Athenaeum* reviewer noted that it was 'intensely modern'.[18] Gissing took considerable interest in the feminist movement. When he was in Paris in the autumn of 1888 he went to hear the feminist Louise Michel lecture at La Salle des Conférences, and a year later he was working at the British Museum reading-room on 'woman literature', in preparation for a novel to be called 'The Headmistress'.

It was rare for Gissing to view historical change with anything other than alarm and despondency. The emotional deadlocks become familiar: present existence is hell, but change is catastrophe. The remark of one character to another in *The Emancipated* catches perfectly this sense of poised trauma: 'You are a sort of Janus, with anxiety on both faces.' It is all the more striking, therefore, to find him for once so far suppressing his anxiety as to pledge positive faith in the historical process. In June 1893, he wrote to his friend Bertz, with reference to the recently published *The Odd Women*:

> My demand for female 'equality' simply means that I am convinced there will be no social peace until women are intellectually trained very much as men are. More than half the misery of life is due to the ignorance and childishness of women. The average woman pretty closely resembles, in all intellectual considerations, the average male *idiot* — I speak medically . . . I am driven frantic by the crass imbecility of the typical woman. That type must disappear, or at all events become altogether subordinate. And I believe that the only way of effecting this is to go through a period of what many people will call sexual anarchy. Nothing good will perish; we can trust the forces of nature, which tend to conservation.[19]

The confidence with which Gissing faces the prospect of 'sexual anarchy' is in startling contrast to the dismay with which he viewed the whole 'democratic question' (though later in this same letter he seems to recognise the anomalies in his attitude). 'Nothing good will perish' is a remark that one would instinctively attribute to Morris rather than Gissing, in the context of a discussion of historical change. It certainly seems likely that the urgency of his own problems in his second marriage to Edith contributed to his enthusiasm for the prospect of a general transformation of relationship.

The theme of the novel is explicit. The 'odd women' are the unwanted, unmarried minority, being quietly crucified on the social fiat that a woman's role is marriage and mother-hood. They are represented by the Madden sisters, Alice, Virginia and Monica, three survivors out of an original impossible complement of six, fortunately whittled down by consumption, accident and suicide. For women excluded from marriage by deficiency of money and looks as the two elder ones are, there remain only the most menial of social roles — at best, the governess, teacher or companion, at worst the prostitute ('a not unimportant type of the odd woman', Gissing comments). Alice and Virginia take refuge in religion and alcohol respectively. In its deliberate eschewal of the opportunities for irony, let alone comic relief, the portrayal of Virginia is affecting in a way not normally associated with the English novel. There is neither revulsion nor humorous distancing from the fragile gentility driven, blushing, to the surreptitious companionship of the gin bottle. One remembers Orwell's shrewd remark about Gissing's lack of 'that curse of English writers, a "sense of humour" '.[20]

It is the youngest sister, Monica, however, whose marriage to Widdowson constitutes one of the two main relationships in the novel. Here we see the ideal of marriage propagated by society being tested against the actuality. Not that it is a conventional match, by any means. Widdowson is a dour, awkward city clerk, elevated into relative prosperity by a brother's legacy, but without the social qualifications to find a wife through the regular channels of social intercourse. He is reduced, in fact, to chance encounters on park benches, which he conducts, nevertheless, with 'scrupulous modesty'. But after their marriage, it becomes clear that Widdowson is the precise embodiment of the conventional, 'Ruskinian' attitude towards woman, that ostensibly enthrones and idolises her as queen of the domestic virtues, and in actuality censors brutally any attempt to transgress the narrow limits of the domestic prison. His whole emotional capacity is devoted to the reduction of Monica to a *type*. Like Casaubon and Phillotson, he is obsessed by punctiliousness, routine, formality. The sterility of his life is suggested by the very syntax of a description such as this:

> He had always two or three solid books on hand, each with marker; he studied them at stated hours, and always sitting at a table, a note-book open beside him.[21]

The repetition of those clipped 'st's' ('studied', 'stated') and the vacancy of that merely 'open' note-book emphasise the man's meticulous bloodlessness. From his white hairy hands to the sombre glee with which he pads over the bare boards of his new house, he is felt as a detailed, totally convincing presence.

The motives behind Monica's acceptance of him are quite blatantly economic. *She* does not subscribe to the Ruskinian fictions as her sisters do, but is merely innocent of their teeth. She is imprisoned in the drapery establishment where she works, economically, socially and personally — the familiar triad, of money, class and sex. Widdowson offers her release from the pointless monotony of her daily labour and pursuit by pimply, indigent drapers' assistants. Undazzled by any sentimentality about marriage with an older man, she imagines (like Gwendolen Harleth and Sue Bridehead) that she can accept the material security he offers without surrendering a fraction of her cherished autonomy. The subsequent drama of mistaken identity develops into characteristically authentic scenes of niggling and wrangling, as the two fight desperately over the definition of each others' roles. They culminate in the classic Gissing tableau — husband and wife staring at each other in total estrangement.

> Both panting as if after some supreme effort of their physical force, they stood and looked at each other. Each to the other's eyes was incredibly transformed. Monica could not have imagined such brutal ferocity in her husband's face, and she herself had a wild recklessness in her eyes, a scorn and abhorrence in all the lines of her

countenance, which made Widdowson feel as if a stranger were before him.[22]

This is the moment of vertigo in which the fixed image of the Other splinters.

But the patterns of conventional definition are quick to provide a negative image as soon as the positive is contradicted. As Kate Millett points out, the inverse image of Ruskin's 'queen of the garden' is the prostitute of the city street. In fact, Widdowson is grasping a smouldering brand marked 'whore' behind his back even as he makes the positive identification of 'angel in the house', since he is suspicious to the point of paranoia about Monica's sexual allure. So Monica finds herself forced to choose between the definitions of wife or whore for herself, and of husband or adulterer for the Other. The hapless, soft-hearted Bevis, himself trapped by the economic and emotional demands of a dependent mother and sisters, gallantly but foolishly volunteers for a role in this drama before reading the script. He is understandably horrified to find that Monica has taken his merely sentimental posturing for a firm contract to play the part of the daring adulterer who will sweep her away, reckless of husband, society and convention. Again the image shatters.

> Her lover, as she had thought of him for the past two or three months, was only a figment of her imagination; Bevis had proved himself a complete stranger to her mind; she must reshape her knowledge of him.[23]

And yet, though this is effectively the end of Monica (she dies in child-birth at the end of the novel), the fact that she does produce a child is important, for it is the child that Rhoda Nunn will never have.

Rhoda Nunn, the central character in the novel, has affinities with many of Gissing's other aggressive young women, such as Ada Warren, Clara Hewett and Nancy Tarrant, but she is unique in the energy and articulacy with which she challenges society's conventions, as she feels them threatening her right to self-determination. She knows from an early age that she will be forced to support herself unless or until saved by marriage, but the prospect of her personal

redemption does not obscure her feeling of identification
with all those single women doomed as a statistical fact to
spinsterhood. Rejecting the available roles of teacher and
governess, she procures for herself a training in shorthand,
typing and book-keeping, and then joins an organisation
devoted to the similar training of young girls for clerical
work. These are perhaps modest beginnings, but Rhoda has
made an advance on Gissing's previous 'exiles'. Before this,
they have had great difficulty in focusing their protest on to
specific injuries, and even when, as in *New Grub Street*, these
can be identified, it is apparently impossible to enact a
positive challenge within the narrative. Rhoda's energy is
therefore all the more welcome, though it is a pity that more
is not seen of the actual day-to-day details of the organisation
for which she works. But Rhoda does at least *work* for
change — and for the tough change of consciousness, rather
than the flaccid change-of-heart. When Virginia Madden
comes to visit her in London and recounts the lamentable
story of her life as a companion, all the assumptions she has
so placidly accepted as given conditions of her social identity
crumble before Rhoda's brisk response.

> 'I wished to leave again and again. But at the end she
> always begged me not to desert her — that was how she
> put it. After all, I never had the heart to go.'
> 'Very kind of you, but — these questions are so difficult
> to decide. Self-sacrifice may be quite wrong, I'm afraid.'
> 'Do you think so?' asked Virginia anxiously.[2 4]

So might a whole era of Victorian womanhood, raised on the
ethics of self-sacrifice, have trembled at the daring Rhoda.
Mill had excited horror and abuse when he had made a
similar challenge about woman's 'selflessness'.

> All the moralities tell them that it is the duty of women
> and all the current sentimentalities that it is their nature,
> to live for others; to make complete abnegation of
> themselves, and to have no life but in their affections.[2 5]

And narrowly circumscribed 'affections' at that.
    In the contrast between Rhoda and Mary Barfoot, the head
of the organisation, Gissing is reflecting one of the crucial

divisions in the actual feminist movement of the time: Mary's
'gradualist' approach to change is a deliberate foil to Rhoda's
'revolutionary' militancy. Unlike Mary, Rhoda actively
encourages the girls in the organisation to forgo the prospect
of marriage, and sets herself up as an example of militant
chastity. Compassion for the women not strong enough to
resist the security of marriage is a confirmation of their
weakness. There is harshness as well as nobility in her
belligerence: 'Human weakness is a plea that has been much
abused, and generally in an interested spirit'. Her aim is to
'make women hard-hearted'. In the test-case of a girl who has
run off with a married man and now wishes to return to their
community, she holds to her hard logic. Unfortunately, in
this particular case, the result of her therapeutic severity is
that the rejected girl commits suicide. And the severity
suggests the involvement of personal motivations informing
and perhaps distorting the appearance of impersonal idealism.
For Rhoda *resents* the fact that woman is dependent on man
for both the facts and images of relationship, and this drives
her towards a fanatical rejection of *all* relationship. Although
she commits herself publicly to communal activity, she
attempts to insulate her inner Self from all personal
entanglements. Now, for the first time, Gissing is examining
with true impartiality and acuteness, the psychology of
change, social and personal. In her vigorous rejection of the
identity that society would impose on her, Rhoda lays claim
to a total self-determination that will result in an equally
disastrous rigidity of type. It is the most profound and
balanced study of the values and dangers inherent in the
impulse towards radical change that Gissing ever achieved.

Rhoda can no more retain that deep inner privacy than
Monica (or Godwin Peak), as soon as she finds herself the
object of another's desire. Her relationship with Everard
Barfoot is schematically opposed to the conventional
marriage and estrangement of the Monica—Widdowson
relationship. Everard's name seems to complement the
belligerence of her own ('Nunn'), in its intimation of
masculine obstinacy ('Ever-hard Bar-foot'?) But his claims to
sympathy with her cause are not necessarily specious. He
seems genuinely attracted by the possibility of an alternative

to the conventional match with Agnes Brissenden, economically comfortable, culturally refined – and 'Ruskinian'.[26] But from the start, his attraction to Rhoda is contaminated by the element of sexual challenge. Rhoda carries with her 'a suggestiveness directed not solely to the intellect, of something like an unfamiliar sexual type . . .' What is, or can be, the quality of his attraction to this 'unfamiliarity', or the degree of sincerity in his statement: 'My own ideal of marriage involves perfect freedom on both sides . . .'?

It will perhaps seem portentous to invoke *Jude the Obscure* and *Women in Love* at this point, but for all the obvious differences, indeed *because* of them, the comparison is worth making. Rhoda and Everard face the same problems in trying to create a *new* basis for relationship beyond marriage, as Jude and Sue, and Birkin and Ursula. The Widdowson marriage does more than vindicate the aspiration to break free of the conventional; it is when the two individuals find themselves at the same time free of the imposed forms and yet unable to create a new form, that we start to explore the deep anomalies. The old issues of domination and submission can be juggled with more freely, but they are still, so it seems, the old issues. It is the same problem that the three writers dramatise, in very different ways: how to create a genuinely new relationship without merely reproducing the old patterns of force? Conditioned by anxiety into a fear of relationship as necessarily based on dependence and domination, how can the individual create a new relationship that will redeem the sterility of singleness without precluding its independence – except through the transcendent images of 'star-like polarity' and the 'polarized sex-circuit'?

Neither Rhoda nor Everard can resist the anxiety that drives them into this power struggle. For though the ostensible issue between them is the denial of convention by living together, the real issues are those of power, of Everard reducing Rhoda to a willed type, and Rhoda resisting. When he is temporarily defeated by Rhoda in his acceptance of her plea for a conventional marriage, Everard suffers the familiar disillusionment, the sense of human flexibility mocking the rigidity of definition.

Free as he boasted himself from lover's silliness, he had
magnified Rhoda's image. She was not the glorious rebel he
had pictured. Like any other woman, she mistrusted her
love without the sanction of society.[27]

But this is not the point; it is the male's rationalisation of
defeat. Rhoda does not regress to the conventional out of
timidity, but because she has no other direction in which to
move when threatened with reduction to a new prescribed
image. Gissing emphasises this, by later showing us their
ostensible positions reversed, she ready to contract a free
union, he insisting on the conventional match. In the end, he
escapes unscathed back to his *pis aller*, Agnes Brissenden, and
Rhoda is left with her work.

The novel ends with one of Gissing's tantalising scenes,
that suggest so much more than is achieved in the narrative as
a whole. Rhoda comes to visit Alice Madden, the eldest sister,
who has now found her vocation in bringing up the dead
Monica's child. Rhoda talks enthusiastically about her work,
but the novel ends on a different note.

Whilst Miss Madden went into the house to prepare
hospitalities, Rhoda, still nursing, sat down on a garden
bench. She gazed intently at those diminutive features,
which were quite placid and relaxing in soft drowsiness.
The dark, bright eye was Monica's. And as the baby sank
into sleep, Rhoda's vision grew dim; a sigh made her lips
quiver, and once more she murmured, 'Poor little child!'[28]

Rhoda's mellowed compassion for the child, for Monica, for
woman's whole entanglement in the processes of relationship,
with birth and death, is balanced by *our* sense of compassion
for her exclusion from these processes. For despite the
horrors, the injustice and suffering of the conventional
marriage, out of it there is created a child. If only the forces
hinted at in the 'dark bright eye' could have reached fuller
expression. The child points to the price Rhoda has to pay
not just in terms of human tenderness and affection, but also
of essential creativity, for her idealism. For is not this the
child that fails to survive the marriage of Jude and Sue, and
the child that can never disturb the perfect sterility of

Birkin's 'polarized sex-circuit'? The child is what the impossible, perfect relationship, in which perfect freedom is mystically reconciled with perfect inter-dependence, can never create.

If we take 'marriage' in a sense that extends to embrace the concept of any consensus between Self and Other, the rejection of 'other-determined' definitions of identity can be seen as the necessary radical impulse in the individual's search for self-determination. But the claim to exclusive self-determination can only lead to a new absolute unless mitigated by a re-engagement with the Other — a re-engagement not merely in terms of public commitment to the redefining of the external forms, but also in terms of active personal relationship. And this in its turn involves some measure of self-surrender in the establishment of a true mutuality. The final perception on which the novel ends is that 'marriage' has the power to create, and that 'separation', in itself, does not.

To pretend that these issues are satisfactorily and dramatically incorporated into the narrative as a whole would be to over-read the novel grossly. But, as often in Gissing — hence his attraction and disappointment — they are 'there', within, behind, beyond. Within its limits, this novel is a remarkable study of the human forces that make for historical change, and of the subsequent difficulties of evolving new forms that can be *lived* as well as spoken.

iii. IN THE YEAR OF JUBILEE (1894)

In the Year of Jubilee is in many ways the most immediately attractive of Gissing's major novels. It offers a sharply observed and panoramic cultural analysis, as rich in the details of contemporary urban life, houses, streets, clothes, fashions, advertisments, as any novel of the time. It attempts to catch the 'essential spirit' of suburban life in Camberwell in the same way as *Thyrza* and *The Nether World* had done for working-class life in the specific localities of Lambeth and Clerkenwell. Gissing himself predicted that this novel would mark 'a reversion to my old style, *without* the socialistic spirit — indeed, I hope without any spirit but that of art'.[29] Yet the impassioned scepticism with which Gissing viewed the rampant cultural degeneration evidenced by the effects of 'sham' education and a 'higher standard of living', points to the novel's continuity with the deep concerns of *New Grub Street*.

Gissing wrote in explanation of the novel's 'satirical' title:

> The year of Jubilee signified so much that is contempt-
> ible — snobbery, blatant ochlocracy, shams gigantic &
> innumerable — all thrown together into an exhibition of
> human folly not often surpassed for effectiveness.[30]

Gissing leaves us in no doubt about his valuation of the social changes that have promiscuously extended to the three French sisters the measure of education and leisure that allows them to buy their children 'elaborate and costly playthings', to wear flashy clothes and speculate in business. There is a violent eruption when Ada, the eldest sister, learns that her husband Arthur has deserted her, and Beatrice tries to stop her tearing the house apart.

> Now indeed the last trace of veneer was gone, the last rag
> of pseudo-civilization was rent off these young women; in
> physical conflict, vilifying each other like the female
> spawn of Whitechapel, they revealed themselves as
> born — raw material which the mill of education is
> supposed to convert into middle-class ladyhood.[31]

Beneath the thin 'veneer' of education and moderate affluence, this is still a 'nether world'. It is no longer physical want that characterises this condition of fallen humanity, in which Samuel Barmby can proudly air his smatterings of 'culture', Stephen Lord rents pianos to those who are 'rabid in the pursuit of gentility', Beatrice French cons customers into joining the 'South London Fashionable Dress Supply Association', and the advertising agent Luckworth Crewe plies his aggressive ingenuity. It is, as always, the casualties of this restless, competitive, pretentious world in whom Gissing is interested. For the same desires and frustrations still burn beneath the surface. There is Arthur Peachey, the victim of one of Gissing's most excruciating married hells. There is the Morgan family, condemned by their desire for respecta-bility to the horrors of a gimcrack desirable residence that is collapsing before their eyes. Above all, there is the Lord family; Stephen the father, taking surreptitiously to drink, Horace the son, infatuated by the pathetically coquettish Fanny French, and Nancy the daughter, the novel's central character.

Nevertheless, there are striking divergences from the ostensible vision of total cultural degeneration — even more so than in *New Grub Street*. The energetic, resourceful advertising agent, Luckworth Crewe, turns out to be quite extraordinarily likeable, and both he and Beatrice French, whom he encourages in business, have a brash, resilient charm, that the offered leading male character, Lionel Tarrant, singularly lacks. More important, however, is the fact that Nancy Lord herself belongs unequivocally to this 'new generation'. Gissing is indeed concerned to attribute a representative status to her belligerent energies.

> Thus, by aid of circumstance, had she put herself into complete accord with the spirit of her time. Abundant privilege; no obligation. A reference of all things to her sovereign will and pleasure. Withal, a defiant rather than a hopeful mood; resentment of the undisguisable fact that her will was sovereign only in a poor little sphere which she would gladly have transcended.[32]

The course of the narrative will dramatise the chastening of this 'sovereign will', and Nancy's consequent development away from 'the spirit of her time'. Yet it is hard to resist the suggestion that it is exactly Nancy's participation in 'the spirit of her time' that endows her with so much charm and engages our sympathies so deeply. Though Gissing is careful to place the 'vulgarity' of her enthusiasm for the Jubilee celebrations, we cannot help sharing the girl's instinctive excitement, the thrill of sudden independence and the gusto with which she throws herself into the occasion. Nancy has grown up with the French sisters and been educated with them, and to some extent she shares Beatrice's aggressive self-confidence and affected masculinity. She is certainly distinguished from the French sisters by the 'innate' quality of her dissatisfaction with the nether world to which she is confined. Yet Gissing refuses to face the unavoidable implication that, for all the liabilities of the 'sham' education so viciously displayed by at least two of the French sisters, it is this same education that allows Nancy even the limited powers of self-expression with which she can explore and challenge the forces obstructing her self-fulfilment.

Nancy continues the efforts of Godwin Peak and Rhoda Nunn positively to *transform* their condition of exclusion or deprivation. Like Godwin Peak, she feels excluded from a sphere of (apparently) superior gentility and 'culture', represented by Lionel Tarrant. Like Rhoda Nunn, she feels the limiting conditions of her role as a woman, and then as a mother.

> Must there not be discoverable, in the world to which she had, or could obtain access, some honest, strenuous occupation, which would hold in check her unprofitable thoughts and soothe her self-respect?[33]

It is a measure of Gissing's scepticism that the only 'honest, strenuous occupation' Nancy can in fact find is (in her case, somewhat implausibly) writing novels. But it is the class tensions between Nancy and Lionel that contain the most penetrating observations in the novel. She is provoked and stimulated by his veneer of leisured elegance, his well-bred languor and suggestion of intellectual reserve. There is an echo of Godwin Peak's great deception, when she experiences the sense of being an 'impostor', by laying claim to a cultural suavity that she cannot sustain. She pretends to intimacy with contemporary periodicals, and dourly insists on reading Helmholtz's 'Lectures on Scientific Subjects' when they go for a country walk. There is an excellent scene in which she blunders with quasi-malicious intent into asking Tarrant if the family is connected with 'Tarrant's Black Lead'. While he is shocked at her tactlessness, she feels simultaneously a 'keen gratification' at the barb, and regret at her conviction of irrevocable vulgarity.

Yet if the class tensions between them are admirably done, the sexual are less so. In Nancy's equivocal attraction to the 'superior' Tarrant and the 'inferior' Crewe, there are hints of a familiar triangular relationship in which some of Gissing's previous women have been trapped, Adela Waltham and

Thyrza Trent for example. More suggestive, however, are the echoes of Hardy's *Tess*. Not only does the central seduction scene, and the aura of reticence that surrounds it, seem to draw on Hardy, but also the whole notion of building a narrative that deliberately goes *beyond* the supposedly crucial cataclysm of the heroine's sexual 'fall'. If the sham gentleman Lionel has some affinities with Alec D'Urberville, he has also some of Angel Clare's social hauteur (and, incidentally, flees in the same direction as Angel). What is unusual for Gissing is his identification with the social and cultural inferior in such a situation; for it is certainly part of the novel's strength that Nancy is *not* specially gifted, like Thyrza, for instance, but, in the word's least pejorative sense, 'ordinary'. It is therefore particularly unfortunate, given the potential of this situation, that their relationship fails to develop with any conviction. One can see Gissing struggling with the same problems so bravely anatomised in *The Odd Women*, the supreme difficulty of moving beyond the conventional basis for marriage, out into the no-man's-land where Jude and Sue, and later Birkin and Ursula will wander. Tarrant expresses some forceful and familiar opinions about conventional marriage:

> Hugger-mugger marriage is a defilement and a curse. We know it from the experience of the world at large, — which is perhaps more brutalised by marriage than by anything else . . .[34]

But given Tarrant's consistent failure in the course of the novel to engender any emotion in the reader other than that of repulsion, we cannot feel that his demand for a new sort of star-like polarity is anything much more than male egotism trying to escape the responsibilities of a truly mutual relationship. Nancy's acquiescence in the maintenance of separate establishments (aided by a legacy that makes her financially independent) does not seem to be undertaken out of a positive desire for experiment, but merely out of weakness. When set beside Rhoda Nunn's continuing vitality, the etiolation of her original bristling self-confidence is deeply disappointing.

But it is in her that the most powerful aspects of the novel

have been concentrated, both in her role as the representative
of a new generation of social and cultural aspirants, and more
specifically in her role as a woman. Nancy is trapped by class,
by sex and by money. Her education has roused aspirations
beyond her apparent station. Her sexual desires land her with
a child, and thus marriage. And, as so often in Gissing, the
sexual desire is complicated by the intrusion of a will (her
father's), designed to inflict the most awkward obstacles
possible in the way of personal fulfilment. We remember the
obstructive will in *Isabel Clarendon*, the legacies that Marian
Yule and Godwin Peak receive in *New Grub Street* and *Born
in Exile*. It is a characteristic and bitter paradox that the lack
of money impedes, but its possession exposes the individual
to even harsher restraints and obligations. It is also a familiar
pattern, that Nancy should find herself burdened with a
secret 'guilt' (the child, and marriage to Tarrant) that
becomes entangled in other people's schemes and desires. It
echoes Peak's great 'secret' in *Born in Exile* — and of course
Gissing's own.

Despite the novel's return from the comparatively narrow
scope of *Born in Exile* and *The Odd Women* to a broader
social analysis, it does not succeed in sustaining a significant
interaction between Nancy's initially attractive and intense
desire and her circumambient conditions and possibilities.

iv. THE WHIRLPOOL (1897)

The *Whirlpool* is Gissing's last major novel. Though it
exhibits the general slackening of tension apparent in all his
work from the mid-nineties on, it dramatises with some
potency a number of his most continuing preoccupations. At
its centre is the study of a particular marriage, between the
sensitive and retiring Harvey Rolfe and the vain and neurotic
Alma Frothingham. But this marriage, distinguished by a
characteristically subtle delineation of jealousies and aspirations, is seen in relation to a general social condition. The
novel, which was unexpectedly successful, elicited a fine
review of Gissing's work by H. G. Wells, in which he praised
Gissing's attempt 'to write novels which are neither studies of
characters essentially, nor essentially series of incidents, but
deliberate attempts to present in typical groupings distinct

phases of our social order'.[35] This particular novel never in fact achieves the solidity of vision that animates *The Nether World* or *New Grub Street*, but as a general characterisation of Gissing's work, Wells's remarks constitute a vital step forward in the recognition of Gissing importance.

Wells defines as 'the structural theme', 'the fatal excitement and extravagance of the social life of London'. The 'whirlpool' of the title is a fine image for that threat of unwanted, resisted absorption, against which all Gissing's central characters struggle. Harvey Rolfe possesses that same stubborn determination to live apart, single and independent, as characterised such different personalities as Waymark, Reardon, Peak and Rhoda Nunn. But the novel is concerned to test the possibility of this perfect autonomy with the same bitter scepticism as permeated *Born in Exile* and *The Odd Women*.

We can perhaps at this stage distinguish three main phases of Gissing's treatment of desire. In its first phase, up until *The Nether World*, the desire for the perfect transcendence of imagination over fact, of inner freedom over outer circumstance, is so intense as to necessitate continuing elements of fantasy release (the endings of *The Unclassed* and *Demos*, in particular). In the two major novels that follow, *The Nether World* and *New Grub Street*, Gissing reaches his most mature and balanced recognition of the inter-penetration of desire and circumstance. In the third phase, from *Born in Exile* onwards, he shifts with some acerbity to a narrower study of the falsifying processes of desire. Yet at the same time, there begins to re-emerge, in stubborn contradiction of this deep scepticism, the indulged fantasy of perfect invulnerability that will reach its consummation in *The Private Papers of Henry Ryecroft*.

The Whirlpool is a parable about the necessary failure of the dream of perfect autonomy. Harvey Rolfe, a leisured, literary bachelor, aims to possess his soul in peace from the 'whirlpool' of modern society. The picture of this society is different from anything Gissing has previously attempted. Its most prominent aspects are those of rapidly acquired wealth, high fashion and intrigue, at a level well above the shabby suburbias of *In the Year of Jubilee*. This is a world of millionaires, speculators, men's clubs and society hostesses. In its intimation of the sexual intrigue, gossip and acquisitiveness of a whole area of society, dominated by the image of new sorts of newly-won wealth, the novel clearly owes something to Meredith's *One of Our Conquerors* (a book that had already influenced Gissing in the writing of *Denzil Quarrier*). The keynote of this world of apparent ease and luxury is a deep, continual anxiety, that erupts into violence in the suicide of Frothingham, Alma's father, and the accidental killing of the flashy millionaire, Cyrus Redgrave. Strange realms for Gissing to move in, one might think. But Gissing understands by now, after the technical proficiency of *New Grub Street*, how to present the picture of a general condition of social malaise by almost entirely oblique perspectives. The millionaires, speculators and hostesses are rarely seen directly. Instead we watch, from a narrow but illuminating angle, the effect on specific but peripheral individuals of the forces and tensions radiating out from the frenetic centre of social activity.

It is in the character of Alma that Gissing succeeds so well in delineating the essential characteristics of this sort of society. For Alma can only sustain her identity through the perpetual playing of roles, the conscious stylisation of personality and mutual corroboration that the dizzy social round provides. Thus is set up the central irony that Rolfe chooses as a partner in his experiment in independence, a woman who *can* only live through other people's confirmation of her poses.

> I don't want to shape you to any model of my own: I want you to be your true self, and live the life you are meant for.[36]

But Alma's raptures over the rural idyll (the cottage in North Wales) are those of the sentimental urbanite. The image of the 'simple life' provides her with a striking attitude in prospect, the proud gesture of renunciation of society's false glamour. Once they settle down to the actuality, the boring and trivial details of everyday life, Alma yearns desperately for her vanished stage, her scripts and props. From then on, her increasing need to embroil herself again in the 'whirlpool' becomes that of the doomed addict.

It is a pattern familiar enough in Gissing, the testing of the
dream against the reality, and the consequent sour, pathetic
or ironic erosion of the former by the latter. Rolfe himself
exhibits some characteristic traits of the confused idealist. At
the start he congratulates himself on his evasion of the snares
of connection, as he notes the ubiquity of disastrous
marriages around him. Yet his position is typically ambiguous. Pride in his apparent independence coexists with
unease amid the glitter of the fashionable society in which he
moves. For his inner autonomy is no more proof against the
tentacular grip of connection than that of the exiled
intellectual trapped in the slums, at the other end of the
social scale. It is precisely the impossibility of Rolfe's fiction
of perfect separateness that Gissing is intent on disclosing. It
is a pity, however, that Alma's personality is so neatly
tailored to the clinching of the ironies; the experiment is
clearly doomed from the start. Gissing's attention is really
concentrated on the process of Rolfe's enlightenment, and
the chastening of his egotism through fatherhood. The
development of the relationship is inconclusive in the
extreme, as Rolfe tries to balance his new sense of responsibility for the child with compassion for Alma's neurotic
traumas and his instinct to regress into male authoritarianism.

This problem of reconciling humanistic ideals of freedom
and independence with the compulsive issues of power in
their relationship, links up with a more general theme.
Throughout the novel there has been reference to an ethos of
physical strength, that is associated with the atmosphere of
the 'whirlpool's' competitive struggle, but also with the
political ethos of aggressive imperialism. For at the centre of
the whirlpool stand the unstable but compelling idols of
personal and national power, the twin figures of the
conquering millionaire and the conquering nation. Rolfe's
own ambiguous attitude towards the ethos of 'strength' is
expressed in a well-known scene at the end of the novel,
when he discusses Kipling's *Barrack-Room Ballads* with his
scholarly friend, Basil Morton. Wells misinterpreted the
import of this scene, mistaking its attitude as one of
uncritical endorsement, and the nature of what it endorsed as
something closer to his own conception of evolutionary
renewal and progress. Yet, though Gissing rightly rebuked

Wells,[37] there is good reason for the misunderstanding, in the depth of Rolfe's sceptical detachment. For Rolfe senses the inevitability, as he sees it, of 'the voice of the reaction', that Kipling incarnates, and to which he himself, under the pressure of his marriage to Alma, has felt a deep, instinctual attraction.

> It's the voice of the reaction. Millions of men, natural men, revolting against the softness and sweetness of civilisation; men all over the world; hardly knowing what they want and what they don't want . . .[38]

It is perhaps the phrase the 'softness and sweetness of civilisation' that misled Wells, for it is indeed a surprise for Gissing to attribute such qualities to a 'civilisation' that has produced the horrors of *The Nether World*. But this 'softness and sweetness' is not that of the 'spacious culture' that Wells imagined Gissing to be at last renouncing. This civilisation is indeed as far away as ever from embodying Gissing's ideal of 'spacious culture'. Its softness and sweetness are those of a decay, that makes the reaction to barbarism inevitable and necessary. Wells projected his own enthusiasm for such a violent renewal of evolutionary energy on to the scene, but Gissing made it clear that he shared with Rolfe the absolute disgust of the detached spectator.

> Thus and thus — says he — is the world going; no refusing to see it; it stares us in the eyes; but what a course for things to take! — He talks with a little throwing-up of the arm, and in a voice of quiet sarcasm. Go ahead! I sit by and watch, and wonder what'll be the end of it all.[39]

But Rolfe *has* been involved, has felt 'the reaction' in himself, even though Gissing refuses to follow the implications through.

This topic of imperialism and the ethos of physical might is a crucial one for Gissing's last years, since it serves to define his increasing detachment and scepticism. He did indeed express horror at the rising tide of militarism and nationalistic fervour, in his article 'Tyrtaeus' for the anti-imperialist journal, *The Review of the Week*,[40] in which he denounced Kipling and Swinburne, and also in his novel of

the same year, *The Crown of Life* (1899). But the symptomatic words in the exegesis of Rolfe's speech quoted above,
are the '*little* throwing-up of the arm', and the 'voice of *quiet*
sarcasm'. For they fix precisely the diminution of energy in
Gissing's protest against 'the world'. From now on, Gissing
will nurture this idiom of world-weary resignation with
disappointing assiduity. In this novel, the culminating
Ryecroftian dream of sceptical seclusion is adumbrated in the
idealised retreat of Rolfe's friends, the Mortons. The 'old-
fashioned stability' their marriage represents may seem like a
'rut' to some, but 'if the choice were between rut and
whirlpool . . .'. Basil Morton and his wife represent the true
ideal of achieved autonomy to replace Rolfe's disappointed
one. Morton's is a life of cultivated leisure, supported by a
moderate income and a model wife. After the sharp analysis
of Rolfe's own marriage, his easy capitulation to this fiction
of tensionless domestic bliss is disappointing in the extreme.
For the 'old-fashioned stability' he finds in their home is as
much an embattled anachronism as the Wanley Valley that
Eldon had temporarily saved from industrialisation in *Demos*.
The outpost of 'culture', as the rest of the novel implicitly
proves, survives only by the most arbitrary of chances. It is a
return, under some pressure, to the fiction of the autonomous 'inner life' that Gissing's finest work had so scathingly
exposed.

Conclusion: Gissing's Great Good Place

The Private Papers of Henry Rycroft (1903) occupies a special place in Gissing's work, as the expression of the dream of perfect release that has haunted all his creative life. Since the present argument has been that Gissing's value lies in the tensions and frictions and unresolved contradictions of his writing, it will be clear that the Utopian calm so affectionately figured here can only be considered as a deplorable but logical capitulation. Nevertheless, if it can be seen in the context of Gissing's work as a whole, it does him no disservice. For it illuminates in retrospect the courage and passion with which his finest writing has *resisted* the deep temptation to indulged withdrawal.

Only two responses are possible to *Ryecroft*: either you succumb or you resist. Ryecroft's passionless haven is only one of the many Utopian visions produced by the literature of these times. But some distinctions need to be drawn. Can we really consider it, as one critic has done, as the 'new kind of utopia', based on the 'central affective symbol' of Nature, to oppose the hell of modern industrialism and democracy?[1] (*New?*) Ryecroft's cottage belongs less with Morris's *News from Nowhere* than with Henry James's 'The Great Good Place' and H. G. Wells's 'The Door in the Wall'. It represents not so much a 'public' vision of a shared future, as a private, very private, vision of personal release. For this is always the key question about a utopia, or its nightmare counterpart: *how* does the imagined state, desired or feared, relate back to the assumed present from which it is a release? Even beside James's brilliant short story, let alone Morris's provocative vision, *Ryecroft* will seem lacking in all but the thinnest emotions, of self-indulgent, self-caressing sentimentality.

The argument about the extent to which Ryecroft *is*

Gissing need not detain us. The key statement offered by Gissing himself is that 'The thing is much more an aspiration than a memory'.[2] In his unfinished novel *Veranilda*, the refuge of the main character Basil at the Benedictine monastery at Monte Cassino produces a response that seems close to Gissing's own. Basil, and Gissing, admire this enclave of calm unworldliness, but cannot suppress their own instinctual need for continued engagement with 'the world'.

> He could approve the wisdom of those who renounced the flesh, to be rewarded with tranquillity on earth and eternal happiness hereafter; but his will did not ally itself with his intellect.[3]

(In James's 'Great Good Place', the monastic calm is reminiscent of 'some great abode of an Order, some mild Monte Cassino . . .'.) Henry Ryecroft does indeed express some of Gissing's most specific aspirations during his last rootless years in France, travelling vainly from place to place in search of health. Ryecroft's celebration of 'Home', of English food and the English countryside draws on Gissing's own deep wants. The lyricism of the passages on English food may strike us as comic now, but Gissing had been involved in almost catastrophic arguments with his French mother-in-law over the meagreness of the continental diet.

Jacob Korg has shown that the decisive difference between fiction and reality is Ryecroft's possession of a mellow resignation and tolerance that the 'real' Gissing did not quite share,[4] and that this creates a qualifying distance within an essential identification. Ryecroft embodies Gissing's image of satisfied desire. That this represents a sort of death, or posthumous release, is made clear by Ryecroft himself: 'I speak as one who has quitted the world.' The lines are cut, the tensions dissolved. Here in the perfect rural peace of Devon, free from economic need (the releasing legacy) and the exigencies of human relationship (the one miraculous housekeeper), Ryecroft, 'the egoist in grain', is alone with himself, his books and 'Nature'. H. G. Wells was indeed privileged to be the only human being, in the person of 'N—', really allowed to intrude into Ryecroft's perfect solitude. Even the housekeeper is effectively archaicised out of human contact, by her 'festal mien'. It is the fantasy fulfilled, of the perfect autonomous 'inner life', swathed from all rude contact with external reality. For this external reality is now, in such contrast to Gissing's early novels, divested of all but the most deferential, soothing characteristics, the well-loved books, the flowers and hedgerows — and the memories. For the characteristic dissolve back through an incident of the present to one in the past (the countryman's song, for instance, that leads back to the peasant's song heard in the ruins of Paestum), celebrates the ease with which the currents of thought and emotion can slip and slide, weaving out of the controlled, harmless stores of memory the comfortable tapestry of Self. This is certainly where the reason for the book's popularity is to be found, in its extraordinary capacity to catch the idiom of *relief*, the relief of a perfectly defined distance between Self and the World. Ryecroft presents us with a sharply marked out circle, within which objects and thoughts (my home, my books, my memories) provide an endless satisfaction of secure possession, and without which, the world (democracy, industrialism, militarism) can go hang.

The secret of *Ryecroft's* peculiar 'magic' is that it relies on an alternating rhythm around this central security of Self. First there is the rhythm of absorption, of the relapse into the calm, affectionate enthusiasm for an ordered private world, sanctioned by the images and movements of 'Nature' (the seasons of the year that structure the book). It is of course a 'Nature' neutralised of all threat or disruptive energy. Yet against this private, present world is set another past, urban world of labour, poverty and frustration — past as far as Ryecroft is concerned, that is: 'the life . . . which had to be supported by anxious toil; the life which was not lived for living's sake, as all life should be, but under the goad of fear'. It is this 'other world', in spite of Ryecroft's personal escape, still going on its heedless, egalitarian way, that initiates the second rhythm, of consolidation, of confirmed distance. 'I am no friend of the people'. (Gissing is deliberately echoing his beloved Horace: 'Odi profanum vulgus et arceo'; and Horace was undoubtedly in Gissing's mind as he shaped the general conception and style of the book.) It is the tone of haughty, magisterial judgement on a world that can provide only objects for ironic, self-satisfied contemplation. Ryecroft's opinions, his 'philosophy', tastes and shibboleths, may be considered instructive in themselves, but the real interest is in this shallow but seductive structure of desire. For it reflects, even in its state of advanced debility, that same pattern of conflict between the desire to resist and the desire to relapse that had at its fiercest animated Gissing's best work. But now the tensions between Self and the World are those only of pastime.

It is, therefore, a sardonic but not unexpected irony that the significance of Gissing's most popular book, according to the present argument, should consist entirely in the retrospective valuation it confers on his earlier writing. For it is *against* the voluptuous relaxation of *Ryecroft* that we should measure the fierce tenacious endurance that characterises Gissing's finest work. It is the quality of this grim energy that has rarely received recognition; yet it is central to an understanding of these late-Victorian years. Gissing's stature deserves to gain not in size, but in solidity. We can do no better than to close with the testimony of one of the 'few lonely watchers', who perceived this solidity of creative achievement at the time.

In such novels as *The Nether World* and *New Grub Street*, he penetrated to an expression of fortitude in poverty and privation, the force and truth of which have given him a place in English literature. *Such books are representative: they make a part of the essential record of our generation.* (my italics)[5]

Notes

(The name of the publisher is given only when it varies from the original; unless otherwise stated, the place of publication is London.)

INTRODUCTION

1. Virginia Woolf, 'George Gissing', *Collected Essays*, I (1966) p. 297.
2. *George Gissing's Commonplace Book*, ed. Jacob Korg (New York Public Library, 1962) pp. 23—4; hereafter abbreviated to *CBk*.
3. A *comparative* absence; if desired, the reflections and influences can of course be ferreted out. See Gillian Tindall, *The Born Exile* (1974), and Pierre Coustillas, 'Gissing's Feminine Portraiture', *English Literature in Transition*, VI, 3 (1963) 130—41.
4. *CBk*, p. 23.
5. Letter to Bertz, 24 November 1894; *George Gissing: Letters to Eduard Bertz*, ed. Arthur C. Young (1961) p. 191; hereafter abbreviated to *LEB*.
6. Quoted by B. Dobell, Introduction to James Thomson ('B.V.'), *Poetical Works*, ed. Dobell (1895) I, pp. lii—liii.
7. *Modern Painters*, IV, pt V, ch. II.
8. John Spiers and Pierre Coustillas, *The Rediscovery of George Gissing* (1971) p. 16. See also Tindall, *Born Exile*, pp. 47—56.
9. *CBk*, p. 26.
10. Gillian Tindall argues for the likelihood of Gissing having enjoyed a more positive sense of well-being in his family relationships than has usually been recognised. *Born Exile*, pp. 56—69.
11. See Pierre Coustillas, 'George Gissing à Manchester', *Etudes Anglaises*, XVI (July-Sep 1963) 254—61.
12. Rutherford wrote: 'We were not told what was the charge against us, nor what were the terms of the trust deed of the college, if such a document existed; . . . yet the council must have been aware that nothing less than our ruin would probably be the result of our condemnation.' *The Early Life of Mark Rutherford*, by himself (1913) pp. 68—9.
13. Austin Harrison, 'George Gissing', *Nineteenth Century*, LX (Sep 1906) 458—9.
14. *The Bookman*, XLVII (Jan 1915) 119.
15. *George Gissing and H. G. Wells: Their Friendship and Correspondence*, ed. Royal A. Gettmann (1961) facing p. 99.
16. Diary, 14 October 1888; quoted in *The Letters of George Gissing to Members of his Family*, ed. Algernon and Ellen Gissing (1927) p. 227; hereafter cited as *Letters*.

17. Diary, 8 July 1888.
18. John Gross, Introduction to *New Grub Street* (Bodley Head, 1967) p. v; hereafter abbreviated to *NGS*.
19. Asa Briggs notes that these missionary images were used in relation to provincial towns earlier in the century, and then more consistently in relation to London's East End in the 1880s — marking an important shift of focus. The images reveal 'the deep gulf in experience and values between observers and observed in the late nineteenth century'. *Victorian Cities* (rev. ed., 1968) p. 315.
20. *Our Mutual Friend*, Book the Fourth, ch. XV.
21. Letter to Ellen Gissing, 30 August 1888; *Letters*, p. 222.
22. Wanda Neff, *Victorian Working Women* (1929) ch. V, 'The Governess'.
23. Letter to Margaret Gissing, 12 April 1887; *Letters*, p. 191.
24. *CBk*, p. 29.
25 *Villette*, ch. XXV.
26. 'Address to Working Men, by Felix Holt', *Essays of George Eliot*, ed. Thomas Pinney (1963) p. 429.
27. *Middlemarch*, Book II, ch. XX.
28. 'The Progress of the Intellect', *Essays of George Eliot*, p. 31.
29. 'Address to Working Men', *Essays of George Eliot*, p. 429.
30. *Beauchamp's Career*, ch. IV.
31. *One of Our Conquerors*, ch. V.
32. Ibid., ch. XLI.
33. Max Nordau, *Degeneration* (Popular ed., 1913) p. 39.
34. Letter to Havelock Ellis, 20 January 1886; *Letters of Olive Schreiner*, ed. S. C. Cronwright-Schreiner (1924) p. 92.
35. Letter to Bertz, 26 October 1902; *LEB*, p. 312.
36. Guinevere Griest, *Mudie's Circulating Library and the Victorian Novel* (Indiana, 1971).
37. Letter to Bentley, 27 September 1853; quoted in Griest, *Mudie's*, p. 95.
38. The selection includes stories by James, Gissing, Symons, Morrison, Crackanthorpe, Dowson, Henry Harland, Frederick Wedmore and H. D. Lowry.
39. See John Goode's exploration of this issue in 'William Morris and the Dream of Revolution', *Literature and Politics in the Nineteenth Century*, ed. John Lucas (1971).
40. Oscar Wilde, *De Profundis* (Collected ed. 1908–22, ed. Robert Ross; repr. 1969) p. 30.
41. For Gissing's temporarily warm embrace of Schopenhauer see his essay 'The Hope of Pessimism', written in autumn 1882, but unpublished until *George Gissing: Essays and Fiction*, ed. Pierre Coustillas (Baltimore and London, 1970).

CHAPTER 1

1. Henry Mayhew and John Binny, *The Criminal Prisons of London and Scenes of Prison Life* (Frank Cass, 1968) p. 4.

2. Pierce Egan, *Life in London* (1821) pp. 20—1.
3. Mayhew and Binny, *Criminal Prisons*, p. 7.
4. *A Tale of Two Cities*, Book the First, ch. III.
5. *Dombey and Son*, ch. XLVII.
6. Letter to Ellen Gissing, 23 November 1881; *Letters*, p. 106.
7. Note for 28 March 1888; Florence Emily Hardy, *The Life of Thomas Hardy 1840—1928* (1962) p. 207.
8. Arthur Symons, *Spiritual Adventures* (1905) p. 101.
9. Hardy, *Life*, p. 207.
10. Preface to *The Princess Casamassima* (New York ed., 1909) p.v.
11. Ibid., p.xxii.
12. Ibid., p. xxiii.
13. Thomson, *Poetical Works*, II, 109—90. For Raymond Williams's discussion of the poem, see *The Country and the City* (1973) pp. 235—7.
14. Ibid., II, pp. 31—43.
15. Meredith, *Poems* (1851) pp. 16—22.
16. *Workers in the Dawn* (1880) III, p. 42.
17. Letter to W. R. W. Stephens, 16 June 1867; quoted in Horatio F. Brown, *John Addington Symonds: A Biography* (1895) II, p. 119.
18. Thomson, *Poetical Works*, I, pp. 173—82.
19. *The Autobiography of Sir Walter Besant* (1902) pp. 275—6.
20. Ibid., p. 277.
21. H. G. Wells, *Experiment in Autobiography* (Gollancz and Cresset, 1966) I, p. 245.
22. *The Private Papers of Henry Ryecroft* (Everyman ed., 1964) p. 54.
23. *Demos: A Story of English Socialism*, ed. Pierre Coustillas (Brighton: Harvester Press, 1972) pp. 220—1; hereafter abbreviated to *D*.
24. *D*, pp. 453—4.
25. Richard Le Gallienne, *The Romantic '90's* (1925) p. 208.
26. See Jackson's whole excellent chapter on 'The New Dandyism', *The Eighteen-Nineties* (1913) pp. 126—40.
27. P. J. Keating, *The Working Classes in Victorian Fiction* (1971).
28. H. J. Dyos, 'The Slums of Victorian London', *Victorian Studies*, XI, 1 (Sep 1967) 23—4.
29. Keating, *Working Classes*, p. 258.
30. Barry Pain, *De Omnibus* (1901) p. 1.
31. W. Somerset Maugham, *Liza of Lambeth* (Penguin, 1967) pp. 65—6.
32. *Charles Booth's London*, ed. Albert Fried and Richard Elman (Pelican, 1971) p. 48.
33. *Booth's London*, p. 49.
34. Jack London, *The People of the Abyss* (1903) pp. 36—7.
35. George Orwell, *The Road to Wigan Pier* (Uniform ed., 1959) p. 20.
36. Arthur Symons, *London: A Book of Aspects* (1909) p. 5.
37. Milton Chaikin, 'George Moore's Early Fiction', *George Moore's Mind and Art*, ed. Graham Owens (Edinburgh, 1968) p. 44.

38. Graham Hough, 'George Moore and the Novel', *George Moore's Mind and Art*, p. 174.
39. George Moore, *Confessions of a Young Man* (Heinemann, 1917) p. 184.
40. Moore revised the novel for a new edition by Heinemann in 1918, tightening the narrative almost word by word, and producing an extraordinary before-and-after effect in the two versions. In the particular scene referred to here, the vision is kept much closer to Kate herself by the addition of such phrases as 'it amused her to stand gazing', 'it seemed to her that . . .'. This produces a gain in concentration, but the loss of that movement, away and back, that characterised the original version.
41. George Moore, *A Mummer's Wife* (1885) p. 68.
42. Ibid., p. 69.
43. Stephen Crane, *Bowery Tales: Maggie, George's Mother*, ed. Fredson Bowers (Charlottesville, 1969) p. 21.
44. Crane, *Maggie*, p. 23.

CHAPTER 2

1. *Workers in the Dawn*, I, p. 1.
2. Beatrice Webb, *My Apprenticeship* (Penguin, 1971) p. 214.
3. Edith Sichel, 'Two Philanthropic Novelists: Mr. Walter Besant and Mr. George Gissing', *Murray's Magazine*, III (Apr 1888) 506—18; reprinted in *Gissing: The Critical Heritage*, ed. Pierre Coustillas and Colin Partridge (1972) pp. 114—26.
4. Walter Besant, *The Art of Fiction* (1884) p. 30.
5. 'The Natural History of German Life', *Essays of George Eliot*, p. 270.
6. Coustillas and Partridge (eds), *Critical Heritage*, p. 121.
7. 'The Sins of the Fathers', *Chicago Tribune* (Saturday supplement, 10 Mar 1877) unsigned; reprinted in *The Sins of the Fathers and Other Tales* (Chicago, 1924).
8. Frederic Harrison, *The Present and the Future: A Positivist Address* (1880) p. 41.
9. Raymond Williams, *Culture and Society, 1780—1950* (1958) pp. 175—6.
10. *The Unclassed* (1884) III, p. 7.
11. Letter to Frederic Harrison, 29 June 1884; quoted in Harrison, 'George Gissing', 460.
12. Letter to Algernon Gissing, 18 July 1883; *Letters*, p. 128.
13. Ibid., 12 June 1884; *Letters*, p. 139.
14. Harrison, 'George Gissing', 462.
15. John Goode, 'Gissing, Morris and English Socialism', *Victorian Studies*, XII (Dec 1968) 201—26; Alan Lelchuk, '*Demos*: The Ordeal of the Two Gissings', *Victorian Studies* XII (Mar 1969) 357—74; Goode and Lelchuk, 'Gissing's *Demos*: A Controversy', *Victorian Studies*, XII (June 1969) 431—40.
16. Letter to Algernon, 31 October 1885; *Letters*, p. 172.
17. Ben Tillett, *Memories and Reflections* (1931) p. 77.

18. *D*, p. 461.
19. Paul Sporn, 'Gissing's *Demos*: Late Victorian Values and the Displacement of Conjugal Love', *Studies in the Novel*, I (fall 1969) 335.
20. *D*, p. 89.
21. 'On Battersea Bridge', *Pall Mall Gazette*, 30 November 1883; reprinted in *Selections Autobiographical and Imaginative from the Works of George Gissing*, ed. A. C. Gissing (1929) pp. 54—8.
22. *D*, p. 350.
23. Ibid., p. 370.
24. *The Egoist*, ch. XXI.
25. Letter to Algernon, 22 September 1885; *Letters*, p. 169.
26. *Thyrza* (Eveleigh, Nash and Grayson, 1927) p. 136; hereafter abbreviated to *Th*.
27. Keating, *Working Classes*, p. 61.
28. Letter to Ellen, 31 July 1886; *Letters*, p. 184.
29. *Th*, p. 41.
30. Ibid., p. 259.
31. Ibid., p. 108.
32. Ibid., p. 113.
33. Ibid., pp. 111—2.

CHAPTER 3

1. Diary, 26 March 1888.
2. *Victorian Cities*.
3. Letter to Margaret Harkness, April 1888; *Karl Marx and Friedrich Engels: Selected Correspondence* (1956) p. 480.
4. Gareth Stedman Jones, *Outcast London: A Study in the Relationship between Classes in Victorian Society* (Oxford, 1971) p. 14.
5. Arnold White, *Problems of a Great City* (1886) p. 13.
6. Jones, *Outcast London*, p. 93.
7. Ibid., p. 342.
8. *The Nether World* (Everyman ed., 1973) p. 1; hereafter abbreviated to *NW*.
9. *NW*, p. 2.
10. See Paul Elmer More's fine appreciation of the quality of energy that animates Gissing's writing, and of the way in which we slowly become aware '. . . of the vast, dumb, tumultuous *will to live* that is struggling into consciousness through all these horrors and madnesses. The very magnitude of the obstacles, the unreason of endurance is witness to the unconquerable energy of this blind will.' 'George Gissing', *Shelburne Essays*, 5th ser. (1908); reprinted in Coustillas and Partridge (eds), *Critical Heritage*, p. 523.
11. *NW*, p. 2.
12. John Goode, 'Gissing's *The Nether World*', in D. Howard, J. Lucas and J. Goode, *Tradition and Tolerance in Nineteenth-Century Fiction* (1966) p. 211.
13. As Goode notes, *Tradition and Tolerance*, p. 212.

14. *NW*, p. 345.
15. Ibid., p. 67.
16. Ibid.
17. Ch. XXI, 'Woman and Actress'.
18. Tillett, *Memories and Reflections*, pp. 75—6.
19. Ibid., p. 76.
20. *NW*, p. 392.
21. Ibid., p. 104.
22. Jacob Korg, *George Gissing: A Critical Biography* (1965) p. 114.
23. *NW*, p. 274.

CHAPTER 4

1. Letter to Algernon, 11 February 1881; *Letters*, p. 92.
2. Letter to Bertz, 31 December 1899; *LEB*, p. 271.
3. *CBk*, p. 56.
4. *CBk*, p. 40.
5. Letter to Bertz, 2 June 1889; *LEB*, p. 60. 'The "Carlyle" seems to be admirably written; an excellent résumé of his professional life; old as the matter is to me, I read it with keen interest . . .'
6. Journal, 22 June 1832; quoted in J. A. Froude, *Thomas Carlyle* (Longman's, Green and Co., 1903) II, p. 294.
7. *On Heroes, Hero-Worship and the Heroic in History* (Centenary ed., 1898) p. 162.
8. Froude, *Carlyle*, II, p. 200.
9. Ibid., II, p. 236.
10. Letter to John Carlyle, 27 September 1824; Froude, *Carlyle*, I, p. 247.
11. Froude, *Carlyle*, I, p. 312.
12. Letter to Dr Carlyle, 23 September 1835; *Selected Works, Reminiscences and Letters*, ed. Julian Symonds (Reynard Library, 1955) p. 730.
13. 'Dickens in Memory', *Literature* (21 Dec 1901); reprinted in *Critical Studies of the Works of Charles Dickens*, ed. Temple Scott (New York, 1924) p. 156.
14. 'Mr. Kitton's Life of Dickens', *Times Literary Supplement* (15 Aug 1902); reprinted in Pierre Coustillas, *Gissing's Writings on Dickens* (Enitharmon Gissing series, no. 2, 1969) p. 25.
15. *CBk*, p. 34.
16. Coustillas, *Gissing's Writings on Dickens*, p. 4.
17. *Forster's Life of Dickens*, abridged and revised by George Gissing (1902) p. 49.
18. *Charles Dickens: A Critical Study* (1898) p. 95; hereafter cited as *Dickens*.
19. *Dickens*, p. 130.
20. Preface to *Tess of the D'Urbervilles* (July 1892, 5th and later eds); reprinted in *Thomas Hardy's Personal Writings*, ed. Harold Orel (Kansas, 1966) p. 26.

21. Letter to William Gissing, 26 February 1880; *Letters*, p. 59.
22. Letter to Edmund Gosse, 10 November 1895; Hardy, *Life*, p. 271.
23. *Dickens*, p. 90.
24. *CBk*, p. 34. The note runs on: 'To realize the inferiority of Dickens to Thackeray, it is enough to compare Major Bagstock with Major Pendennis, & Toots with Foker . . .' (note made some time between March and October 1889).
25. Coustillas, *Gissing's Writings on Dickens*, p. 1.
26. Letter to Wells, 3 October 1897; Gettmann (ed.), *Gissing and Wells*, p. 61.
27. Letter to Clodd, 1 September 1898; *Letters of George Gissing to Edward Clodd*, ed. Pierre Coustillas (Enitharmon Gissing series, no. 7, 1973) p. 51.
28. Thackeray wrote: 'Since the author of *Tom Jones* was buried, no writer of fiction among us has been permitted to depict to his utmost a MAN. We must drape him, and give him a certain conventional simper. Society will not tolerate the Natural in our Art.' Preface to *The History of Pendennis* (1849–50).
29. Letter to *Pall Mall Gazette* (15 Dec 1884) 2.
30. 'Gissing the Rod', *Punch* (3 Jan 1885) 1.
31. *CBk*, p. 69.
32. James Thomson, 'Bumble, Bumbledom, Bumbleism', *National Reformer*, (5 Nov 1895); reprinted in *Selected Prose of James Thomson ('B.V.')*, ed. W. D. Schaefer (Berkeley and Los Angeles, 1967) p. 123.
33. *Pall Mall Gazette* (10 Dec 1884) 1.
34. Letter 3 July 1895; quoted in Royal A. Gettmann, *A Victorian Publisher: A Study of the Bentley Papers* (Cambridge, 1960).
35. Quoted by Gissing in a letter to Algernon, 20 September 1882; *Letters*, p. 119. For a full account of the saga of *Mrs. Grundy's Enemies*, see Gettmann, *Victorian Publisher*, pp. 196–7, 215–22.
36. Quoted in Reginald Pound, *The Strand Magazine 1891–1950* (1966) p. 25.
37. Quoted in Louis Dudek, *Literature and the Press: A History of Printing, Printed Media, and their Relation to Literature* (Toronto, 1960) p. 129.
38. Letter to Algernon, 12 June 1884; *Letters*, pp. 38–9. 'When I am able to summon any enthusiasm at all, it is only for Art — how I laughed the other day on recalling your amazement at my theories of Art for Art's sake!'
39. 'The Place of Realism in Fiction', *Humanitarian* (July 1895); reprinted in *Sections*, p. 220.
40. Letter to Algernon, 14 March 1885; *Letters*, p. 155.
41. *CBk*, p. 37.
42. Letter to Bertz, 15 January 1892; *LEB*, p. 142.
43. Diary, 18 March 1888.
44. Letter to Hardy, 10 August 1868; quoted in C. L. Graves, *Life and Letters of Alexander Macmillan* (1910) p. 290.

45. Hardy, *Life*, p. 104.
46. Letter to *The Bookman* (Dec 1891) 98.
47. Quoted in Leon Edel, *Henry James: The Conquest of London 1870–1883* (1962) p. 178.
48. *Complete Tales of Henry James*, ed. Leon Edel, XI (1964) p. 32.
49. Ibid., Introduction; see also Edel's essay, 'Henry James: The Dramatic Years', a biographical introduction to *Guy Domville* (1961).
50. Letter to William James, 2 February 1895; *Letters of Henry James*, selected and ed. Percy Lubbock (1920) I, p. 240.
51. Letter to W. D. Howells, 22 January 1895; *Letters*, I, p. 237.
52. Besant, *Art of Fiction*, p. 31.
53. Letters to Bertz, 24 November 1894; *LEB*, p. 190, and 27 August 1895; p. 204.
54. [Marie Corelli], *The Silver Domino* (1892) p. 295.
55. Jane Helen Findlater, *Stones from a Glass House* (1904) p. 119.
56. John Gross, *The Rise and Fall of the Man of Letters* (1969) p. 215.
57. Arnold Bennett, *The Truth about an Author* (1903) p. 150.
58. For a discussion of the significance of this novel's radical difference from the subsequent Edwardian novels of 'self-therapy', see William Bellamy, *The Novels of Wells, Bennett and Galsworthy, 1890–1910* (1971) pp. 71–87.
59. Wells, *Experiment in Autobiography*, II, p. 506.
60. *Ryecroft*, p. 59.
61. Wells, *Experiment in Autobiography*, II, p. 507.
62. Diary, 10 October 1888.
63. Letter to Clodd, 8 January 1902; Coustillas (ed.), *Letters to Clodd*, p. 78.
64. Letter to Ellen Gissing, 1 April 1890; Jacqueline Steiner, 'George Gissing to his Sister', *More Books* (Bulletin of the Boston Public Library) XXII (Nov 1947) 335.

CHAPTER 5

1. Diary, 19 October 1888.
2. *Letters*, p. 228.
3. Letter to Bertz, 3 January 1889; *LEB*, p. 33.
4. *NGS*, pp. 361–2.
5. Bennett, *The Truth about an Author*, *passim*, and Walter Besant, *The Pen and the Book* (1899) p. 25.
6. Dudek, *Literature and the Press*, p. 116.
7. Letter to Hardy, late June 1886; quoted in Hardy, *Life*, p. 182.
8. *NGS*, p. 370.
9. I am indebted to some of the evidence collected and argument forwarded by V. K. Daniels, 'New Grub Street 1890–96' (unpublished Ph.D. thesis, University of Sussex, 1966).
10. Frederic Whyte, *William Heinemann: A Memoir* (1928) p. 57.
11. P. J. Keating, *Gissing: New Grub Street* (1968) p. 12.

12. Ibid., p. 54.
13. *NGS*, p. 54.
14. Ibid., p. 306.
15. Korg, *George Gissing*, p. 161.
16. *NGS*, p. 341.
17. 'The Son's Veto', written late 1890 to early 1891, first published *Illustrated London News* (1 Dec 1891); collected in *Life's Little Ironies* (1894).
18. Letter to Algernon, 22 September 1895; R. L. Purdy, 'George Gissing at Max Gate, 1895', *Yale University Library Gazette,* XVII (Jan 1943) 52.
19. *NGS*, p. 74.
20. Robert L. Selig, 'The Valley of the Shadow of Books: Alienation in Gissing's *New Grub Street*', *Nineteenth Century Fiction*, XXV (Sep 1970) 188—98.

CHAPTER 6

1. *Isabel Clarendon*, ed. Pierre Coustillas (Brighton: Harvester Press, 1969) I, p. 124.
2. Ibid., II, p. 103.
3. See Coustillas's introduction to the Harvester Press ed., for the instructive contemporary reception of the novel.
4. Letter to Bertz, 20 May 1892; LEB, p. 153.
5. Ibid., 8 April 1891; *LEB*, p. 120.
6. Letter to Morley Roberts, 10 February 1895; published in *The Bookman*, XLVII (Jan 1915) 123—4.
7. Letter to Bertz, 21 October 1889; *LEB*, pp. 76—7.
8. Letter to Ellen, 20 January 1891; *Letters*, pp. 312—13.
9. Diary, 20 June 1890.
10. *Born in Exile* (Gollancz, 1970) p. 57; hereafter abbreviated to *BE*.
11. M. C. Donnelly, *George Gissing: Grave Comedian* (Cambridge, Mass., 1954) p. 165.
12. *BE*, p. 81.
13. Ibid., p. 66.
14. This is in contrast to Gissing himself, whose own scholastic bent is represented rather by Earwaker, another of Peak's friends, who wins the Poem and Essay prizes.
15. *BE*, p. 67.
16. Ibid., p. 169.
17. Ibid., p. 148.
18. *CBk*, p. 58.
19. Jacob Korg, 'The Spiritual Theme of *Born in Exile*', *Collected Articles on George Gissing*, ed. Pierre Coustillas (1968) pp. 131—41.
20. Ibid.
21. Ibid., p. 139.
22. Ibid., p. 135.
23. *BE*, p. 156.

24. Jens Peter Jacobsen, *Niels Lyhne*, trans. Hanna Astrup Larsen (New York, 1919) p. 48.

CHAPTER 7

1. 'Queen Bees or Working Bees?', *Saturday Review*, XLVII (12 Nov 1859) 576.
2. Eliza Lynn Linton, 'Woman's Place in Nature and Society', *Belgravia* (May 1876) 349—63.
3. Kate Millett, *Sexual Politics* (1971) pp. 88—108.
4. *Sesame and Lilies* (1865). Kate Millett notes that this was Ruskin's most popular volume.
5. J. S. Mill, *On the Subjection of Women*, ed. Stanton Coit (1924) p. 105.
6. *The English Wife: A Manual of Home Duties* (1843) p. 13.
7. Friedrich Engels, *The Origin of the Family, Private Property and the State*, trans. Alick West, rev. Dona Torr (1940) p. 69.
8. Ibid., p.79.
9. *Commonweal* (18 Feb 1888); quoted in *Labour's Turning-Point: 1880—1900*, ed. E. J. Hobsbawm (1948) p. 62.
10. See T. F. Eagleton, 'Nature and Spirit: A Study of Edward Carpenter in his Intellectual Context' (unpublished Ph.D. thesis, University of Cambridge, 1968).
11. Olive Schreiner, *The Story of an African Farm* (Penguin, 1971) p. 188.
12. MS. letter to Edmund Gosse, 5 March 1890; quoted in Phyllis Grosskurth, *John Addington Symonds: A Biography* (1964) p. 282.
13. MS. letter to H. G. Dakyns, 19 May 1867; quoted in Grosskurth, *Symonds*, p. 103.
14. *[Westward Ho!* and *Constance Herbert]*, *Essays of George Eliot* p. 135.
15. *Middlemarch*, Book III, ch. XXVIII.
16. *The Egoist*, ch. VII.
17. Ibid., ch. XIII.
18. *Athenaeum*, Cl (27 May 1893) 667.
19. Letter to Bertz, 2 June 1893: *LEB*, p. 171.
20. George Orwell, 'George Gissing', *Collected Articles*, ed. Coustillas, p. 56.
21. *The Odd Women* (Anthony Blond, 1968), p. 154; hereafter abbreviated to *OW*.
22. *OW*, p. 250.
23. Ibid., p. 242.
24. Ibid., pp. 21—2.
25. Mill, *On the Subjection of Women*, p. 43.
26. Agnes Brissenden performs the same function as the heiress Constance Asper in Meredith's *Diana of the Crossways* (1885), which clearly had a diffused influence on Gissing's novel.
27. *OW*, p. 269.

28. Ibid., p. 336.
29. Letters to Bertz, 2 June 1893; *LEB*, p. 172.
30. Unpublished letter to Clara Collet, 26 August 1894; quoted in Spiers and Coustillas, *The Rediscovery of George Gissing*, p. 99.
31. *In the Year of Jubilee* (Lawrence and Bullen, one vol. ed., 1894) p. 253; hereafter abbreviated to *IYOJ*.
32. *IYOJ*, p. 96.
33. Ibid., p. 276.
34. Ibid., p. 411.
35. H. G. Wells, 'The Novels of Mr. George Gissing', *Contemporary Review*, LXXII (Aug 1897); reprinted in Gettmann (ed.), *Gissing and Wells*, p. 245.
36. *The Whirlpool* (Watergate Classics, 1948) p. 118.
37. Letter to Wells, 7 August 1897; Gettmann (ed.), *Gissing and Wells*, pp. 47–9.
38. *Whirlpool*, p. 449.
39. Letter to Wells, 7 August 1897; Gettmann (ed.), *Gissing and Wells*, p. 48.
40. 'Tyrtaeus', *The Review of the Week* (4 Nov 1899) 6–7; reprinted in *Gissing Newsletter*, X, 3 (July 1974) 2–3.

CONCLUSION

1. Jackson I. Cope, 'Definition as Structure in *The Ryecroft Papers*', *Collected Articles*, ed. Coustillas, p. 154.
2. Letter to Frederic Harrison, 11 February 1903; quoted in Harrison, 'George Gissing', 463.
3. *Veranilda* (World's Classics, 1929) p. 301.
4. Jacob Korg, 'The Main Source of *The Ryecroft Papers*', *Collected Articles*, ed. Coustillas, pp. 168–78.
5. Allan Monkhouse, 'George Gissing', *Manchester Quarterly* (April 1905); reprinted in Coustillas and Partridge (eds), *Critical Heritage*, p. 467.

Selected Bibliography

(The name of the publisher is given only when it varies from the original; unless otherwise stated, the place of publication is London.)

SECTION A. GEORGE GISSING

1 Gissing's Writings
Dates in parentheses on the left are those of original publication.

(a) Novels
(1880) *Workers in the Dawn.* 3 vols.
(1884) *The Unclassed.* 3 vols.
        The Unclassed. Lawrence and Bullen, revised ed., 1895.
(1886) *Demos: A Story of English Socialism,* ed. Pierre Coustillas. Brighton: Harvester Press, 1972.
(1886) *Isabel Clarendon,* ed. Pierre Coustillas. 2 vols. Brighton: Harvester Press, 1969.
(1887) *Thyrza.* Eveleigh, Nash and Grayson, 1927.
(1888) *A Life's Morning.* 3 vols.
(1889) *The Nether World.* Everyman ed., 1973.
(1890) *The Emancipated.* 3 vols.
(1891) *New Grub Street.* Bodley Head, 1967.
(1892) *Denzil Quarrier.*
(1892) *Born in Exile.* Gollancz, 1970.
(1893) *The Odd Women.* Anthony Blond, 1968.
(1894) *In the Year of Jubilee.* Lawrence and Bullen, one vol. ed., 1894.
(1895) *Eve's Ransom.*
(1895) *The Paying Guest.*
(1895) *Sleeping Fires.*
(1897) *The Whirlpool.* Watergate Classics, 1948.
(1898) *The Town Traveller.*
(1899) *The Crown of Life.*
(1901) *Our Friend the Charlatan.*
(1904) *Veranilda: A Romance.* World's Classics, 1929.
(1905) *Will Warburton.*

(b) Short Stories and Miscellaneous
For a detailed bibliographical study of Gissing's short stories, see Pierre Coustillas, 'George Gissing's Short Stories: A Bibliography', *English Literature in Transition,* VII, 2 (1964) 59—72.

(1880) 'Notes on Social Democracy', *Pall Mall Gazette,* 9, 11 and 14 Sep 1880; reprinted in Enitharmon Gissing series, no.1. 1968.

(1898) *Human Odds and Ends: Stories and Sketches.*
(1898) *Charles Dickens: A Critical Study.*
(1901) *By the Ionian Sea: Notes of a Ramble in Southern Italy.* Richards Press, 1956.
(1903) *Forster's Life of Dickens*, abridged and revised by George Gissing.
(1903) *The Private Papers of Henry Ryecroft.* Everyman ed., 1964.
(1906) *The House of Cobwebs, and other stories.*
(1924) *The Sins of the Fathers, and other tales.* Chicago.
(1924) *Critical Studies of the Works of Charles Dickens*, ed. Temple Scott. New York.
(1925) *The Immortal Dickens.*
(1927) *A Victim of Circumstances, and other stories.*
(1929) *Selections Autobiographical and Imaginative from the Works of George Gissing*, ed. A. C. Gissing.
(1931) *Brownie.* New York.
(1938) *Stories and Sketches.*
(1962) *George Gissing's Commonplace Book*, ed. Jacob Korg. New York Public Library.
(1970) *George Gissing: Essays and Fiction*, ed. Pierre Coustillas. Baltimore and London.

(c) Letters
Letter to Morley Roberts, 10 February 1895; published in *The Bookman*, XLVII (Jan 1915) 123–4.
The Letters of George Gissing to Members of his Family, ed. Algernon and Ellen Gissing. 1927.
Seventeen letters to Ellen Gissing; published in Jacqueline Steiner, 'George Gissing to his Sister', *More Books* (Bulletin of the Boston Public Library) XXII (Nov and Dec 1947) 323–36 and 376–86.
The Letters of George Gissing to Eduard Bertz, ed. A. C. Young. 1961.
George Gissing and H. G. Wells: A Record of their Friendship and Correspondence, ed. Royal A. Gettmann. 1961.
The Letters of George Gissing to Gabrielle Fleury, ed. Pierre Coustillas. New York Public Library, 1964.
Six letters to Thomas Hardy; published in Pierre Coustillas, 'Some Unpublished Letters from Gissing to Hardy', *English Literature in Transition*, IX, 4 (1966) 197–209.
Fifty-four letters, all but two to Henry Hick; published in *Henry Hick's Recollections of George Gissing*, ed. Pierre Coustillas. Enitharmon Gissing series, no.3. 1973.
The Letters of George Gissing to Edward Clodd, ed. Pierre Coustillas. Enitharmon Gissing series, no.7. 1973.

(d) Unpublished material
Gissing's Holograph Diary, 1887–1903. 3 vols. Berg Collection, New York Public Library.

2 *Writings about Gissing: Biography and Criticism*
The following recent publication provides the most complete check-list
available of Gissing criticism (from 1880 to 1970): *George Gissing: An
Annotated Bibliography of Writings about Him*, compiled and ed.
Joseph J. Wolff. DeKalb, Ill., 1974.

Bookman, The, 'George Gissing', XLVII (Jan 1915) 117—125. (Collection of notes and reminiscences by various writers.)

Coustillas, Pierre, 'George Gissing et H. G. Wells', *Etudes Anglaises*, XV
(April—June 1962) 156—66.

'George Gissing à Manchester', *Etudes Anglaises* (July—Sep 1963)
254—61.

'Gissing's Feminine Portraiture', *English Literature in Transition*, VI,
3 (1963) 130—41.

Gissing's Writings on Dickens: A Bio-Bibliographical Survey. Enitharmon Gissing series, no.2. 1969.

George Gissing at Alderley Edge. Enitharmon Gissing series, no.4.
1969.

Coustillas, Pierre (ed.), *Collected Articles on George Gissing*. 1968.

Coustillas, Pierre and Partridge, Colin (eds), *Gissing: The Critical
Heritage*. 1972.

Donnelly, Mabel C., *George Gissing: Grave Comedian*. Cambridge,
Mass., 1954.

Gissing, Ellen, 'George Gissing: A Character Sketch', *Nineteenth
Century*, CII (Sep 1927) 417—24.

'Some Personal Recollections of George Gissing', *Blackwood's
Magazine*, CCXXV (May 1929) 653—60.

Gissing Newsletter, The, Vols I—X, 3 (Jan 1965—July 1974).

Goode, John, 'George Gissing's *The Nether World*', *Tradition and
Tolerance in Nineteenth-Century Fiction*, by D. Howard, J. Lucas
and J. Goode. 1966. Pp. 207—41.

'Gissing, Morris and English Socialism', *Victorian Studies*, XII, 2
(Dec 1968) 201—26.

Introduction to *The Nether World*, ed. Goode. Brighton: Harvester
Press, 1974.

Gordan, John D., *George Gissing 1857—1903: An Exhibition from the
Berg Collection*. New York, 1954.

Harrison, Austin, 'George Gissing', *Nineteenth Century*, LX (Sep 1906)
453—63.

Hick, Henry, *Henry Hick's Recollections of George Gissing*, ed. Pierre
Coustillas. Enitharmon Gissing series, no.3. 1973.

James, Henry, 'London Notes, July 1897', *Notes on Novelists*. 1914.
Pp. 346—51.

Keating, P. J., *George Gissing: New Grub Street*. 1968. (Studies in
English Literature, no.33.)

Korg, Jacob, *George Gissing: A Critical Biography*. 1965.

Leavis, Q. D., 'Gissing and the English Novel', *Scrutiny*, VII (June
1938) 73—81.

Lelchuk, Alan, *'Demos:* The Ordeal of the Two Gissings', *Victorian Studies*, XII, 3 (March 1969) 357—74.

Murry, John Middleton, 'George Gissing', *Katherine Mansfield and Other Literary Studies*. 1959. Pp. 3—68.

Nicoll, Sir William Robertson, *A Bookman's Letters*. 1913. Pp. 289—96.

Purdy, R. L., 'George Gissing at Max Gate', *Yale University Library Gazette*, XVII, 3 (Jan 1943) 51—2.

Roberts, Morley, *The Private Life of Henry Maitland*, ed. Morchard Bishop. 1958.

Seccombe, Thomas, Introduction to *The House of Cobwebs*. 1906.

Selig, Robert L., 'The Valley of the Shadow of Books: Alienation in Gissing's *New Grub Street*', *Nineteenth Century Fiction*, XXV, 2 (Sep 1970) 188—98.

Spiers, John and Coustillas, Pierre, *The Rediscovery of George Gissing*. 1971. (Reader's Guide to National Book League Gissing Exhibition, 1971.)

Swinnerton, Frank, *George Gissing: A Critical Study*. 1912.

Tindall, Gillian, *The Born Exile: George Gissing*. 1974.

Ward, A. C., *George Gissing*. 1959. (Writers and their Work, no.111.)

Wells, H. G., *Experiment in Autobiography*. Gollancz and Cresset, 1966. Vol.II, pp. 567—81.

Woolf, Virginia, 'George Gissing', *Collected Essays*, I (1966) 297—301.

SECTION B. GISSING'S LITERARY CONTEXT

In the interests of concision, I have not included here any works of those major mid-Victorian authors (Carlyle, Dickens, George Eliot, etc.) who may be assumed to have made a diffused contribution to the establishment of Gissing's 'literary context'. Of the major figures writing between 1880 and 1900 (Meredith, Hardy, James), I have listed only those works most relevant to the shaping of the presented argument.

Adcock, Arthur St John, *East End Idylls*. 1897.

Bennett, Arnold, *A Man from the North*. 1898.
   Fame and Fiction: An Enquiry into Certain Popularities. 1901.
   The Truth about an Author. 1903.

Besant, Walter, *All Sorts and Conditions of Men*. 3 vols. 1882.
   The Art of Fiction. 1884.
   The Pen and the Book. 1899.
   Autobiography. 1902.

Bookman, The, Vols I—VIII (Oct 1891—Mar 1895).

Booth, Charles, *Charles Booth's London*, selected and ed. Albert Fried and Richard Elman. 1969.

Brown, Horatio F., *John Addington Symonds: A Biography*. 2 vols. 1895.

[Corelli, Marie], *The Silver Domino: or Side Whispers, Social and Literary*. 1892.

Crane, Stephen, *Bowery Tales: Maggie, George's Mother*, ed. Fredson Bowers. Charlottesville, 1969.

Findlater, Jane Helen, *Stones from a Glass House*. 1904.

Froude, J. A., *Thomas Carlyle*. 4 vols. Longman's, Green and Co., 1903.

Hardy, Florence Emily, *The Life of Thomas Hardy, 1840–1928*. 1962.

Hardy, Thomas, *The Mayor of Casterbridge*. 2 vols. 1886.
    Tess of the D'Urbervilles. 3 vols. 1891.
    Jude the Obscure. 1896.
    Thomas Hardy's Personal Writings: Prefaces, Literary Opinions, Reminiscences, ed. Harold Orel. Kansas, 1966.

Jacobsen, Jens Peter, *Niels Lyhne*, trans. Hanna Astrup Larsen. New York, 1919.

James, Henry, *The Princess Casamassima*. 2 vols. New York, 1909.
    The Tragic Muse. 2 vols. New York, 1909.
    The Letters of Henry James, selected and ed. Percy Lubbock. 2 vols. 1920.
    The Complete Tales of Henry James, ed. Leon Edel.
    'The Author of Beltraffio', vol.V. 1963.
    'The Lesson of the Master', vol.VII. 1963.
    'The Private Life', vol.VIII. 1963.
    'The Middle Years', vol.IX. 1964.
    'The Death of the Lion', vol.IX. 1964.
    'The Coxon Fund', vol.IX. 1964.
    'The Next Time', vol.IX. 1964.
    'The Figure in the Carpet', vol.IX. 1964.
    'John Delavoy', vol.IX. 1964.
    'The Great Good Place', vol.XI. 1964.

Keating, P. J. (ed.), *Working Class Stories of the 1890s*. 1971.

Kipling, Rudyard, *Plain Tales from the Hills*. 1890.
    The Light that Failed. 1891.
    Soldiers Three and Other Stories. 1895.
    Kim. 1901.

London, Jack, *The People of the Abyss*. 1902.

Maugham, William Somerset, *Liza of Lambeth*. Penguin, 1967.

Meredith, George, *Beauchamp's Career*. 3 vols. 1876.
    The Egoist. 3 vols. 1879.
    Diana of the Crossways. 3 vols. 1885.
    One of Our Conquerors. 3 vols. 1891.

Moore, George, 'A New Censorship of Literature', *Pall Mall Gazette*, 10 Dec 1884, 1–2.
    Literature at Nurse or Circulating Morals. 1885.
    A Mummer's Wife. 1885.
    Esther Waters. 1894.

Morris, William, *Selected Writings*, ed. G. D. H. Cole. Nonesuch Press, Centenary ed., 1948.

Morrison, Arthur, *Tales of Mean Streets*. 1894.
    A Child of the Jago, ed. P. J. Keating. Panther, 1971.
    To London Town. 1899.
    The Hole in the Wall. 1902.

Nevinson, H. W., *Neighbours of Ours*. Bristol, 1895.

Pugh, Edwin, *A Street in Suburbia*. 1895.

Ridge, William Pett, *Mord Em'ly*. 1898.

Rook, Clarence, *The Hooligan Nights*. 1899.

Rutherford, Mark, *The Autobiography of Mark Rutherford*. 1881.
  Mark Rutherford's Deliverance. 1885.
  The Revolution in Tanner's Lane. 1887.

Schreiner, Olive, *The Story of an African Farm*. Penguin, 1971.

Stanford, Derek (ed.), *Short Stories of the 'Nineties*. 1968.

Symons, Arthur, *Spiritual Adventures*. 1905.
  London: A Book of Aspects. 1909.

Thomson, James ('B.V.'), *Poetical Works*, ed. Bertram Dobell. 2 vols.
  1895.
  *The Speedy Extinction of Evil and Misery: Selected Prose of James
  Thomson ('B.V.')*, ed. William D. Schaefer. Berkeley and Los
  Angeles, 1967.

Turgenev, Ivan, *Fathers and Sons*, trans. R. Edmonds. Penguin, 1965.

Wells, H. G., *The Time Machine*. 1895.
  *Experiment in Autobiography: Discoveries and Conclusions of a
  Very Ordinary Brain (Since 1866)*. 2 vols. Gollancz and Cresset,
  1966.

Whiteing, Richard, *No.5 John Street*. 1899.

Wilde, Oscar, *The Picture of Dorian Gray*. Collected ed. 1908–22, ed.
  Robert Ross, repr. 1969.
  De Profundis. Collected ed. 1908–22, repr. 1969.

Zola, Emil, *L'Assommoir*, trans. L. W. Tancock. Penguin, 1970.
  Germinal, trans. L. W. Tancock. Penguin, 1968.

SECTION C. CRITICISM, BIOGRAPHY, MISCELLANEOUS

Altick, R. D., *The English Common Reader: A Social History of the
  Mass Reading Public, 1800–1900*. Chicago, 1957.

Banks, J. A. and Olive, *Feminism and Family Planning in Victorian
  England*. Liverpool, 1964.

Bradbury, Malcolm, *The Social Context of Modern English Literature*.
  Oxford, 1971.

Briggs, Asa, *Victorian Cities*. Revised ed., 1968.

Coleman, B. I. (ed.), *The Idea of the City in Nineteenth-Century
  Britain*. 1973.

Daniels, V. K., 'New Grub Street 1890–96: Publication of Novels'.
  Unpublished Ph.D. thesis, University of Sussex, 1966.

Dudek, Louis, *Literature and the Press: A History of Printing, Printed
  Media, and their Relation to Literature*. Toronto, 1960.

Dyos, H. J. and Wolff, Michael (eds), *The Victorian City: Images and
  Realities*. 2 vols. 1973.

Eagleton, T. F., 'Nature and Spirit: A Study of Edward Carpenter in his
  Intellectual Context'. Unpublished Ph.D. thesis, University of
  Cambridge, 1968.

Edel, Leon, *The Life of Henry James*, vols.II, III, IV:
   The Conquest of London, 1870—1883. 1962.
   The Middle Years, 1884—1894. 1963.
   The Treacherous Years, 1895—1901. 1969.
Egan, Pierce, *Life in London*. 1821.
Eliot, George, *Essays of George Eliot*, ed. Thomas Pinney. 1963.
Engels, Friedrich, *The Origin of the Family,Private Property and the State*, trans. Alick West, rev. Dona Torr. 1940.
Fletcher, Ian (ed.), *Meredith Now: Some Critical Essays*. 1971.
Gettmann, Royal A., *A Victorian Publisher: A Study of the Bentley Papers*. Cambridge, 1960.
Goode, John, "'Character" and Henry James', *New Left Review*, no.40 (Nov—Dec 1966) 55—75.
Graham, Kenneth, *English Criticism of the Novel 1865—1900*. Oxford, 1965.
Griest, Guinevere L., *Mudie's Circulating Library and the Victorian Novel*. 1971.
Gross, John, *The Rise and Fall of the Man of Letters: Aspects of English Literary Life Since 1800*. 1969.
Grosskurth, Phyllis, *John Addington Symonds: A Biography*. 1964.
Hobsbawm, E. J., *Industry and Empire*. 1968.
Hobsbawm, E. J. (ed.), *Labour's Turning Point: 1880—1900*. 1948. (History in the Making: Nineteenth Century, vol.III.)
Howard, D., Lucas, J., and Goode, J., *Tradition and Tolerance in Nineteenth Century Fiction*. 1966.
Jackson, Holbrook, *The Eighteen-Nineties*. 1913.
Jones, Gareth Stedman, *Outcast London: A Study in the Relationship between Classes in Victorian Society*. Oxford, 1971.
Keating, P. J., *The Working Classes in Victorian Fiction*. 1971.
Lucas, John (ed.), *Literature and Politics in the Nineteenth Century*. 1971.
Lynd, Helen Merrell, *England in the Eighteen-Eighties: Towards a Social Basis for Freedom*. 1945.
Mayhew, Henry, *Mayhew's London*, ed. Peter Quennell. 1969.
Mayhew, Henry and Binny, John, *The Criminal Prisons of London and Scenes of Prison Life*. Frank Cass, 1968.
Mill, John Stuart, *On the Subjection of Women*, ed. Stanton Coit. 1924.
Miller, J. Hillis, *The Form of Victorian Fiction*. Indiana, 1968.
Millett, Kate, *Sexual Politics*. 1971.
Neff, Wanda F., *Victorian Working Women*. 1929.
Nordau, Max, *Degeneration*. Popular ed., 1913.
Rutherford, Andrew (ed.), *Kipling's Mind and Art*. Edinburgh, 1964.
Sheppard, Francis, *London 1808—1870: The Infernal Wen*. 1971.
Thompson, E. P., *William Morris: Romantic to Revolutionary*. 1955.
Tillett, Ben, *Memories and Reflections*. 1931.
Webb, Beatrice, *My Apprenticeship*. Penguin, 1971.

Whyte, Frederic, *William Heinemann: A Memoir*. 1928.
Williams, Raymond, *Culture and Society 1780—1950*. 1958.
    The Long Revolution. 1961.
    The English Novel from Dickens to Lawrence. 1970.
    The Country and the City. 1973.

Index